SATURN CYCLES

ABOUT THE AUTHOR

Wendell C. Perry, a writer and artist living in Lexington, Kentucky, has been researching astrology and related subjects for nearly forty years. A member of the International Society for Astrological Research, he is co-author, with his wife Linda Perry, of *The Mars/Venus Affair* (Llewellyn, 2000), and has written a number of articles for *Mountain Astrologer* and *Dell Horoscope* magazines.

TO WRITE TO THE AUTHOR

If you wish to contact the author or would like more information about this book, please write to the author in care of Llewellyn Worldwide and we will forward your request. Both the author and publisher appreciate hearing from you and learning of your enjoyment of this book and how it has helped you. Llewellyn Worldwide cannot guarantee that every letter written to the author can be answered, but all will be forwarded. Please write to:

Wendell C. Perry
℅ Llewellyn Worldwide
2143 Wooddale Drive, Dept. 978-0-7387-1493-6
Woodbury, Minnesota 55125-2989, U.S.A.
Please enclose a self-addressed stamped envelope for reply,
or $1.00 to cover costs. If outside U.S.A., enclose
international postal reply coupon.

Many of Llewellyn's authors have websites with additional information and resources. For more information, please visit our website at http://www.llewellyn.com

WENDELL C. PERRY

MAPPING CHANGES IN YOUR LIFE
SATURN CYCLES

Llewellyn Publications
Woodbury, Minnesota

Saturn Cycles: Mapping Changes in Your Life © 2009 by Wendell C. Perry. All rights reserved. No part of this book may be used or reproduced in any manner whatsoever, including Internet usage, without written permission from Llewellyn Publications, except in the case of brief quotations embodied in critical articles and reviews.

First Edition
First Printing, 2009

Book design by Donna Burch
Cover design by Kevin R. Brown
Editing by Connie Hill
Llewellyn is a registered trademark of Llewellyn Worldwide, Ltd.

Chart wheels were produced by the Kepler program by permission of Cosmic Patterns Software, Inc. (www.AstroSoftware.com)

Library of Congress Cataloging-in-Publication Data
Perry, Wendell.
　Saturn cycles : mapping changes in your life / Wendell C. Perry. — 1st ed.
　　　p. cm.
　Includes bibliographical references (p.　　).
　ISBN 978-0-7387-1493-6
　1. Human beings—Effect of Saturn on.　2. Astrology.　I. Title.
　BF1724.2.S3P47 2009
　133.5'37—dc22

2008032668

Llewellyn Worldwide does not participate in, endorse, or have any authority or responsibility concerning private business transactions between our authors and the public.

　All mail addressed to the author is forwarded but the publisher cannot, unless specifically instructed by the author, give out an address or phone number.

　Any Internet references contained in this work are current at publication time, but the publisher cannot guarantee that a specific location will continue to be maintained. Please refer to the publisher's website for links to authors' websites and other sources.

Llewellyn Publications
A Division of Llewellyn Worldwide, Ltd.
2143 Wooddale Drive, Dept. 978-0-7387-1493-6
Woodbury, Minnesota 55125-2989, U.S.A.
www.llewellyn.com

Printed in the United States of America

OTHER BOOKS BY WENDELL C. PERRY

The Mars/Venus Affair with Linda Perry
(Llewellyn, 2000)

CONTENTS

Introduction xiii

PART 1: THE SAINTS

*People Who Made Good Use
of Their Saturn Transits*

1: The Dalai Lama 3
*Tibetan religious leader who was forced to flee
his country after it was invaded by the Chinese*

2: Oprah Winfrey 13
*African-American TV personality who has made the role
of talk show host a force for social and cultural progress*

3: Thomas Merton 23
*Catholic monk noted for his writings on the power
of religious devotion and the ills of modern civilization*

4: Bruce Lee 33
*American-born actor and martial arts master who brought
Chinese martial arts and Taoist philosophy to American movies*

5: Albert Einstein 43
*German scientist whose theory of relativity changed
the way we understand time and space*

6: Malcolm X 53
*African-American leader who became the angry public face
of the Black Muslim movement until he was expelled
from that organization and assassinated*

7: Bono (Paul Hewson) 63
*Irish rock star who has become a respected activist
for such causes as African debt relief*

8: Jimmy Carter 73
American politician who followed a disappointing single term as president of the United States with a long career as a peacemaker and moralist

9: Michael J. Fox 83
Canadian-born actor whose personal battle with Parkinson's disease has made him a symbol of hope and courage for the entire world

10: Ralph Nader 95
Consumer advocate who rose to fame as the champion of automobile safety and for his opposition to corporate influence on American government

11: Gloria Steinem 105
American writer and magazine editor who has become one of the intellectual leaders of the feminist movement in the United States

12: Carl Gustav Jung 117
Swiss psychoanalyst who broke with Sigmund Freud and developed a new approach to the unconscious

PART 2: THE SINNERS

People Who Made Poor Use of Their Saturn Transits

13: Britney Spears 129
American pop singer whose personal life has become a textbook for celebrity meltdown

14: O. J. Simpson 141
African-American football great who seemed to be living a charmed life until the day his wife and a man who was visiting her were brutally murdered

15: Mata Hari (Margaretha Zelle MacLeod) 153
Dutch-born courtesan who faked her way to international fame as a dancer, only to be falsely accused and executed as a spy during World War I

16: Hermann Göring 163
Nazi leader who became the head of the German Air Force and the Gestapo under the regime of Adolf Hitler

17: Janis Joplin 173
American singer who came to personify the "sex, drugs, and rock-and-roll" era, and died accordingly

18: Paul Gauguin 183
French painter famous for his paintings of Tahiti and his love for Tahitian women

19: Lee Harvey Oswald 195
Alleged assassin of President John F. Kennedy, although he did not live long enough to stand trial

20: Bill Clinton 205
President of the United States whose many accomplishments were largely overshadowed by his sexual improprieties while in the White House

21: Andrew Cunanan 217
A charming California-born hustler who went on a five-week killing spree that ended after he murdered fashion mogul Gianni Versace, and then committed suicide

22: Jerry Siegel 227
Comic book writer who invented Superman, only to see his publishers take all the glory and the profits

23: Jim Bakker 239
American TV evangelist who built an empire with the faith and the money of other people

24: Jayne Mansfield 249
American actress who used every means to become the next great "blond bombshell," but never quite got there

PART 3: SATURN AT WORK FOR YOU

25: Saturn at Work on the Midheaven 261

26: Saturn at Work on the Ascendant 267

27: Saturn at Work on the Imum Coeli 273

28: Saturn at Work on the Descendant 277

29: Saturn Conjunct Natal Saturn 283

30: Saturn Opposed Natal Saturn 287

31: Saturn Square Natal Saturn 291

Appendix: Abbreviated Ephemeris for Saturn 1990–2020 295

Bibliography 305

INTRODUCTION
Saturn at Work

Of all the predictive tools and techniques that are available to astrologers, few are as universally accepted and reliable as are the cycles of Saturn. Saturn's transits relative to its natal place map the step-by-step development of the individual into adulthood and beyond. Saturn's transits across the angles of the horoscope, the Ascendant, *Imum Coeli*, Descendant, and Midheaven, signal important changes in the areas of self, home, relationships, and career, respectively. If an astrologer wants to know when something important is going to happen in a person's life, the first thing that he or she is going to look at is the location of transiting Saturn.

For this reason it is not surprising that there are many books about Saturn and its transits. Many of these books do an excellent job of describing Saturn, the archetype, and of relating the mythological and conceptual basis for our understanding of the astrological Saturn. Some also provide generalized, "cookbook" explanations of what we can expect from different Saturn transits.

That is not what this book is about.

This is a book about how Saturn works. It is about specific, real-life experiences of Saturn transits. It is a book that takes complex, abstract concepts like individuation and self-discovery, and demonstrates how they actually happen through real events happening to real people. We will see how transiting Saturn challenges us, how it forces us to make hard choices and dares us to create our destinies. And we will see how, in successive Saturn transits, these challenges and changes are woven into a personal history—how they create the story of our lives.

We will demonstrate how Saturn creates life stories by following the progress of transiting Saturn through the lives of twenty-four people. Our examples are all famous people whose lives have been extensively studied and recounted. Their lives were and are, to one extent or another, lived in the public arena and are open to our examination. This means that anyone who wishes to check our facts and the timing of events used in this book is free to do so. This also means that a reader who finds any particular Saturn passage in any particular example relevant to his or her situation has the ability to study the period further through biographies, autobiographies, published letters, and other materials.

SAINTS AND SINNERS

Our examples are divided into two groups. The first we call "Saints." This tag has less to do with their morality than it does with the fact that these are people who, in general, made good use of their Saturn cycles. Some of them are spiritual people with deep religious convictions. Others are people who have devoted themselves to public service and the advancement of human knowledge. They come from a variety of backgrounds and disciplines, but they all share a willingness to put the welfare of humanity and the search for truth ahead of their own personal needs.

The second group we call "Sinners." These are people who failed to make the best use of their Saturn transits. These are people who placed short-term comfort and pleasure before long-term goals, people who sought to aggrandize their own egos at the expense of broader, more altruistic concerns. Many of them were people with extraordinary talents who fought their way to successful careers but, in the process, were crippled and destroyed. All of them have, in one way or another, impressed themselves on the public mind as cautionary examples of the perils of a life poorly lived.

Comparing these saints and sinners will help the reader to understand how crucial Saturn transits are and that the passages they suggest represent more than a natural growth into adulthood—they are the building blocks of the person we are to become. We will see that making the right choice during a Saturn transit and embracing the challenges and hard lessons these aspects so often bring us are crucial, not just to development into responsible, moral, and successful members of the social order, but also to the development of our character at every level.

TWO WAYS OF LOOKING AT SATURN

These biographies will give us an opportunity to see how Saturn transits work in an individual life, how one Saturn passage and the choices and challenges it brings relate to the next Saturn transit and the next. It will allow us to see how Saturn weaves our strengths and weaknesses, our errors and successes into a life story, into a destiny. In order to understand this fully, we must see in it the context of a single life. In this context, your Saturn transit is like no one else's. It is particular to you and your life experience. No cookbook explanation of what a Saturn return or a Saturn passage over the Ascendant should be like can account for what you did or didn't do during your last Saturn transit. Nor can it account for the context of your expectations, your talents, and your individual horoscope. By examining the way in which Saturn worked in other people's lives, you will gain a sense of how these powerful transits adapt themselves to the individual.

Though it is crucial to understand how Saturn functions in the context of a particular life's story, it is also necessary to understand the general characteristics of each Saturn crossing. For this reason, the third part of the book contains the traditional "cookbook" explanations of each aspect of transiting Saturn to its natal position and of transiting Saturn's passage over each of the cardinal points of the horoscope. Here you will see what *typically* happens when Saturn makes its first return or crosses the Ascendant. The difference between the explanations offered here and descriptions offered in other books, however, is the fact that our descriptions are based on what we saw happen in our examples, and we will use events from the lives of our examples to illustrate the various influences of these Saturn transits.

This dual approach will give you, the reader, two ways of looking at each Saturn transit and two ways to achieve a clearer understanding of what you can expect during your next Saturn crossing. You will have the opportunity to observe what these transits mean in the context of a particular life's story and in the generalized context of several life stories.

WHAT DOES SATURN WANT FROM US?

Too often Saturn is tied in with our climb up the social ladder, with success and failure, fame and fortune, and events in our lives that make the newspapers or, at least, company newsletters. We forget that the real significance of Saturn transits lies in what they bring us on an internal, spiritual level. Saturn transits provide the rhythm and the structure of our lives. They ask the questions and bring forth from us the answers that are crucial to building character and virtue. If we choose to evade these questions or if we fail to come up with the right answers, then Saturn transits can be every bit as hard and unhappy as they are often reputed to be. If we embrace this process, if we face squarely the questions asked of us and learn from the answers, then we can make something positive, edifying, and even triumphant of even the most dire of circumstance.

There is always an element of trial and testing when Saturn transits one of the angles or aspects its natal place. We are often called upon to provide proof of our competence, talent, and character. If we have the goods, if we possess the ability and the strength to pass these tests, then a Saturn transit can actually be a happy time, a time when we see our hard work and good planning validated by the authority and by the outside world. And yet, even when a Saturn passage brings us joyous news and well-deserved victory, there is always a test hidden within the celebration. Winning brings its own challenges—and triumphs can often test our virtue and challenge our judgment even more severely than defeat.

Because our primary concern during a Saturn transit has to be with this process of building and testing one's character, there will naturally be Saturn passages that are quiet and seemingly uneventful. The hard questions, the big tests do not always have to come from major events in our lives. Unspoken realizations, spiritual revelations, private conflicts with family and friends, and other processes that take place outside of the public purview can become just as significant in the building of virtue as any public event. As we have said, the important work of these passages takes place at a psychological and spiritual level, and sometimes the process of building character and putting together a well-lived life has to take place behind closed doors.

DESTINY

It is impossible to discuss Saturn and its transits without also discussing the concept of destiny. Some people respond to this concept with hostility. They like to think that fate is entirely the product of the decisions and choices we make in life, that luck is simply an excuse, and that the power of the will can overcome any obstacle. For such people, Saturn transits can become painful lessons in the limitations of human intelligence, understanding, and willpower.

At the other end of the spectrum, we have people who think that destiny is a puzzle that they can somehow master. Many people enter into the study of astrology with the notion that it will help them solve the puzzle of fate and give them control over uncontrollable circumstances. The truth of the matter is that the proper study of astrology only deepens our awareness of the mystery of destiny and fate. Instead of giving us the means to control our destinies, astrology provides us with an even keener awareness of just how unpredictable fate can be. In some cases, it also allows time to prepare ourselves for the twists and turns of unruly circumstances and the means to ameliorate bad luck, but the most valuable thing we gain from astrology is the opportunity to place this ill fortune, or good fortune for that matter, in a broader context and use these experiences to increase our understanding of life.

This is why the cycles of Saturn are so important. They describe the intersection between our choices, our natural abilities, and our will with the remorseless forces of history, circumstance, and fate. You must be alert during these transits. You must be mindful of even the most insignificant changes and events. Written within the cadence of these happenings, you will find the secret to understanding who you are and who you will become. You will gain a deeper awareness of the role this slippery and mysterious concept called destiny might play in your life. Don't expect to understand it all. Don't expect to solve the puzzle. But, very often, a properly used Saturn passage does provide us with just the beginnings of an understanding of the relationship between our personal will and the larger workings of destiny. Achieving this, we could hardly hope for anything more.

PART 1
THE SAINTS
*People Who Made Good Use
of Their Saturn Transits*

THE CHOICE

In October 1951, three thousand Chinese troops marched into Lhasa, the capital of Tibet. Watching their advance was a nervous sixteen-year-old, the newly ordained fourteenth Dalai Lama. The young man was a political innocent who had spent most of his life under the care of monks and government officials, whose fervent attention to the lad's religious instruction had left him virtually ignorant of the world outside his palace. Still, even this sheltered youth could see that, with those advancing phalanxes of grim-faced foreign troops, a wave of irrevocable change was sweeping over his country. At that moment **Saturn was crossing the Dalai Lama's Ascendant** and he was facing one of the most important choices of his life.

The fourteenth Dalai Lama had begun life as Lhamo Dhondup, a simple lad with an undistinguished pedigree. Then, when he was three years old and **Saturn was crossing his Descendant**, it was decided that little Lhamo was the reincarnation of the recently deceased thirteenth Dalai Lama and therefore the rightful ruler and ultimate religious authority of all Tibet. At that point, Lhamo Dhondup became Tenzin

Gyatso, the incarnate or the Kundun. He also became the object of the intense religious devotion of the Tibetan people and the focal point of political intrigue that he was far too young to understand.

Such an emphasis was placed on Tenzin's religious education that he was shocked when, in 1950, he learned that his country was being invaded by China. His regent and other high officials took the unprecedented step of ordaining Tenzin as the fourteenth Dalai Lama immediately, instead of waiting until his eighteenth birthday. Then Tenzin was removed from Lhasa and the government was transferred to a town closer to the border with India. During this period, Uranus was crossing his natal Midheaven, an indication of radical, even violent change.

The situation had seemed to improve early in 1951 when a Chinese general came to Tenzin and assured him that his government had no territorial designs on Tibet and that the government of Tibet would not be disturbed. The general had also reassured the fourteenth Dalai Lama with regard to his personal safety and invited him to return to his palace in Lhasa. Tenzin complied with the general's wishes but, once he was reinstalled in his palace in Lhasa, the young ruler found that he was simply being used as a figurehead. The Chinese had no intention of loosening their grip on Tibet. As **Saturn crossed his Ascendant,** the youthful fourteenth Dalai Lama had to decide whether to acquiesce to the invaders and the radical changes they were bringing into his country or join many of his countrymen, including members of his own family, and resist.

THE HOROSCOPE

Astrology was one of the tools used to determine that Tenzin Gayatso was the reincarnation of the Dalai Lama, so it is no surprise that the dominating feature of his horoscope is a Grand Trine with Saturn, Jupiter, and his Cancer Sun in the 10th House just a few degrees past the Midheaven. These aspects all but cry out, "Wise and benevolent leader!" At first glance, the rest of the horoscope seems to bear out this initial judgment. The Rising Sign is calm and judicious Libra, with its ruler, Venus, in Leo forming a nice sextile to a strong Mercury in Gemini. This

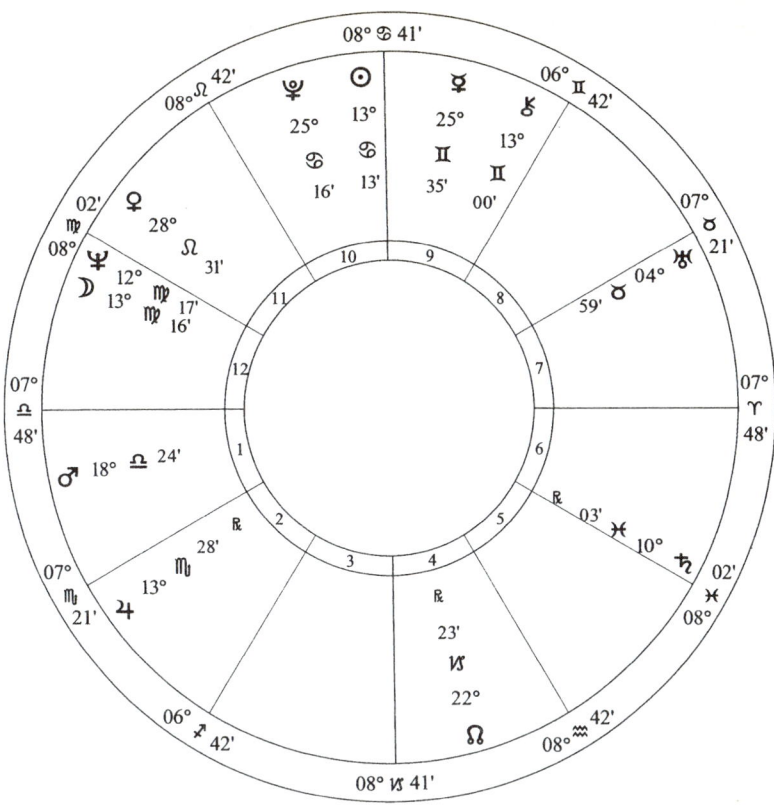

The Dalai Lama XIV
July 6, 1935, 11:45 AM local time
Tengster Village, Tibet, 36N32 101E12

is definitely a person who expresses himself with grace and clarity, a natural communicator and facilitator. The Moon is in Virgo in the 12th House where it conjuncts Neptune. In terms of purely worldly concerns this is not altogether a positive placement, but it is certainly appropriate for someone who would be expected to spend a great deal of his time in seclusion and meditation. More importantly, this conjunction of the Moon and Neptune forms a close sextile to both the Sun and Jupiter, adding spiritual weight to that benevolent combination.

And yet, as with any horoscope, there are some bad aspects mixed with the good. Mars, though weak by sign, is strongly placed in the 1st House and square to the Sun. This is an odd situation for a religious man. Were it not for the wealth of aspects and placements indicating a calm, peace-loving nature, we might say this aspect would produce a quick temper and tendency toward violence and contention. Instead, we will have the reverse equation. The violence and conflict will be directed toward the individual and it will be a pervasive issue in his life. On the positive side, this is an aspect that indicates courage in the face of conflict and adversity, and the ability to act quickly and decisively.

The second bad aspect in the horoscope is the opposition of both his Moon and his Neptune to natal Saturn. In some ways this is a more worrisome situation than the Mars to Sun square. It shows us a strong tendency toward depression and escapism. It would be very easy for this person to push unpleasant realities and responsibilities aside for the sake of experiences of a religious or mystical nature. The aspect also carries a potential of self-delusion and self-doubt, insecurity and discontent. A strong effort to emphasize the more positive elements of the horoscope will be needed to avoid these pitfalls.

THE LIFE

Even though religion appeared to be the chief function of the Dalai Lama, the position had also been a political one for centuries. In fact, the office was so politically charged that many of the young men being groomed as the Dalai Lama had been assassinated before they were old enough to assume their duties. Tenzin's predecessor, the thirteenth Dalai Lama, had been canny enough to avoid this fate and he had enjoyed a long and eventful reign. During the time of the thirteenth Dalai Lama, the Chinese empire—which had always played an important, sometimes destructive, role in Tibetan affairs—was falling into anarchy and the colonial powers of Europe were becoming the major players in the region. The British had entered Tibet with a small army and the 13th had been forced to open his tightly closed nation to Western influence. The opening had been minor, however, and even in Tenzin's time Tibet was still considered a place of mystery.

By the time that the fourteenth Dalai Lama came on the scene, the political dynamic had changed. Britain had ceased to be a major influence in the Far East and the government of China had undergone a radical transformation. Mao Tse Tung was now the ruler of China, and the Buddhist religion was viewed with great suspicion by his Communist regime. Perhaps more importantly, modern technology was piercing the precious isolation of Tibet on multiple fronts.

Unlike many in his country, Tenzin readily embraced modernity. Even as a small child he had been fascinated by the old automobiles and other Western gadgets that had been collected by his predecessor, so his attitude toward the invading Chinese was uncertain. On the one hand, he recoiled at the notion of an occupying army in his capitol city. On the other hand, he was open to the new ideas and modern improvements the Chinese could offer.

So whatever misgivings the fourteenth Dalai Lama felt that day in October 1951, Tenzin decided to put them aside and acquiesce to the superior forces of the Chinese. After all, he was still just a teenager with much to learn, and there seemed to be little that his people could do to resist the invading army. He concentrated on his religious studies and on preparing for the various initiations and rites that would complete his preparation for the lofty office for which he had been born. In 1954, not long after he turned eighteen, Tenzin was invited by the Chinese government to visit Beijing (then Peking). He spent the next year touring China and had several meetings with Mao Tse Tung.

At first the youngster was thrilled by the opportunity to travel and see new things. He was not put off by Communism and the vast restructuring of Chinese society that it had wrought. Compared to the practically medieval economy of his country, the revamped and modernized China he saw seemed like a paradise in the making. But soon Tenzin began to notice how his Chinese handlers struggled to prevent him from having private conversations with the everyday people. Likewise, though he was at first impressed by Chairman Mao's charm and intelligence, Tenzin later was made aware of the utter contempt the great helmsman held for Buddhism and for the people, like the Dalai Lama, who devoted their lives to its beliefs and practices. The reality of his situation and the situation of his country was made even clearer when he learned that China and India, Tibet's other powerful neighbor, had signed a treaty in which India essentially recognized China's control over Tibet.

Meanwhile the resistance of Tibetan people against the Chinese army of occupation had intensified. Armed with little more than their courage and antiquated weapons left behind by the British, the Tibetans fought a guerilla war against their oppressors. The Chinese responded to this resistance with terrific brutality. They killed without compunction, and then wreaked terrible vengeance on the families and villages of the rebels.

Having returned to his capital, the Dalai Lama searched for some way to stop the bloodshed. He recognized that the Tibetans were completely overmatched in their war against the Chinese and decided that he had to persuade the prime minister of India, Jawaharlal Nehru, to come to the aid of his beleaguered nation. With great difficulty, he talked the Chinese into allowing him to visit holy sites in India in December 1956. While he was there, the young man arranged a meeting with the Indian prime minister. Tenzin begged Nehru to help him save Tibet, but his request was refused. Nehru was not about to go to war with China over Tibet. Four months later, Tenzin faced the choice of staying in India where he would be out of the reach of the Chinese, or returning to Tibet where his life would be in constant jeopardy. **Transiting Saturn was making its square aspect to natal Saturn** at this time and he felt the call of responsibility. Ignoring the objections of his family and many of his advisers, the fourteenth Dalai Lama returned to Lhasa, intent on doing what little he could to help his people.

The Dalai Lama stayed in war-torn Tibet until 1959. By this time, a rumor that the Chinese were planning to murder the Dalai Lama had inflamed the countryside. Tibetans jammed into the capitol in order to protect their leader. The Chinese army in the city was on the verge of slaughtering the frantic demonstrators. During the previous years, Tenzin had consulted an oracle about his plight. Each time, the oracle had advised the Dalai Lama to stay in Tibet. On March 31, 1959, the oracle suddenly changed his opinion. He told the fourteenth to get out of the country immediately, and the young religious leader was quick to follow this advice. He escaped across the border into India with about eighty members of his family and court.

In many ways, the Dalai Lama's escape from Chinese control was only the beginning of his story. His party was followed within a few months by streams of Tibetan refuges, as the Chinese brought the full force of their military might against Tibetan resistance. Tenzin was able to persuade Nehru to give the Tibetan refugees parcels of land where they could live and preserve the distinctive traditions of their nation. As **Saturn reached the Dalai Lama's IC** in December 1959, the first of these settlements was established, and with it a new Tibet began to take root.

By the time **Saturn made its first conjunction to its natal place** in Tenzin's horoscope, he was the leader of an archipelago of Tibetan communities spread across eastern India. The transition was not easy. The climate of India was much hotter and damper than that of Tibet, and the labor the Tibetans had to undertake in order to establish their new homes was daunting. Many died because of the heat and because of diseases. The Dalai Lama did all he could to coax financial aid from India and other sources and to encourage his people. In the meantime, he revamped the structure of the Tibetan government, making it a modern, democratic state in which the needs of the people came before religious tradition. He also removed the strict code of deference that surrounded the Dalai Lama in Tibetan society, demystifying his position and allowing him more direct communication with his people.

But more than anything else, the Dalai Lama struggled to maintain the identity of his people and to keep the plight of Tibet alive in the public mind. Not only was he the leader of a government in exile, he also became the living representation of Tibet's centuries-old traditions and religious faith. Previous incarnations of the Dalai Lama had fought to keep foreign influences from contaminating and diluting the rich religious culture of Tibet and its special place in the Buddhist world. Now that situation was reversed. With the Chinese doing everything they could to uproot Tibetan culture and destroy those ancient traditions in Tibet, the preservation of the great Buddhist traditions of that nation came to depend on the benevolent scholarship of foreigners and the determined faith of an exiled people, the most prominent of whom is the fourteenth Dalai Lama himself.

The Dalai Lama's battle for Tibet and the Tibetan people continues even today. In the process, he has made himself a public figure, a bestselling author, and a spiritual advisor to the entire world. One full Saturn cycle after he established the first Tibetan settlements in India, when **Saturn returned to his IC** in 1989, Tenzin Gyatso was awarded the Nobel Peace Prize.

SATURN AT WORK

For most of us, the earliest transits of Saturn are relatively mundane. The changes they bring have to do with our relationship with our parents and families, and with our developing awareness of ourselves. They concern the inevitable transformation from childhood to adulthood and have little influence on our standing in the world outside our home. This is not the case for the Dalai Lama. With the first contact of Saturn to one of the angles of his horoscope in 1937, he became a public figure. For him, every Saturn passage became a crucial phase, not just in his development as a person but for the fate of his nation.

If we assume that the choice Tenzin Gyatso faced when the Chinese troops marched into Lhasa was a choice between acquiescence to the invaders or joining the resistance and fighting against them, then it would have truly been an impossible choice. Complete surrender was unthinkable—and resistance, particularly for an unworldly, pacifist sixteen-year-old, was equally out of the question. But this was not the choice Tenzin was facing. What Saturn was telling him during this passage was that his country was already lost. His choice was how to deal with this loss.

The Dalai Lama chose to return to his religious studies and complete the rituals that prepared him to fulfill the role of religious leader of his people. This choice could have become an irresponsible escape into mysticism and an evasion of the pressing problems facing his country. But for Tenzin, now that he had been stripped of his temporal authority, the realization of his full spiritual and moral authority became a matter of great importance. The Dalai Lama was no longer preparing himself to be the autocrat of Tibet; he was preparing himself to be a spiritual leader to the Tibetan people, wherever they might be.

This is why the conjunction of Saturn with the next angle in his horoscope coincided, not with his dramatic escape from Lhasa, but with the establishment of the first Tibetan communities in India. This would be the beginning of the Dalai Lama's new temporal state. But more importantly, it was the beginning of his appearance on the world stage. His persistent, articulate, yet gentle protest of the Chinese occupation of his nation quickly made him widely known and accessible in ways that his secretive predecessors could not have imagined. With the publication of many books, concerning both the plight of his country and popularized interpretations of his Buddhist philosophy, and his winning of the Nobel Peace Prize, the Dalai Lama has taken on the role of spiritual leader for all of us, and we are so much richer for it.

SOURCES

Barbara Foster and Michael Foster, *Forbidden Journey: The Life of Alexandra David-Neel* (San Francisco: Harper Row, 1987).

Dalai Lama XIV, *Freedom in Exile: The Autobiography of the Dalai Lama* (New York: Harper Collins, 1990).

2

OPRAH WINFREY

African-American TV personality who has made the role of talk show host a force for social and cultural progress

THE CHOICE

On the evening of March 24, 1986, a budding actress named Oprah Winfrey sat nervously in the audience of the Academy Awards ceremony. The actress had much to be happy about. She had been nominated for an Oscar for best supporting actress for her very first movie. Things weren't going so bad on her day job, either. Her Chicago-based talk show had become a local phenomenon and soon it would be syndicated and broadcast across the nation. And yet, Oprah Winfrey was not happy and the source of her discontent was close at hand. It was packed around her thighs, her buttocks, and her belly. It was all over her body and wrapped in a tight designer dress that showed off every bulge. In a room full of some of the most attractive and slender people in the world, Oprah Winfrey was a fat woman. With a sigh of relief, she greeted the announcement that someone else had won the Oscar, that someone else would have to rise from her seat and parade her body before this elite crowd and the television cameras.

Saturn was just a degree beyond Winfrey's IC on March 24, moving retrograde. It would pass over that degree again in April and

then again in November 1986, by which time Winfrey's newly syndicated talk show would prove to be just as popular nationally as it had been in the Chicago market. This Saturn passage would not only leave Oprah Winfrey very wealthy; it would mark the beginning of her phenomenal rise as an icon of American popular culture. For Winfrey, these massive successes were meager compensation for the battle she was losing with her weight. Winfrey had not always been fat. As a teenager, she had won beauty pageants. It was only after she had been removed as the news anchor of a Baltimore TV station and demoted to an early morning slot (one of the few defeats she suffered during her adult life) that Oprah began this fight against overeating and excess weight. Now, with an ever-growing national audience watching her every weekday, millions of people were seeing her fat, and millions of people were listening when she talked frankly about her efforts to manage her weight. And, more importantly, millions of people would feel themselves a part of Winfrey's battle to lose her excess pounds. The ups and downs of her bathroom scale would become a part of the pulse of America: Oprah Winfrey versus Fat; the Battle of the Decade (and a little more) was starting.

THE HOROSCOPE

The horoscope of Oprah Winfrey is complex, with several dynamic aspect patterns that often seem to work in opposite directions. One of the most worrisome of these aspects is the very close (within a degree) square between her natal Saturn and Sun. This is a classic aspect of hardship, limitation, and sadness—particularly early in life. It is an aspect often associated with an absent father and with difficulties with male authority figures. It many cases, this hard connection between the Sun and Saturn seems to force people to become tough, disciplined, and goal-conscious, just as a survival mechanism, but even the toughest of those who live with this aspect carry a residual of insecurity, self-doubt, and harsh, unrelenting self-criticism.

In Winfrey's case, the hard, judgmental qualities of this square are softened by the exact conjunction of the Sun and Venus. This also places Venus in a tight square with Saturn, an aspect that can severely

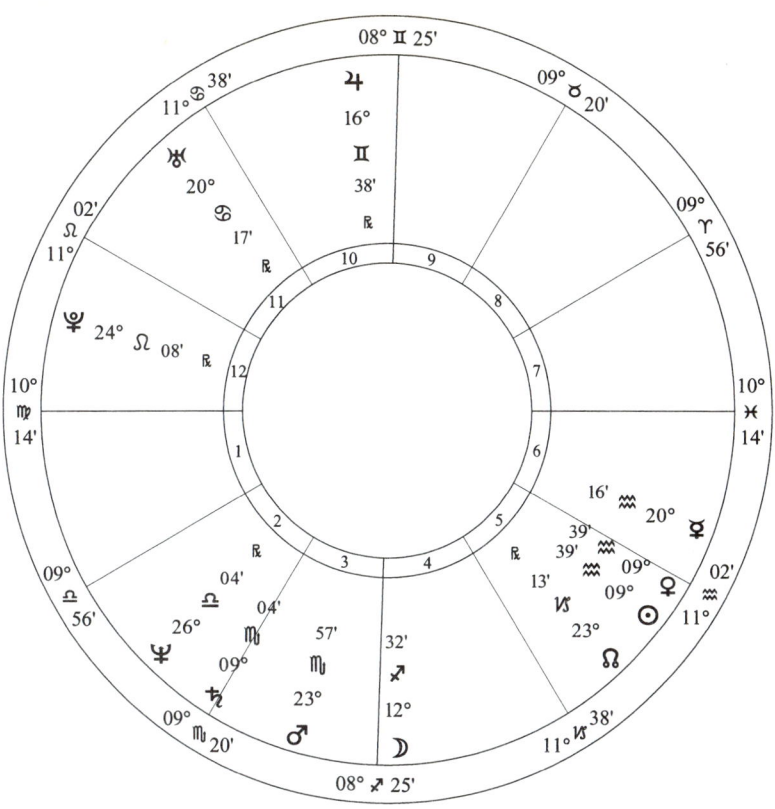

Oprah Winfrey
January 29, 1954, 7:50 PM CST
Kosciusko, MS, 33N03'27 89W35'15

hobble one's ability to love and to make a happy marriage, but the presence of Venus in this aspect also adds a touch of sweetness and charm to the mix. The close conjunction of the Sun and Venus typically marks someone who is, for better or worse, always lovable—indicating that, though the burdens represented by Saturn may be very real and debilitating, the subject will be able to find people to help her bear them.

The second aspect of note is the opposition of Winfrey's Moon in Sagittarius with Jupiter. What makes this aspect so crucial is the fact that it is close to the angle of the MC and IC, indicating that the qualities represented by these two planets will be highly visible to the public. The prominence of the Moon provides for a high degree of empathy and emotional sensitivity. Since the Moon is in Sagittarius, it also brings a light-hearted, engaging curiosity to the fore. The opposition to Jupiter might be viewed as a bad aspect, but here it will probably seem more like a blessing. Jupiter expands the sympathetic energy of the Moon without increasing the emotional vulnerability that so often makes a prominent Moon problematic. With Jupiter placed in the 10th House so close to the MC, it would be hard not to predict great success or at least extraordinary ambitions. This is an aspect that promises great popularity and a high public profile.

The last strong aspect system in this chart is hardly the least. It is a T-square featuring Pluto and Mercury on the wings and Mars in Scorpio at the center. Taken by itself, this system gives us an extremely serious, deep, and argumentative personality, and a mind that is always suspicious of simple answers or surface appearances. It is a rather morose and introspective aspect system, contrasting sharply with the jolly openness of Winfrey's Moon to Jupiter opposition. Fortunately both Mercury and Mars make very positive aspects outside this T-square. Mercury trines Jupiter, placing it in sympathy with Winfrey's Sagittarius Moon and countering much of the fixity and closed-mindedness otherwise indicted by the T-square. Mars trines Uranus, again indicating an openness to new ideas that contrasts with the T-square, and taking the natural curiosity and intellectual energy reflected by her Sagittarius Moon and Aquarian Sun up a couple of notches. Still, the emotional depth and introspection of this T-square cannot be discounted. There will always be a tendency to dwell on the negative and hold on to feelings of anger and guilt.

THE LIFE

It is difficult to imagine a childhood more fraught with hardship and sadness than that of Oprah Winfrey. Her father left her mother before she was born, and, when Oprah was only four, her mother also abandoned her. Winfrey spent her earliest years with her grandmother in Mississippi. It was only after her grandmother became too ill to care for her that Oprah joined her mother, who was working in Milwaukee. There the six-year-old Winfrey found herself competing with another, younger daughter for her mother's affection, and generally losing. In 1962, Winfrey's mother became pregnant again and she sent Oprah to live with her father, who had moved to Tennessee and remarried. In the household of this father, who was a stranger to her, Winfrey was met with a surprising amount of affection and a structured lifestyle that she enjoyed. Then, in the summer of 1962, Winfrey was taken back to Milwaukee to visit her mother, who was now struggling to support and care for two children, one of them an infant. At this point Winfrey made a fateful decision. She decided to stay with her mother in order to help her and, perhaps, earn her affection. **Saturn was squaring her natal Saturn and conjuncting her Sun.** Winfrey felt the call to be responsible and useful to the people she loved, but it would turn out to be an unfortunate decision.

In 1963, Uranus began a long transit of Winfrey's Ascendant. Sometime during that year, she was left alone with an older cousin who sexually abused her. Winfrey was traumatized. Two years later, as Uranus completed its crossing of her Ascendant and **Saturn contacted her Descendant,** she was molested again by another man, and this time the abuse became continual. Winfrey apparently told no one about the abuse until much later in her life. Her reaction was typical. She understood that she was a victim, but she also felt somehow complicit in the acts that were being carried out on her body, and burdened by shame and guilt.

Also in 1965, as Saturn crossed her Descendant, Winfrey had a much more typical experience for this transit. She had always been a good student. She had learned to read even before she was in kindergarten and continued to love books, even though her mother frequently chided her for being such a bookworm. One of her teachers took note of this and had Winfrey transferred to an all-white school. Winfrey performed well at her new school and made many friends, though her status as an outsider was always evident. Finally, however, the terrible situation she was enduring at home began to influence her behavior. By 1968, she was skipping class, lying, stealing, and running with boys. Winfrey's mother didn't know what to do with this new, rebellious Oprah. She considered putting her in a reform school, but decided to send her back to Nashville and her father instead. Oprah arrived at her father's house with a grave secret. She was pregnant. Once again her father and stepmother proved amazingly supportive. The baby was born prematurely and died two days later.

Oprah Winfrey entered the Nashville school system with a resumé in life experiences that few of her fellow students could equal or would envy. Now, with a stable and loving home behind her, Winfrey seemed determined to make the most of those experiences and her natural gifts. **In 1970, the same year that Saturn opposed her natal Saturn and squared her Sun**, Winfrey won a speech contest and was given a scholarship that would allow her to attend college. The next year she began classes at Tennessee State College and, after winning a local beauty contest, got a part-time job reading the news on a Nashville radio station. A year later, as **Saturn crossed her Midheaven**, Winfrey won the Miss Black Nashville and the Miss Black Tennessee beauty pageants. These accomplishments brought her to the attention of Nashville's CBS television affiliate. They offered Winfrey a job as their news anchor. At first, Oprah turned the offer down. Her dream was to finish college and to have a career as an actress. But the television people kept asking and finally one of Winfrey's teachers told her to forget about college and take the job. Oprah Winfrey followed his advice.

Not surprisingly, considering her subsequent career, Winfrey was a great success in Nashville and, as is the way of these things, her success in her father's hometown soon brought an offer from a larger market. **In August 1976, just as Saturn opposed her natal Saturn and squared her Sun**, Winfrey made her debut as a newscaster on a Baltimore TV station. This time, however, Oprah was not a hit. In Nashville, her warm, folksy style had been seen as engaging. In Baltimore, it was viewed as unprofessional. Winfrey was quickly removed from the news anchor position and given an early morning show. Moreover, the management of the station seemed intent on changing Winfrey's look as well as her broadcasting style. Suddenly this erstwhile golden girl was cast back to the worst days of her childhood, and she reacted by overeating and gaining weight.

Fortunately, Winfrey's next Saturn transit brought a new opportunity to display her talent. In 1978, **the same year that Saturn transited her Ascendant**, Winfrey was given a chance to do a television talk show. She immediately understood that she had finally found a medium that would allow both her curiosity and her humanity to shine forth. The show proved highly successful in the Baltimore market and, after a while, Winfrey began to scout around for opportunities to bring her gifts before a larger audience. As it turned out, Winfrey had to wait until **Saturn reached its natal place in 1984** to make the next step up in her career. **In September of that year, three months after Saturn made its last contact with her natal Saturn**, Oprah Winfrey debuted as the new host of *Chicago AM*.

Winfrey proved so popular and her new show so successful that the next year its name was changed to the *Oprah Winfrey Show*. This was only the beginning of Winfrey's good luck. Quincy Jones saw her on the talk show and decided she would be perfect to play a part in a movie he was producing. The movie was based on *The Color Purple*, a novel by African-American writer Alice Walker. Winfrey, who had never retired her early ambitions to be an actress, jumped at the chance and nailed the role. Her performance earned her a nomination for an Academy Award. The problem was that in order to play the character, Winfrey had to be overweight; long after her performance and its glorious reception was over, the excess weight remained.

The year after her Oscar nomination saw continued success for Winfrey. Using the money she got from her syndication deal, she started her own production company called Harpo. That year she also began her long-standing relationship with Stedman Graham and won her first daytime Emmy award. But her weight was still very much on her mind. In December 1987, she began a radical liquid diet that promised quick results and it seemed to work. Within a year, she was able to proclaim on her show that she had lost over twenty-five pounds and was down to a size ten. A year later, however, the diet was over and she quickly gained back her lost twenty-five pounds. A year after that, she gained another twenty-five. Now over two hundred pounds and still gaining weight, Winfrey had reached a personal low, even as her professional life continued its phenomenal rise.

In February 1992, Saturn squared Winfrey's natal Saturn and aligned with her Sun. Around this time, Winfrey began work on an autobiography, an exercise that caused her to ruminate on the connection between the sexual abuse she suffered as a child and her weight problems. By this time her weight was up to 237 pounds. The autobiography was never published. Apparently, Winfrey came to the conclusion that she was not yet ready for an overall assessment of her life's story. Also in 1992, while visiting a health spa, Winfrey met a young fitness guru named Bob Greene, who advocated a challenging and highly disciplined exercise routine in order to lose weight. One year later, Green was hired as her personal trainer. **By the time Saturn reached her Descendant in 1994**, Winfrey was running fifty miles a week and losing weight at a remarkable rate. Fitness became the new watchword on her talk show as she sought to get America moving.

Also in 1994, Winfrey hired a new producer for her show and became more personally involved in the show's production. She had grown tired of the typical talk show format of bringing on ordinary people with shocking problems and listening to them either cry and moan about their bad luck or rage against the system. Winfrey wanted her show to be more uplifting. She wanted it to help people take charge of their lives and take responsibility for their choices (very much the values one would expect from someone with a strong Sun square Saturn aspect). After 1994, *The Oprah Winfrey Show* moved from being just another TV talk show toward becoming a moral and intellectual force in American culture.

Meanwhile, Winfrey's personal battle with her weight continued. Though she did not suffer the terrible relapse into overeating that had followed the liquid diet, her enthusiasm for Greene's demanding exercise regimen began to waiver. Even in 1994, Greene had complained that Winfrey was finding excuses such as her birthday or an office party to skip her daily run. In 2001, **as Saturn neared her Midheaven**, Winfrey began suffering from heart palpitations and high blood pressure. Concerned about her health, Oprah began a new exercise routine, this time emphasizing weight training. Again she lost weight, but her main concern now was maintaining a healthy body. Her efforts apparently paid off. By **April 2006, when Saturn squared her natal Saturn and opposed her Sun,** Winfrey was able to tell *Shape* magazine that, even though it was hard work and she was denied many foods that she loved, she had finally found an exercise and eating routine that she could maintain over the long haul (Robbins, 2006).

SATURN AT WORK

Considering the many important subjects that Oprah Winfrey has dealt with on her show, the magnitude of her success, and her far-reaching influence, it might seem trivial to concentrate on her weight problems. What these excess pounds have come to represent, however, is the rise and fall of Winfrey's self-image. They are, in a manner of speaking, lingering evidence of the anger, the guilt, and the hunger for love that she had been made to feel during her childhood, and that she carried with her even into her amazingly fortunate and successful adulthood.

Aside from her weight issues, the list of Winfrey's adult Saturn transits reads like a step-by-step guide to success. At each juncture, Winfrey made the right decision, the decision not to give into the traumas she suffered in the past and her self-criticism, and to let her natural talent and charm shine. Even when she was demoted in Baltimore, Winfrey did not give up. She did the best she could do with the opportunity she had, and eventually found the role that best suited her ability. It was only with her excess weight that Winfrey revealed the price at which her wisdom and admirable self-discipline had been gained.

Winfrey's first major effort to gain control over her weight began outside her Saturn transits and, predictably, it not only failed, it made her situation worse. It was only after a period of self-examination undertaken as Saturn squared its natal position, when she came to understand the relationship between her overeating and her childhood trauma, that Winfrey was truly prepared to change her way of living. It is interesting that when Saturn made its last exact connection with Winfrey's Descendant, in January 1995, she was running a marathon in Washington, D.C., proving to the world that she had gained control over her body.

Of course, extraordinary efforts are rarely sustained and in the years after she completed the marathon, Winfrey's commitment to running wavered. Then Saturn came visiting again in 2001, and her excess pounds were not just a matter of vanity; they also represented a threat to her health. It was at this point that Winfrey seemed to gain a more perfect mastery of her personal demons and her physical fitness. This mastery continues, although the demons, represented in her horoscope by the Pluto, Mars, Mercury T-square, are not likely to ever leave her.

SOURCES

Sarah Robbins. "Oprah Winfrey: Issues and Answers? She Gives Voice to Both," *People Weekly* (March 15, 1999): 143.

Katherine Krohn, *Oprah Winfrey* (Minneapolis, MN: Lerner Publications, 2005).

Sarah Robbins, "A Look Back With Oprah," *Shape* 25 (April 8, 2006): 32.

Jennifer Harris and Elwood Watson, editors, *The Oprah Phenomenon* (Lexington, KY: University Press of Kentucky, 2007).

3

THOMAS MERTON

Catholic monk noted for his writings on the power of religious devotion and the ills of modern civilization

THE CHOICE

In February 1937, a Columbia University student named Thomas Merton made the most momentous decision of his life. It was in a bookstore in Manhattan. Searching for something to read during a train trip, he happened on *The Spirit of Medieval Philosophy*, by Etienne Gilson. The book had little to do with Merton's studies in literature or his life up until this point, but he bought it anyway. For some time, this intellectually gifted and highly cultured young man had been developing a keen curiosity about religion. He had recently begun attending services at a Protestant church, and he had fond memories of exploring old cathedrals in France, where he had spent his boyhood. To Merton, the book must have seemed like an innocuous way of satisfying his voracious intellectual curiosity and killing a few dull hours. We must add that at the time he purchased and read this book, **Saturn was crossing his Ascendant and squaring his natal Saturn.**

Thomas Merton was hardly a typical student. He was a citizen of the world, born in France to an American mother and a New Zealander father, and he had already lived in three different countries by the time he was seven. He was fluent in several languages, had traveled throughout Europe, and had spent a year as a student at Cambridge University. His interests were wide-ranging and highly cultivated. At Cambridge, he had begun a course of study that would have launched him into the diplomatic corps. At Columbia, he switched his attention to literature. He was due to receive his BA the next year.

Upon opening *The Spirit of Medieval Philosophy*, Merton's first inclination was to toss it out the window of the train. It was introduced with a statement that the book had been approved by the censors of the Catholic Church. For a youngster like Merton, who had been brought up in a world in which the free expression of ideas was taken for granted, the very notion that an author could be forced to submit his work for censorship was nauseating. And yet, the young scholar decided to choke back his disgust and read on. Very soon, he found himself engrossed in Etienne Gilson's description of the philosophical underpinnings of the medieval Catholic Church.

Merton later wrote that what he found in *The Spirit of Medieval Philosophy* was an alluring explanation of the spiritual structure of the Catholic faith, a structure that to Merton's mind was every bit as strong, elegant, and awe-inspiring as any of the great cathedrals he had visited in Europe. At the time Merton read the book, he had never heard a Catholic mass. He was curious about religion and was perhaps beginning to become a spiritual seeker, but his options were still wide open. Reading Gilson's book gave the eager student a sense of direction and served as the starting point for his long love affair with the doctrine and the faith of the Catholic Church.

During the weeks and months that followed, **as transiting Saturn continued to move over his Ascendant and into his 1st House**, the direction Merton had found in *The Spirit of Medieval Philosophy* was reinforced by other factors. A friend introduced him to a book by Aldous Huxley titled *Ends and Means* which, though written from a largely non-Christian point of view, presented Merton with an erudite defense of pacifism, mysticism, and ascetic living. Another friend introduced Merton to a traveling Hindu monk who both impressed the young man with his quiet, nonjudgmental grace, and surprised him

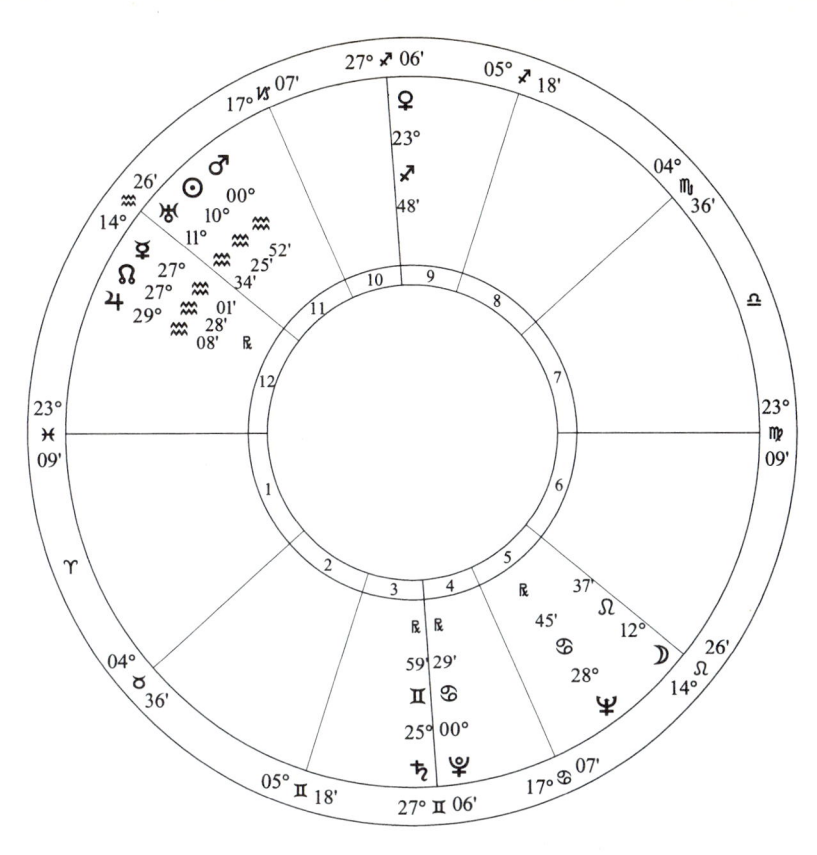

Thomas Merton

January 31, 1915, 9:00 AM GMT

Paris, France, 42N37 02E26

by telling the young seeker that he should read Christian writers like St. Augustine. Finally, there was Merton's encounter with the work of the British poet and artist, William Blake. Blake was the subject of Merton's thesis and he quickly developed a deep admiration of that eighteenth-century genius' defiant spirituality. Blake would serve as an example for Merton of a mystic thriving in an era of rampant materialism. But, in the end, all these influences brought Merton back to Gilson's book and the Catholic Church. Four years after his momentous reading of *The Spirit of Medieval Philosophy,* as mystical Neptune crept near his Descendant, Thomas Merton was baptized into the Catholic Church.

THE HOROSCOPE

Merton's natal horoscope is full of dramatic aspects. First of all, we have the opposition between Venus in Sagittarius at the Midheaven and Saturn on the IC. The Saturn to Venus opposition indicates difficulty in expressing and responding to affection, a quality supported by the absence of water sign placements in the horoscope. It describes a distaste for the trappings of romance and an emotional nature that often seems distant, judgmental, and even selfish. It is a poor aspect for a lover, but a rather positive one for a man expecting to become celibate.

Then we have the opposition between Mars in Aquarius and Neptune. This is a rather slippery aspect. It certainly helps explain Merton's interest in the mystical, but it also describes a tendency to ignore boundaries and to act in a duplicitous and insincere manner. In the context of these two strong aspects, the equally strong combination of a conjunction between his Aquarian Sun with Uranus in the 11th House and an opposition between the Moon and Uranus (along with the Sun), while showing great originality and creative zeal, is troubling. Great originality is not a good quality in a self-centered personality intent on slipping by the rules.

Fortunately, there are other, much more hopeful aspects in Merton's chart. His Aquarius Mercury conjuncts Jupiter in his 12th House and these two planets are both trined by Saturn and Pluto at the bottom of the chart and sextiled by Venus at the top. His Mercury to Jupiter conjunction thus taps into the energy of the angular Venus to Saturn opposition, adding much optimism, artistry, and openness to this otherwise emotionally restrictive aspect. This arrangement definitely marks Merton as a potential writer, although the placement of Mercury and Jupiter in the 12th House foretells some sort of duress affecting his writing; something like imprisonment. Merton was, of course, a brilliant writer, even though he did most of his writing under a vow of silence, inside a shed (the only place he could find the necessary privacy) on the grounds of the monastery. Much of his work, in particular his long autobiography, featured himself and his intellectual odyssey as the central theme. By turning this bold and incisive mind on himself and his own actions, Merton was able to transform the dissolute qualities of his Mars to Neptune opposition into mysticism and a desire to surrender his will to a higher power. He was able to resolve the emotional restriction represented by his Venus to Saturn opposition by choosing a life of celibacy. And he was able to bring out the best of his Sun to Uranus conjunction by giving full flight to its idealism. He was not going to waste his time rebelling against authority. He rebelled against the world.

THE LIFE

For Merton, encounters with transiting Saturn would always mean double trouble because of the conjunction between his natal Saturn and his IC. Therefore, it is not surprising that his first two Saturn passages coincided with very dramatic events. **When he was seven years old and Saturn crossed his Descendant and squared his natal Saturn**, his mother was diagnosed with stomach cancer and died. Merton's mother had been a strong and independent woman who had shocked her well-to-do American family by marrying a foreign-born painter and living in France. Losing her was a tremendous blow to her first-born son. Then, **when transiting Saturn reached Merton's Midheaven and opposed his natal Saturn**, another horrifying blow was struck. Merton's father was diagnosed with a brain tumor. Soon afterward he was placed in a hospital where, within a year, he died. Owen Merton had never gained much success as a painter but Thomas had great respect for him. He could have been the anchor that the youthful Merton needed so badly, with all the uncertain aspects in his horoscope.

One of Owen Merton's friends took over as guardian of the youngster and he arranged for Merton to complete his education at Cambridge University. Here Merton had ample opportunity to test many of the worst qualities of his problematic Neptune and Uranus aspects. Though his own account of these adventures in his autobiography, *The Seven Storey Mountain*, was highly censored by the Church, it is clear that the youthful Merton ran with a wild crowd while at Cambridge. He drank, he caroused, and he was, at least to some degree, sexually promiscuous. There were rumors of one, maybe two, illegitimate children fathered by Merton during this period. Merton's guardian, a respected London doctor, was thoroughly disappointed and offered no objection when the misguided youngster decided to quit Cambridge and resume his studies in New York. Thomas Merton, the monk, recalled this time in his life with disgust. To him it would remain the slimy bottom of the worldly barrel from which he would one day emerge, transcendent.

Merton's religious conversion came at a particularly ominous point in history. The threat of Nazi Germany was rising in Europe and, having traveled through Germany in the early 1930s, Merton was keenly aware of the nature of this threat. He understood that war was nearing and this knowledge made him even more determined to escape the world. Soon after he became a Catholic, Merton made the decision to become a monk. After being rejected by the Franciscans (when Saturn squared his Sun), he was finally accepted into the Trappist order and joined Gethsemani, a monastery in Kentucky.

In many ways, Merton was not cut out to be a monk. His Aquarian Sun and Leo Moon were not much given to humility. Though he embraced the physical hardships of a novice's life, he often balked at the psychological discipline. He needed privacy, he needed some degree of personal autonomy, and he needed an outlet for his expansive and highly creative mind. Fortunately, the head of Gethsemani Monastery understood the potential of Merton's remarkable mind and made allowances for him. Very soon, the new Trappist monk was granted special permission to publish his work.

Merton began with a book of poetry, which was published **when Saturn crossed his IC**. Then, when transiting Uranus arrived at his IC, he published the work that would make him famous, *The Seven Storey Mountain.* In this long, soul-searching book, Merton gave an account of his early years and his conversion to the Catholic faith. To everyone's surprise, it became a bestseller and established Merton as a prominent spokesman, not only for the Church, but for spirituality in general.

With the Moon in Leo, we can't say that Merton suffered because of his notoriety. Still, for a man who had come to the Catholic Church seeking an escape from the world, it was a bit awkward. He continued to publish both poetry and prose. Meanwhile, his rejection of materialism and support of pacifism made the literary monk a darling of the counterculture during the 1960s. By the time he died in 1968, Merton was probably one of the most widely read and sought-after religious hermits of all time.

When we consider Thomas Merton, it is hard not to wonder how a mind so free and open could submit itself to the strictures of Catholic doctrine, and how a writer of such remarkable talent could allow his work to be censored by narrow-minded bishops. But the most outstanding aspect of Merton's horoscope gives a definite answer to this question. Saturn and Pluto bracket his IC in a conjunction. At first glance, this is a very negative aspect. Even mitigated by the influence of the trine these two planets make to Jupiter, this dual placement at the base of the horoscope forecasts much hardship and pain. Certainly the fifteen-year-old, newly orphaned Merton would have attested to this prediction. And yet, this is not what is important about the aspect.

What is important about this aspect is what it reveals on a more psychological level. Here, this dire conjunction represents a strong, life-altering need for hard, clearly defined structure (Saturn), and a deep, gut-level contact with a great overwhelming power (Pluto). To live without this structure or this power, as Merton had done at Cambridge, was more than just a waste of time. It was an exercise in emptiness and futility. What Merton found in his reading of *The Spirit of Medieval Philosophy* was a system, a worldview, in which these two concepts were beautifully intertwined. He found an awareness of God as love and as mercy that obliterated all his intellectual doubt and, growing out of this awesome faith, an intricate web of doctrine, of rules and wisdom, that could give form and structure to an otherwise formless life. No, Merton would never be the perfect monk. He complained and rebelled and occasionally made a nuisance of himself. But his faith in the power and the discipline of his Church never wavered.

The combination of Pluto and Saturn also seems to have played a major role in Merton's untimely end. In 1968, while traveling in the Himalayas on his way to a religious conference in Thailand, Merton had his first encounter with Tibetan Buddhism. He was thrilled at the possibilities this new approach to spirituality offered and was preparing to remain in the East for a year in order to study it further. But on December 10, 1968, Merton stepped out of the shower soaking wet and accidentally touched a badly wired electric fan. He was instantaneously electrocuted to death. At this time, transiting Pluto was crossing his Descendant, indicating a transforming experience, but it was also square to his natal Saturn. The ill fortune symbolized by the joining of these two fateful planets once again asserted itself into Merton's destiny.

SATURN AT WORK

Merton's case presents us with an excellent example of how the little things, decisions and influences that seem insignificant can change the course of a person's life. If we did not have his detailed account of the years prior to his conversion, the importance of that 1937 train ride might be totally missed. We would wonder why Saturn seemed so quiet when Merton finally made his commitment to the Church four years later. This is why it is necessary to be alert to what is happening at all levels of our consciousness during important Saturn aspects. It is always a time when the little things can make a big difference.

At the opposite end of the scale, we have the events that coincided with Merton's two earlier Saturn passages when he lost first his mother and then his father. The tragedy of these events cannot be overstated. Few people are challenged so immensely by Saturn at such a tender age. Yet, as terrible as they were, these events had no more influence on the course of Merton's life than did his reading of *The Spirit of Medieval Philosophy*.

Merton's next big Saturn transit came when he published his first book of poetry. Here he was able to join his two vocations, to be both a monk and a writer. The fact that publication of *The Seven Storey Mountain* did not fit into this pattern should not be surprising. Merton did not set out to become a famous author. He didn't even set out to be a profitable one. He was simply seeking, with both Neptune and the Moon strongly aspected in the 5th House, a means of expressing his enormous creative energy. The fact that he became famous along the way was largely superfluous and often a severe irritation.

After Merton entered the monastery, it was conflicts between his creative and naturally rebellious nature and the strictures of the Catholic Church that dominated his Saturn crossings. His vacillating relationship with the abbot of Gethsemani and the censors of the Church were a constant source of challenge. One passage that stands out came **in 1966 when Saturn crossed Merton's Ascendant once more and squared his natal Saturn**. At this time, Merton fell in love with a nurse almost half his age. Though not fully consummated, the relationship shook Merton's conception of himself as a monk and a solitary. For months Merton struggled with his infatuation with this young woman, until finally he was forced to make a choice and he chose to abide by his vows and withdraw from the relationship.

This would turn out to be the last major Saturn passage of Merton's life. Only two years later he would be dead. In many ways, Merton's decision to forego his sexual longings and maintain his position as the Catholic Church's most famous monk was just as significant to the fulfillment of his destiny as was his reading of Gilson's book. It allowed his reputation as one of the greatest Catholic poets and intellectuals to reverberate throughout the world, undiluted by scandal or betrayal.

Many years later, when his private journals were published (according to arrangements Merton had made shortly before his death), this interruption of his celibacy only functioned to make Gethsemani's resident genius more human, and further cement his position as one of the most important and alluring Christian thinkers of the twentieth century.

SOURCES

Michael W. Higgins, *Heretic Blood: The Spiritual Geography of Thomas Merton* (New York: Stoddart Publishing Co. Ltd., 1998).

Thomas Merton, *The Seven Storey Mountain* (San Diego: Harcourt, Brace, 1999), c. 1948.

4

BRUCE LEE

American-born actor and martial arts master who brought Chinese martial arts and Taoist philosophy to American movies

THE CHOICE

In early 1966, a young martial arts instructor who went by the Americanized name of Bruce Lee got an offer he could have easily refused, even though it was the kind of offer that many people dream of. He was asked to play a secondary role in an upcoming television series. The series was a television version of a radio show called *The Green Hornet*. Patterned after the campy hit series *Batman*, it featured a masked crime fighter and his trusty Oriental sidekick. Lee was to play the trusty sidekick.

The problem was that Bruce Lee was not the sidekick type. He was born, after all, with the Sun on his Ascendant, an almost certain indicator of a star mentality. Though he had come to the United States with virtually nothing, sent there by his mother both to preserve his United States citizenship (he had been born in San Francisco) and to escape pressure from the police after he injured another boy in a fight, Bruce Lee had never lacked confidence. He began giving martial arts lessons even while he was working in the restaurant of a family friend and completing his last year of high school. His own instruction in this art had come from impeccable sources: an elderly master, Yip Man, who represented the last link in a chain of kung fu masters stretching back centuries to the Shaolin monks of China. Lee had started studying kung fu with Yip Man in his early teens and by the time **Saturn crossed his Ascendant near his sixteenth birthday**, it had become the passion of his life.

Not that his life was without other diversions. Lee's father was a veteran actor, both on the stage and in movies in Hong Kong, where Bruce was raised. Through him, Lee had begun a career in motion pictures when he was still an infant. By the time he reached his teens, Lee had worked in several pictures, including one where he played a street-fighting juvenile delinquent. This last role was not too much of a stretch for the youngster. Hong Kong was a tough town. It was also a colonial town with a history of the Chinese majority suffering under the domination of other nations, most recently the British. Boys from the Chinese high school that Lee attended often engaged in turf wars with boys from the British high school. It was one of these fights that earned Lee the unwelcome attention of Hong Kong's police force.

As a result of these experiences, Lee arrived in California with a deep and substantially wounded sense of pride concerning his Chinese heritage. Studies in philosophy at the University of Washington had tempered the combative edge of his wounded pride, and the young kung fu master decided to make it his task to enlighten the West as to the beauty and value of Chinese culture through the vehicle of martial arts. With one student at a time, first in San Francisco, then during his college years in Seattle, and finally in his studio in Oakland, Lee was making converts to both the art of kung fu and the Taoist philosophy. Lee augmented his understanding of this ancient school of thought with the study of Western philosophers. He also paid close attention to the artistry of Western fighters, particularly Muhammad Ali. Other practitioners of kung fu objected to Lee's attempt to share this knowledge with non-Orientals, but Lee remained adamant. Legend has it that he even defeated an objecting kung fu master in individual combat to win the right to teach occidentals.

So the man who was approached to play the Green Hornet's high-kicking assistant, Kato, was not the typical Hollywood wannabe. He was a man with principles, a man with a deep sense of mission. The thought of playing an Oriental version of Tonto (The original *Green Hornet* scripts had been written by the same man who had developed *The Lone Ranger*) filled him with disgust. It was an insult, both to his pride in his Chinese ancestry and to the prestige of the martial art which he practiced and taught. Still, there were other concerns. Two years earlier, Lee had married a white American girl he had met at the University of Washington. The following year they'd had their first child, a boy named Brandon, and Lee's own father had died. More to the point, **Saturn was crossing Lee's IC** just as he was being asked to take the part of Kato. With this Saturn passage, the burden of his new responsibility as a parent and as the head of a household began to weigh on Lee. More importantly, perhaps, Lee realized that the role as Kato would give him an opportunity, albeit a limited one, to bring his ideas and his skills to the attention of a mass audience. With some trepidation and silent apologies to his esteemed Chinese ancestors, Lee took the job.

THE HOROSCOPE

The placement of his Sagittarian Sun so near the ascending degree is certainly the most striking part of Bruce Lee's horoscope. The fact that the Sun is not afflicted and receives a close trine from Pluto seems auspicious. Still, behind this bright and sunny exterior, with its Sagittarian expansiveness and love of fun, there are forces of a much darker and potentially violent nature. Lee has Venus conjunct Mars in Scorpio square to his Pluto and opposed to his Jupiter and Saturn. This powerful T-square also includes the Moon, which is seven degrees separated from his nearly exact square of Mars and Pluto but much closer in its opposition aspect to Jupiter and Saturn. Even his Mercury, also in Scorpio, is within a six-degree orb of an opposition to Saturn. In total, the systems involve the Moon and six planets, making it the dominant feature of the horoscope.

The incredible focus, drive, and potential for violence indicated by the central aspect of this system can certainly be taken as the outstanding theme of Lee's life. In 1964, at a martial arts conference in California, Lee demonstrated a special technique he had developed called the "one-inch punch." He would strike a blow into a man's chest with his hand, starting only one inch from its target. Without the benefit of momentum the power of the blow depended solely on Lee's ability to instantaneously concentrate all the strength of his body into one small motion. In the demonstration, the target, a sturdy karate master, was knocked off his feet by the force of Lee's blow. This was an apt demonstration of both Lee's martial arts skill and the way in which a strong Mars to Pluto square can be used to focus both the mind and the body.

Scorpio is the predominant sign in Lee's T-square. The Moon, Venus, Mars, and Mercury are all in this sign, and the central arm of the T-square is Pluto, which, in the Koch system of houses, is late in his 8th House (Scorpio's house). The contrast between the weighty emotionalism of Scorpio, with its stubborn irrationality and its dark and mysterious ways, and the fiery openness of Sagittarius is striking. Obviously Lee's Sagittarius Sun and Ascendant provided a front, a public face that was quite different from the psychological engine that powered his remarkable personality. On one level he was the perfect Sagittarian, quick-witted, charming, and easy-going. He had a Sagittarian love of both philosophical speculation and stale jokes, and his athleticism had its ultimate source in this Fire sign's love of movement and physical exertion. The deep emotionality of Scorpio, with its emphasis on obsession, rage, sex, and power became the subterranean dynamo of his personality, one he was able to express fully and openly only in the characters he played in the movies.

THE LIFE

Lee's role in the *The Green Hornet* proved to be everything Lee had dreaded. He was given few lines and no opportunity to develop Kato into more than a cardboard cutout of the mysterious Oriental. The only saving grace was the fact that Lee was allowed to choreograph all his fight scenes in such a way as to display all the grace and awesome power of his art. His athletic leaps and remarkable kicks attracted some attention, but not enough to save the show from cancellation after one season.

Bruce Lee

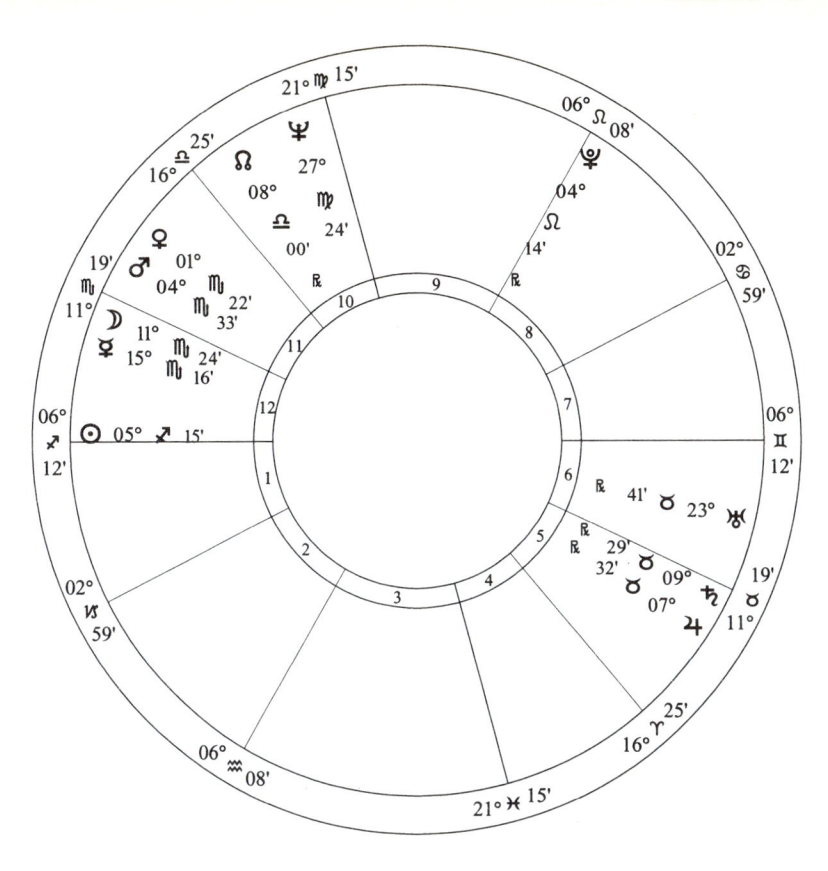

November 27, 1940, 7:12 AM PST

San Francisco, CA, 37N46 122W25

After the cancellation of *The Green Hornet,* Lee worked as a supporting player in TV and movies, but the small taste of Hollywood success that he had enjoyed playing Kato had left him with higher ambitions. Lee was convinced that he could become a leading man in films. The problem was that the movie-making establishment felt that American audiences would not pay to see a movie with an Asian star. Lee, with the aid of some sympathetic Hollywood professionals, even went so far as to develop a script for a TV show featuring a Shaolin priest and kung fu master wandering through the American Old West. They found producers who loved the idea enough to offer the role to an American actor named David Carradine. The TV show later aired under the title *Kung Fu.* Pluto was making a long transit of Lee's Midheaven during this period, indicating frustration and transformation with regard to career goals.

In 1970, when Saturn reached its first conjunction with Lee's **natal Saturn**, he encountered a new obstacle. During one of his regular training routines, a regime that normally went on for at least two hours a day, he injured his back. The injury proved to be so serious that one doctor advised him to give up martial arts altogether. Saturn, it appears, had called for a time out and, at least for a while, Lee listened. He spent several months letting his body heal itself. He relied on the resiliency of the Scorpio level of his personality to accomplish a recovery that seemed to prove the nay-saying doctors wrong. During this period, he worked on the philosophical side of his martial arts training. He completed a book summing up his ideas about Taoism and his style of kung fu.

By the later part of 1970, Lee had finally come to the conclusion that the American entertainment establishment would never accept a Chinese leading man. He decided it was time to move on and he prepared to relocate his family to Hong Kong. To his surprise, when he arrived in his hometown he was greeted as a major celebrity. *The Green Hornet* had been playing in Asian markets for several years under the title *The Kato Show,* and it had become wildly popular. The failed TV show that had once appeared to be a dead end and a dubious decision had made Lee a famous man.

Hong Kong moviemakers were anxious to sign Lee to star in action films. The movies were low budget and quickly made. The first, *The Big Boss* (called *Fists of Fury* when it was released to the U.S. market) premiered in October 1971, just as **Saturn crossed Lee's Descendant (and opposed his natal Sun) for the first time**. **When Saturn made its final pass across Lee's Descendant in May of 1972**, he had completed another film and was working on a third.

All of Bruce Lee's Hong Kong films were enormously successful with Asian audiences. They were also popular in the United States. In fact, these hastily made action movies were soon outgrossing major motion pictures like *The Godfather*. It finally began to dawn on the major film studios in the United States that an Oriental leading man could draw an American audience. In 1972, Warner Brothers agreed to join Lee's own production company in making a film that would be called *Enter the Dragon*. Just two years after he had given up hope of achieving his ambition of becoming the male lead in an American-made action movie, Lee was on his way to becoming a Hollywood star.

More importantly, Lee had gained the most grandiose stage imaginable from which to demonstrate his singular approach to both Taoist philosophy and the martial art called kung fu. Soon the influence of Lee's expression of these age-old disciplines would be felt across America, even across the world. At the same time, Lee engendered a new awareness of and respect for the Chinese culture that he had seen denigrated while growing up in Hong Kong. Bruce Lee's fame not only put a martial arts studio in virtually every town in the United States, it also brought about a grassroots détente between the ancient East and the raw, unruly West.

Unfortunately, Lee would not live to see *Enter the Dragon* released. In May 1973, while putting the final touches on the film, Lee collapsed. Doctors in Hong Kong detected a swelling of his brain. Lee recovered swiftly but he was concerned enough to consult a doctor in the United States. His U.S. physician found nothing wrong and Lee quickly returned to work. Then on July 20, in Hong Kong, Lee developed a sudden headache. An actress who was with him at the time gave him a medication that had been prescribed for her. Lee stretched out on her bed to take a nap and never woke up.

At the time of his death, his secondary progressed Sun was trine to his natal Saturn. The trine (120-degree) aspect is generally considered a good aspect, but any time the Sun, the symbol of vitality and ego, meets Saturn, the symbol of limitation and endings, there is cause for concern.

At the same time, transiting Neptune was moving back and forth across Lee's Ascendant and natal Sun. This aspect would indicate deception, errors in judgment, and a general blurring of boundaries. The relevance of shifty Neptune to Lee's sudden death, or at least the period immediately afterward, is unmistakable. The coroner's report, which blamed a rare reaction to the medication Lee took, satisfied no one and a variety of conspiracy theories began to crop up. Some held that Lee was assassinated by the Hong Kong criminal syndicate. Others claimed that other martial artists who abhorred the way Lee had revealed their secrets to the West had killed him through mysterious means. In typical Neptunian fashion, few of the theories that arose after Lee's tragic death could be either proved or disproved. They persist even today, as does the legend of this charismatic man.

SATURN AT WORK

Here we see an example of how good decisions made during a Saturn passage can lead to unexpected and unforeseen benefits. Bruce Lee made the decision to take the role of Kato in *The Green Hornet* because he was responding to Saturn's call to behave responsibly and place the financial security of his family ahead of his own ego. For a time, this decision seemed to have accomplished nothing else. It was only five years later, when he learned that *The Kato Show* had made him a star in Asian markets, that the true benefits of Lee's decision became evident. The fame he achieved in Hong Kong as Kato laid the groundwork for the incredible advances his career would make when Saturn reached his Descendant.

The 1970 return of Saturn to its natal place brought Lee to another crucial turning point that may have had far-reaching influence. In its classic form, one's first Saturn return is the time when we are forced to grow up and take on the full responsibilities of adulthood. It is also the Saturn transit that shows us the limitations of our bodies as we begin to display the first signs of aging. Bruce Lee got a big dose of this interpretation when he suffered a serious back injury.

On one level, this injury was a challenge to which Lee responded as only he could. He recovered from this injury, confounding the dire predictions of his doctors, and resumed the demanding physical training that made him such an astounding athlete. But, on another level, this Saturn passage was also a warning, a warning that there was a limit to what even Bruce Lee could get from his body. The physical challenges Lee faced two years later while making his Hong Kong movies were formidable. The filming often took place under difficult conditions and in equatorial heat. Given the high level of athletic prowess Lee was expected to display and the breakneck shooting schedule, the situation must have been extremely taxing. Add to this the work and stress that went into putting these films together (Lee suffered his first collapse while editing one of his movies in a room where the temperature was over one hundred degrees) and managing his burgeoning career, and we have a situation in which the absolute limitations of Lee's body could have easily been breached.

On the other hand, by choosing to give all his physical and mental energy to the task of making his movies, Lee was able to achieve the goal he had set for himself, both as an actor and as an exponent of ancient Chinese culture. This was another choice made under a Saturn passage and it is difficult to categorize it as anything but a good choice, even though it would seem to cancel out the good choice Lee had made during his Saturn return to rest and let his body have time to repair itself. Which was the better choice? Who can say? Lee made his choices in accordance with his own set of priorities and he made the most of each. In the end, that is all Saturn demands of us.

SOURCES

Louis Chunovic, *Bruce Lee: The Tao of the Dragon Warrior* (New York: St. Martin's Griffin, 1996).

Linda Tagliaferro, *Bruce Lee* (Minneapolis, MN: Lerner Publications Co., 2000).

5

ALBERT EINSTEIN

German scientist whose theory of relativity changed the way we understand time and space

THE CHOICE

By the time he was twenty-two, Albert Einstein's life had already developed a distinct pattern. He excelled at the things he did well, the tasks that interested him, and everything else he ignored. He had done this in high school, causing his math teacher to throw up his hands and proclaim he had nothing left to teach the boy, while most of his other teachers were writing off young Albert as either a dunce or an impudent lay-about. Thanks to this attitude, the young genius became perhaps the most brilliant high school dropout of all time. At the Zurich Polytechnic, after he had finessed his way to a high school diploma in Switzerland, Einstein fell into the same easygoing pattern. Some of his professors were dazzled by his remarkable mind, while others hardly ever saw him and, when they did, were more impressed by his slovenly appearance and lack of deference to authority than his intelligence. Einstein still managed to pass his final examination, though only barely. Meanwhile, he remained placidly insulated from his father's many business travails. Young Einstein had once promised to learn his father's electrical engineering business, which was perpetually on the brink of disaster, but he never seemed to get around to it.

Then, in 1901, when **Saturn reached his Descendant** and Uranus opposed his natal Moon, life finally seemed to have the twenty-two-year-old Einstein cornered. He had been a college graduate for almost a year by this time, and was still unable to find a job. He had applied for several positions, mostly as a teacher, and been turned down by everyone. Einstein needed a job badly because he was in love and wanted to get married. His girlfriend was a fellow student named Mileva Maric, the only woman in his class, who had come to the Zurich Polytechnic from Serbia. Einstein had proposed to her soon after he passed his final (and Mileva had failed hers) and he was determined to go through with the marriage despite the strenuous objections of his parents. This determination had turned into outright desperation when Mileva became pregnant. The poor girl had been forced to run home to Serbia to avoid a scandal and Einstein missed her sorely.

Intermixed with all these troubles was some good news for Einstein. Switzerland had approved—against all odds, considering that he was an unemployed Jew—his application for citizenship, and he had a promise of a job at the Swiss patent office in Bern, though he wouldn't actually start work there for another year. More importantly, perhaps, he read a scientific paper by Max Planck that helped kindle his own fascination with the properties of light. Einstein even found work, a temporary teaching assignment, but none of these positives gave the young man the prospects he needed to start a family.

The options facing Einstein were all bad. Help from his family, who had already warned him of the ruin he faced if Mileva became pregnant, was highly unlikely. Mileva's family, though more well-to-do than Einstein's, lived in a part of the world still steeped in medieval traditions. To them her condition was a stain on the entire family, past and future generations included. Early in her pregnancy, Mileva returned to Zurich looking for support from her fiancé, but Einstein's teaching job left him little time to comfort her. Besides, Einstein couldn't allow it to become public knowledge that Mileva's child was his. That might ruin his chances at the patent office and make

Albert Einstein 45

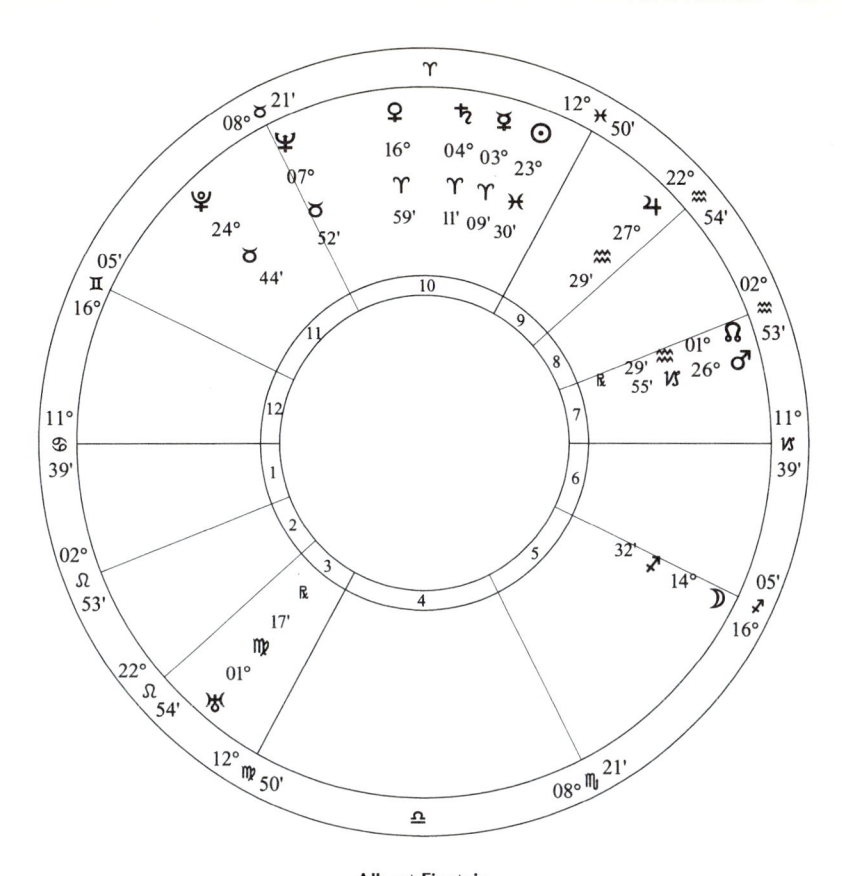

Albert Einstein
March 14, 1879, 11:30 AM local time
Ulm, Germany, 48N20 10E00

the young genius even more unemployable. Likewise, marrying Mileva and claiming the child were out of the question. The Swiss were a conservative people and could be counted on to greet such bohemian courage with stern disapproval.

So Einstein opted for a passive approach. He sent his future wife back to Serbia and wrote her cheery letters full of optimism about the future but, as the pregnancy progressed, mention of the child she was carrying became more infrequent. He even recommended that Mileva talk to her father about what to do about the child, a clear admission that he had no idea what course to take. Meanwhile, **in February 1902, just a few months after Saturn made its last pass across Einstein's Descendant**, Mileva gave birth in her mother's home village. After she recovered from this ordeal, Mileva left her baby in the care of her relatives and returned to Zurich and Albert. It is unclear when or even if Einstein ever saw the child. The last mention of little Lieserl was two years after her birth when Einstein wrote a letter to Mileva, who was back in Serbia, expressing concern at the fact that his daughter had contracted smallpox. Experts on Einstein are still debating what became of Lieserl, whether she died of smallpox or was given up for adoption. The only things that are known for sure is that the child was never a part of the Einstein family, even after he married Mileva in 1903, and that the loss of this child, however it happened, changed the new Mrs. Einstein forever.

THE HOROSCOPE

Albert Einstein was born with a horoscope that seems almost too good. The only hard aspect involving personal planets that is reasonably close in this chart is a sesquiquadrate between Venus and Uranus. Otherwise trines, sextiles, and a close conjunction between Mercury and Saturn in Aries dominate the chart. Hard aspects like squares do present a personality with conflicts and troubles but they also function to activate and inspire the personality. They represent the challenges: the points of pain and discomfort that force us to act on the world around us. With a horoscope like Einstein's, in which such aspects are nearly nonexistent, there is an unhappy potential for passivity and laziness; a tendency to avoid hard work and hard choices, and a general lack of ambition.

In Einstein's chart, however, we have a few saving graces. His Pisces Sun is high in the 10th House, letting us know that this is someone who likes the spotlight, who is a natural performer and perhaps a little bit of an egotist (though, in Pisces, this tendency would be well concealed). Also, one of the trines in the horoscope is from Mars in Capricorn to Pluto. Even though the aspect is easy, the planets involved give us an enormous capacity for hard work, grit, and determination. Overall, the personality may be affable and easygoing, but there is a hard core of effort hidden within the Piscean mists. Finally, the Mercury to Saturn conjunction is a serious aspect providing mental acuity and remarkable powers of concentration.

There are those that would look at Einstein's horoscope, searching for some sign of his genius. In reality, however, the horoscope tells us much less about the source of Einstein's extraordinary IQ than it does about the remarkable way in which he used it. It shows a personality lacking in any hunger for success, with no aching voids that need to be filled with achievement. Rather, this is a personality quite content to work hard outside the limelight, concentrating intensely on problems that captivate his mind—with little concern for fame, monetary compensation, or career goals. Of course, when the spotlight did finally come his way because of his genius, this very solar personality bore the clamor and attention with ease, and even perfected—through a cunning use of the media—the role of the distracted professor that society had assigned him.

All this brings us to that one hard aspect, the sesquiquadrate between Venus and Uranus. In most horoscopes, this is an aspect that would barely rate mention, but in this chart it can't be ignored. On the positive side, it shows an attraction to unusual women. Mileva certainly fitted this description. Not only was she from a place that probably seemed very rustic and foreign to an urbanite like Einstein, she was a woman independent and intelligent enough to compete with men on their own terms. Moreover, she had a physical defect in her hip that caused her to walk with a limp. The negative side of this

Venus to Uranus aspect became apparent, particularly to Mileva, after the two were married. It is always easier for a person with Venus aspecting Uranus to love an abstraction than a reality. Even though Einstein had a strong and extremely down-to-earth sex drive with Mars in Capricorn and the sentimentality and emotional vulnerability of a Pisces Sun with a Cancer Ascendant, his interest in Mileva began to wane soon after the relationship became an established fact. She felt shut out of his life and quickly became aware that he was attracted to other women. The true extent of Einstein's womanizing is unclear. Women certainly found him attractive and he was a tireless flirt, but it is possible (even likely, considering the abstracted nature of Venus to Uranus aspects) that most of these flirtations remained platonic. Still, this would have hardly been a comfort to Einstein's increasingly ignored wife.

THE LIFE

Fame came gradually to Einstein. In 1905, while Uranus was squaring his natal Mercury, Einstein completed several important scientific papers, including one on his theory of special relativity, in one amazing flurry of genius, but even though he published his ideas and sent copies of his papers to important scientists, the work made no immediate impression. **It was only when transiting Saturn crossed his Midheaven, natal Sun, and natal Saturn in 1906 and 1907** that a select few in the scientific community began to notice and appreciate his revolutionary ideas. It was during this period, at the request of one of his supporters, that Einstein penned a review of his special theory of relativity in which he wrote for the first time the formula that would become his signature: $E=mc^2$ or energy equals mass times the speed of light squared. It is likely that even Einstein failed to recognize the ominous potential this formula would soon hold for the world. It was also during this period that Einstein had what he called his "happiest" thought, the beginning of what would become his general theory of relativity (Isaacson, 2007).

By 1908, as Saturn neared its first return, Einstein was growing dissatisfied with his job as a patent clerk. He felt he had earned entry into the exclusive hall of scientific academia. He had applied for a position as a lowly lecturer at the University of Bern the year before, but the hiring committee insisted that he write a thesis before they hired him. After all the papers he had published and all the ground-breaking work he had done, Einstein was stunned. He refused to write the thesis. Now, with Saturn calling him to take on a serious, adult role, Einstein swallowed his pride and wrote the required paper. He got the job in **February, 1908, two months before Saturn reached it first contact with his natal Saturn.** The pay was not enough for him to quit his position at the patent office but, at least, it was a start.

One month after Saturn had passed its last contact with his natal Saturn, in February, 1909, he was recommended to a full professorship at the University of Zurich. At last, he was able to leave his menial job at the patent office and take his place in the scientific community and he quickly advanced. A better position beckoned in Prague and he moved his family to Czechoslovakia. Two years later he was offered an even more prestigious position at the University of Berlin, and once again the Einstein family moved.

Einstein had reasons for moving to Berlin beyond his career. A young widow by the name of Elsa Lowenthall lived in that city. She was a distant relative of Einstein and they had already begun an affair. Einstein felt justified in cheating on his wife because he was no longer in love with Mileva. He confessed to his friends that he found her ugly and shrewish. When transiting Saturn squared Einstein's Sun, Mileva left the professor, taking their two sons with her and returning to Zurich. The separation was reasonably amicable, although Einstein missed his sons and feared his angry wife was poisoning their minds against him. World War I began just a few months after the separation and the shock of the war (Einstein, an avowed pacifist, was one of only a handful of German-born scientists to oppose the war), and the demise of his family life, drove Einstein deeper into his work. When **transiting Saturn crossed his Ascendant in the fall of 1915,** he finally completed and published his general theory of relativity.

Again the impact of Einstein's world-shaking ideas were slow to be felt, largely because the general theory of relativity addressed issues of such enormity that testing it was very difficult. In wasn't until the solar eclipse of 1919, when transiting Uranus was opposed to Einstein's natal Uranus, that English scientists had an opportunity to test Einstein's theory about the relationship between gravity and light. Their findings indicated in a qualified way that Einstein was right. It was at this point that the popular press got hold of Einstein's theories. The accounts they published were often fantastic and only vaguely related to the science, but they captured the public imagination. By the time **Saturn reached his IC,** in December of that year, Einstein had become the most famous scientist in the world.

Einstein's fame did not solve all his problems. To some degree, it was a liability. As the Nazi Party began its rise to power, Einstein found himself in the unenviable position of being a world-famous Jew living in an increasingly anti-Semitic state. At the same time that journalists from around the world were seeking him out for interviews, brown-shirted toughs were harassing him on campus, and anti-Semitic scientists and organizations were attempting to cast doubt on his theories and defame his name. When Germany's first Jewish foreign minister, Walter Rathenau, was assassinated (during **transiting Saturn's opposition to Einstein's natal Saturn**), Einstein feared he would be next.

Einstein dealt with this challenge much as he had dealt with the challenge he faced in 1901. He distanced himself from the trouble. He would reside in Germany for another eleven years, watching the Nazi menace grow and take its horrific final shape. During this period, he arranged to be away from his home in Germany a great deal of the time. He took a visiting professorship in Leyden, he lectured in the Far East, attended meetings and conferences all across Europe, and made multiple trips to the United States. It wasn't until 1933, when the Nazis banned all Jewish students and teachers from the universities, that Einstein and his second wife, the former Elsa Löwenthall, moved to the United States, where he took the post of Professor of Theoretical Physics at Princeton University in New Jersey. It was there, three years later, when **Saturn crossed his Midheaven** and natal Sun a second time, that Elsa died. Einstein remained a widower, though by no means a lonely one, until his death in 1955.

SATURN AT WORK

There are two ways of looking at Einstein's 1901 Saturn transit. On the one hand, it could be said that he was challenged by this Saturn passage to accept responsibility for his actions by marrying his girlfriend and acknowledging his child, and that he failed that challenge in a most dismal and caddish manner. On the other, it could be said that by putting his career aspirations ahead of his loyalty to Mileva, Einstein was able to maintain the fragile toehold he had on the academic career ladder and put himself in as position to bring forth the full potential of his genius.

There is no use in offering conjectures about what might have happened if Einstein had immediately accepted responsibility for his and Mileva's child. He made the decision he made, and his career eventually soared, while at the same time his marriage floundered. It is interesting that Einstein's second marriage was also troubled, mostly because of the famed scientist's relationships with other women, and that after his second wife died, Einstein remained a bachelor for the last twenty years of his life.

Meanwhile, after his dark 1901 Saturn passage, Einstein's subsequent Saturn transits seem to have all represented a ratcheting-up of his fame and success. In Einstein's horoscope, the Midheaven, Sun, and Saturn are positioned relatively close together so that transiting Saturn could contact all three within a three-year period. The seminal period of Einstein's life, the period between 1907 and 1909, occurred during Saturn's conjunct of the MC, his natal Sun, and natal Saturn. During this period he received his doctorate from the University of Zurich, announced the equation that would subsequently be his calling card to the world ($E=mc^2$), achieved the "happiest thought" with regard to the relation of gravity to light that would later form his general theory of relativity, and he was finally able to quit his day job at the patent office and take a position as a lecturer at the University of Zurich.

When Saturn squared his natal Sun and Saturn and reached his Ascendant, Einstein's first marriage ended and he completed his general theory of relativity. When Saturn reached his IC and oppositions with the Sun and Saturn between 1919 and 1922, this theory received an astounding confirmation by British scientists, making Einstein an instant celebrity, and he was awarded the Nobel Prize. Also during this period, Einstein was harassed by anti-Semetic toughs at the University of Berlin, gave a brilliant (and, according to some, self-aggrandizing) defense of his theories in Holland, and married for the second time.

SOURCES

Michele Zackheim, *Einstein's Daughter: The Search for Lieserl* (New York: Riverhead Books, 1994).

Walter Isaacson, *Einstein: His Life and Universe* (New York: Simon & Schuster, 2007).

6

MALCOLM X

African-American leader who became the angry public face of the Black Muslim movement until he was expelled from that organization and assassinated

THE CHOICE

Around 1940, between when Saturn passed over his Descendant and opposed its natal place, a young man named Malcolm Little was asked a question. It was the kind of question any adolescent might be asked. "What do you want to be when you grow up?" Malcolm's answer was immediate. He wanted to be a lawyer. The white teacher who had asked Malcolm Little this question was taken aback. This seemed a very lofty ambition for a young African-American in 1941. Even looking beyond the color of Malcolm's skin, the teacher probably would not have seen much potential. The youngster was living in a foster home, a ward of the state. His father had died (possibly at the hands of the Ku Klux Klan) in 1931, and his mother had been institutionalized. So, the teacher did what, to him, must have seemed the prudent thing to do. He advised the young man to consider a less exalted career, maybe as a cook or a carpenter, something more befitting his race and circumstance in life. Then he walked away, most likely unaware that he had just stoked a fire that had been burning within this young man's breast since the death of his father and the

53

institutionalization of his mother. It was an anger that was directed not just at this teacher, but at all the people like him, and against the entire social structure that he saw as being constructed by whites to keep him and his people subservient.

A year after receiving this priceless advice, young Malcolm dropped out of school and moved from Lansing, Michigan to Boston, Massachusetts, where he lived with an older sister. His sister expected Malcolm to find work in the big city, but Malcolm had other plans. Instead of learning to be a cook or a carpenter, Malcolm learned how to run bootleg whiskey and steal. He found work among gamblers and prostitutes, and was soon on his way to a career as a criminal. Malcolm Little would never forget what his teacher had told him, or the rage that it stirred within his soul, and he would fight back the only way he knew how.

THE HOROSCOPE

Malcolm X's horoscope reveals several strong tendencies that seem very much at odds with one another. First of all, his Sun and Venus are in the 5th House in a rather wide conjunction. The Sun also trines Jupiter and sextiles Uranus. These are all what we might call "playboy" aspects. It is no wonder that young Malcolm Little was so easily seduced by the apparently easy life of a hustler. Even as a Muslim, he spent relatively little time in what we might call a *real* job. Once he was called by Elijah Muhammed to be a minister, his work became the Nation of Islam and a labor of love.

In contrast with these fun-loving aspects, we have Capricorn rising with its ruler, Saturn, strong in Scorpio in the 10th House. Malcolm Little was born with a great deal of personal discipline and a streak of desire, as witnessed by his early ambition to become a lawyer. With a horoscope so dominated by Saturn, Malcolm needed structure and practical goals on which to focus his energy. He was a person who knew how to work within a system and take orders, but he was also a man with his eye always on the top rung of the ladder and a desire to climb.

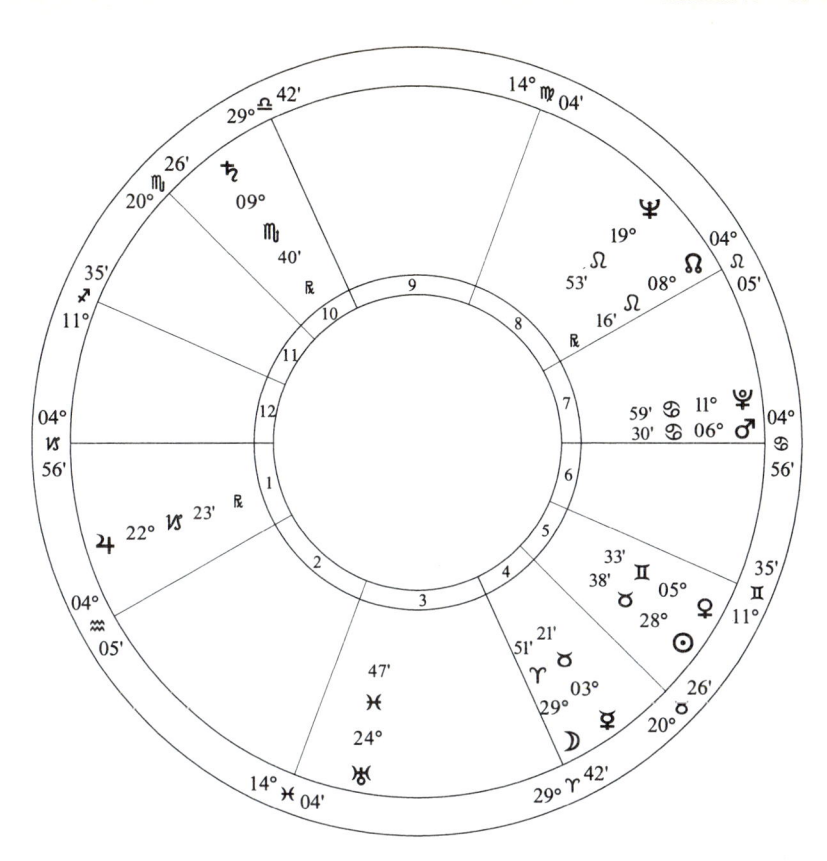

Malcolm X

May 19, 1925, 10:25 PM CST

Omaha, NE, 41N15 95W56

The most ominous feature of Malcolm X's horoscope is the conjunction of Mars and Pluto on the Descendant. It is a powerful aspect, with a strong tendency toward violence and extreme behavior. It is an indicator of a strong personality, a natural leader, and a person who would be hard to please. Malcolm Little had been a tough criminal, with a violent temper. When Malcolm X became a minister, he was equally tough, holding his congregation to the highest standards and then forging them, with military precision, into a force for social change.

Contrasting with the martial tone of his Mars-Pluto conjunction, we have the placement of Malcolm's Moon on the IC in conjunction with his Mercury. The Moon is in the last degree of Aries while Mercury is in Taurus, so we have an odd combination of raw Aries aggression and Taurus sweetness. Again, Malcolm Little was a hustler, a guy who used his gift of gab to run a con or lure prospective customers into a particular house of prostitution. Later in his life, as Malcolm X, he remained a talker, a devastating and extraordinarily articulate debater who knew how to think quickly and speak clearly about the issues that concerned him.

THE LIFE

Malcolm's criminal career was colorful, laced with violence, and short, ending in 1946. **The next year, when Saturn arrived at the age twenty-one square with its natal place**, Malcolm was in prison, beginning an eight-year sentence for burglary. When he was released from prison in August 1952, Malcolm Little emerged a changed man. Even his name was different. From this point on, he would be known as Malcolm X.

While he was in prison, as Uranus crossed his Descendant, Malcolm had undergone a religious conversion. It was just the kind of radical change you might expect from Uranus—a lightning-bolt transformation, complete with visions, mystical revelations, and an intellectual firestorm. This change has also coincided with a 90-degree aspect between transiting Saturn and Malcolm's Sun, so the change came to him when he was under duress, and the change involved a humbling of his ego. The man who walked out of Charlestown Prison that day would come to call himself Malcolm X, and he was on a mission to serve a faith and the "Messenger" of that faith, whom he would forever call "the honorable Elijah Muhammad" (Brown, 1995).

The faith that Malcolm Little had come to embrace in prison was called the Nation of Islam. He had become a Black Muslim. At that time, very little was known about the Nation of Islam. Its founder, Elijah Muhammad, had succeeded in starting mosques in his native Detroit and in Chicago, but his followers were few. However, counted among this small group of followers was one of Malcolm's brothers. This sibling, along with another man Malcolm had met in prison, and, finally, the honorable Elijah Muhammad himself, had gradually brought Malcolm into the fold.

Islam as preached by Elijah Muhammad was not an easy faith to follow. Among the many things it forbade were drugs, alcohol, fornication, gambling, and dancing; all the activities at which Malcolm Little had excelled. But, by his own account, the most challenging requirement for Malcolm had been the act of kneeling in prayer. Malcolm Little was a proud man, and the notion of submitting before any authority, divine or otherwise, did not come easily. This is the part that reflects the influence of his transiting Saturn square to his natal Sun. This is an aspect that frequently forces us to our knees.

The main thing that had attracted Malcolm X to the Nation of Islam, along with many other frustrated African-Americans, was Elijah Muhammad's assertion that black people were superior to whites. Elijah Muhammad claimed he had met a traveling Arab who turned out to be a representative of Allah. This divine being had revealed to Elijah Muhammad the true history of the world, and in that history black people were the original mankind while white people were evil mutants developed by a disaffected black scientist. This idea that white people were "devils" appealed to Malcolm. It fed a fiery rage that had been burning within the young man since his early childhood.

When Malcolm X left Charlestown Prison, Saturn was nearing his Midheaven. He would hold a couple of different jobs during the next two years but they would have little to do with Saturn's passage.

His big break would come during the summer of 1953, **when Saturn was just a few degrees shy of his Midheaven**. At that time, he would be appointed assistant minister for the Detroit mosque. It was hardly an auspicious appointment. He was not even able to give up his day job. But it was an important event for Malcolm, because it showed him that his hard work "fishing" for converts on the city streets was appreciated by the one person he wanted above all others to please, the honorable Elijah Muhammad. It spurred him to work harder and it gave him the chance to speak to the church, revealing his gift for oration. The next year, **when transiting Saturn conjoined his natal Saturn** in the 10th House, he was appointed minister for the mosque in Harlem, one of the most important Black Muslim mosques in the country.

Over the next six years Malcolm continued to work toward making the Nation of Islam a strong voice for the African-American community. In 1957, by a simple but highly organized show of force, he was able to negotiate the release of a Black Muslim who had been beaten and unjustly arrested. In 1958, he married a young woman from the Nation and started a family. Malcolm X seemed to be the rising star of the Nation of Islam. Not only was he an outstanding example of the transforming powers of Elijah Muhammad's philosophy, he was a charismatic leader capable of inspiring his people in a way very few people could manage.

And yet, there were already signs of conflict between Malcolm and the honorable Elijah Muhammad. Malcolm began writing a column in the Harlem newspaper. The column became very popular, thanks to Malcolm's wit and his fierce, take-no-prisoners approach to problems in the black community. Seeing the success of the column, Elijah Muhammad decided to take it over. Malcolm gracefully conceded, but after only a few of Muhammad's rambling homilies were published, the column was quietly discontinued by the newspaper. Then Malcolm began publishing his own newspaper. Again, seeing the success Malcolm was having with *Muhammad Speaks,* the master and his Chicago-based cronies took over this project as well.

By 1959, Malcolm X was quickly becoming a victim of his own success. Within the Nation of Islam, other ministers and longtime followers of Elijah Muhammad were starting to look at Malcolm with jealousy, and even fear. There were whispers that the personality of this young firebrand was beginning to overshadow that of the honorable Elijah Muhammad himself. It was at this point, **with Saturn crossing his Ascendant,** that Malcolm was approached by a representative of Mike Wallace. The journalist wanted to feature the Nation of Islam on his television show. For Malcolm, this offer probably represented nothing more than another opportunity to spread the word. Apparently, Elijah Muhammad agreed. He gave Malcolm permission to do the show. But, under the influence of this powerful Saturn transit, this opportunity to spread the word about the Nation of Islam would become something much more powerful and, for Malcolm, much more dangerous.

Before Wallace's program about the Nation of Islam was aired **in late 1959, just as Saturn made its last contact with his Ascendant,** Malcolm X was famous within the Nation of Islam and well-known in the black community of New York City. And yet, outside of the New York Police Department and possibly the FBI, he was virtually unknown to white America. The Mike Wallace coverage of the Nation of Islam changed all of that. Suddenly the term "Black Muslim" was burned into the psyche of white America as an emblem of fear and hatred. Many white people who watched the program were shocked when they were presented with blacks who abhorred the notion of integration with whites and laughed at the nonviolent protests of such black leaders as Martin Luther King, Jr. More importantly, even though Elijah Muhammad was prominently featured in the program, the face that most of these white viewers came to associate with the defiant new trend within the African-American community was that of Malcolm X.

After the Mike Wallace program was aired, Malcolm X was called upon to lecture at universities and other venues all across the country. He was on TV talk shows and was sought out any time the media needed a witty or controversial quote on matters concerning the black community. Malcolm may have thought that he was advancing the cause of the Nation of Islam when he approached the microphones or stepped up to the podium but, in fact, his rise to national notoriety had all but sealed his fate within the Nation. The jealousy that bubbled beneath the surface for so many years now became outright and vicious. There was evidence that even the honorable Elijah Muhammad was beginning to view his fiery young protégé with a degree of envy and possibly apprehension.

Over the next four years, the relationship between Malcolm X and Elijah Muhammad continued to deteriorate. Rumors were reaching Malcolm concerning the many illegitimate children that the Messenger (as Elijah Muhammad was sometime known) had fathered with various young women. **As Saturn squared its natal place** (in Malcolm's 10th House), the truth of the rumors became evident to Malcolm, and his faith in the man who had been his spiritual mentor and father figure was fatally shaken.

In November 1963, Malcolm X was expelled from the Nation. The next year, with Saturn squaring his Sun, he formed his own church. Now that he was free of the restriction of the Nation of Islam, Malcolm decided to make a pilgrimage to Mecca to see the full glory of Islam firsthand. What he discovered during his visits to several Muslim countries was that Islam was much more than a refuge for African-Americans. It was a worldwide faith that embraced all races. This shocking revelation, so at odds with the teachings of Elijah Muhammad, caused Malcolm to reassess many of his attacks on whites and moderate black leaders. Unfortunately, he was granted little time to preach this new message. On February 21, 1965, when the secondary progressed Sun conjoined his natal Mars, Malcolm X was gunned down in front of his congregation in New York City.

SATURN AT WORK

Given the prominence of Mars and Pluto in Malcolm's horoscope, anger was certainly going to be a major issue in his life story. This anger was first brought into focus for him when Saturn made its first square to its natal place when he was still a child. This occurred just after his father was killed and around the time he was put into foster care. The incident with his teacher provided further focus, and the harsh realities of prison life that he was experiencing during Saturn's second square still more. What Malcolm was going to do with this anger did not become clear until he converted to the Nation of Islam and left prison. When Saturn crossed his Midheaven, he found a way of using his highly focused and controlled anger for the Nation, and he earned the confidence of the man who had become the new figure of ultimate authority in his life, Elijah Muhammad.

For Malcolm, his first Saturn return was more than a call to assume the burdens of adulthood. With Capricorn rising and Saturn in the 10th, Malcolm X had long since grown up. For him, it was a call to become a leader and an inspiration to others. When he was made the head of the Harlem mosque, Malcolm was given an enormous responsibility—particularly for a man so young and so new to the Nation of Islam—but this was just what he needed.

When Saturn crossed Malcolm's Ascendant in 1959, it did not necessarily change his persona. This transit only made that angry yet disciplined persona visible to a much larger audience. What did change, however, was the face of the movement to which Malcolm had devoted so much of his adult life. After 1959, the face of that movement, and the deep-seated anger that drove it, would be his.

Malcolm claimed that he had confirmed the rumors of Elijah Muhammad's philandering for himself in 1963. Saturn made its last square with his natal Saturn in December 1962, indicating that Malcolm's respect for his leader was weakening even before this revelation. In fact, Malcolm told other people that he had noticed an increased concern for money and pretty girls in the Messenger years earlier. This Saturn passage, with transiting Saturn in the 1st House and natal Saturn in the 10th, was a particularly powerful one. Not only did it shake Malcolm free of "the only man he had ever feared," it completed the process begun with Saturn's first return in 1954. It made Malcolm an adult completely independent of his adoptive father figure. Unfortunately, Malcolm's Saturn story was cut short before he had a chance to fully exhibit this new independence.

SOURCES

Alex Haley and Malcolm X, *The Autobiography of Malcolm X* (New York: Ballantine Books, 1973).

Kevin Brown, *Malcolm X: His Life and Legacy* (Brookfield, CT: Millbrook Press, 1995).

Louis A. DeCaro, *On the Side of My People: A Religious Life of Malcolm X* (New York: New York University Press, 1996).

7

BONO (Paul Hewson)

Irish rock star who has become a respected activist for such causes as African debt relief

THE CHOICE

In the autumn of 1974, a teenager in Dublin steeped in a rage against the world—a typical state for a teenager, but this particular young man had good reason for his anger and self-pity. His mother had just died. Suddenly, while attending the funeral of her own father, she had succumbed to a brain hemorrhage. The young man had been close to his mother. He was a Taurus by Sun sign and his Sun was squared by Uranus, so he was more prone than most to battle authority and, at the same time, notably stubborn and irrational. Only his mother had been able to communicate with him when he fought with his strict father, which was often. Now she was gone and this young man, Paul Hewson, seemed to roam the streets of Dublin like a bomb waiting to explode.

The death of Paul's mother had come just as his secondary progressed Sun squared his natal Pluto in the 8th House, but **only a month later Saturn moved opposite his natal Saturn.** This natural period of adolescent adjustment became a cruel test for young Hewson. **A few months after that, transiting Saturn contacted his Descendant,** bringing changes in relationships, the most obvious and tragic of which would be getting used to the absence of his mother. How would this youngster deal with all that pressure? Paul had already shown a penchant for rebellion, and now his rebellions and his fights with his father and older brother became more violent. There were many unfortunate options available to him. The neighborhood in which he lived contained both middle- and working-class elements, and the opportunity to become involved in gangs and crime was certainly there. On the other hand, Hewson had already shown an interest in religion, an issue that was a constant sore spot in his home, since his father was a Catholic and his mother was a Protestant. Paul had spent the summer previous to his mother's death in a bible camp. The possibility of burying his sorrows in an overwrought religious conversion was also there.

In the end, Paul Hewson eschewed both these extremes and did not explode. Instead, he went back to his high school and (with Saturn still hovering close to his Descendant) formed four relationships that would dictate the course of his life. First, he began dating a beauty named Alison Stewart, a girl many thought was too pretty and too smart to waste her time on a guy like Hewson, whose only distinguishing feature in high school was his talent for banter. The other relationships involved three boys around his own age: Larry Mullen, David Evans, and Adam Clayton. The four teens got the entirely unoriginal idea of forming a rock-and-roll band: a decision that was mostly based on the fact that Mullen's parents had given him a drum kit and were not averse to letting the lads practice in their kitchen. During this same period, David Evans was tagged with a new name by some of their friends. He was called "The Edge," and Paul Hewson also gained a nickname. Originally called "Bono Vox" because of his gift for gab, Paul's new moniker was later shortened to Bono. The band went on to become U2.

THE HOROSCOPE

The dominant feature of Bono's horoscope is the conjunction of Saturn with his Capricorn Ascendant. Since Saturn is very strong in its own sign and the Sun is in earthy Taurus, this would generally present us with a very practical but rather dull Saturn-laden personality. When we

Bono (Paul Hewson)

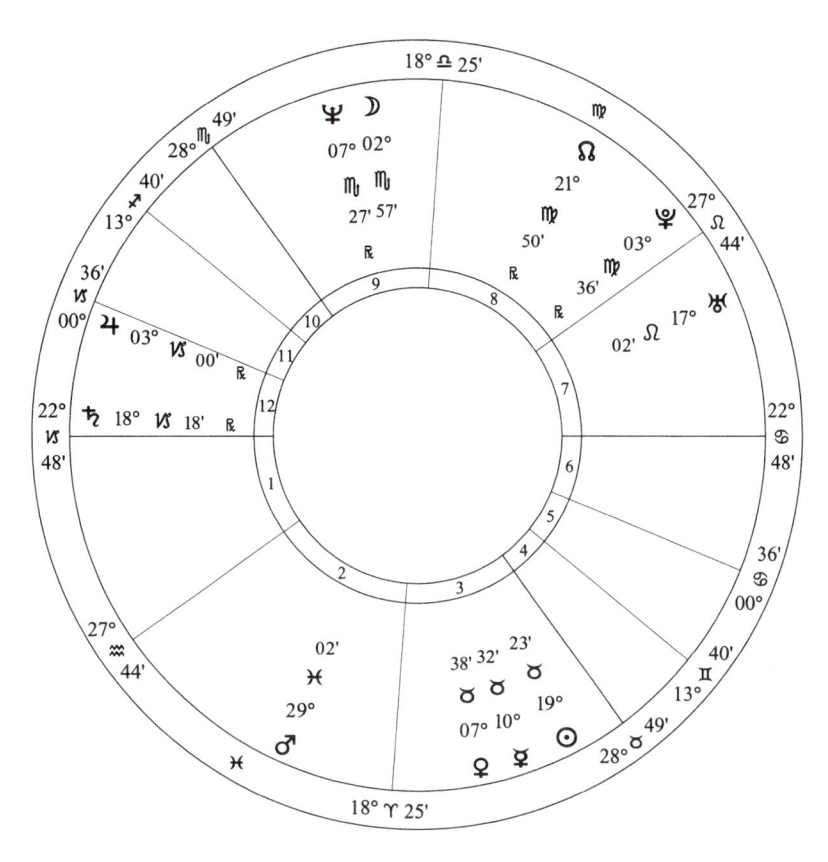

Bono (Paul Hewson)
May 10, 1960, 2:00 AM BST -1 hour
Dublin, Ireland, 53N20 06W15

look closer, we see that Saturn is in a close trine with Bono's Taurus Sun and that the Sun forms a tight square with Uranus, giving him a load of charm and a rebellious and unpredictable streak that is anything but boring. What Saturn and Capricorn rising does add to the personality is the assumption that there is important work to be done. There is weight in this personality, and a need to wrestle with important issues. In some cases, the weight of these issues and the size of the problems Saturn feels it necessary to confront are so overwhelming that despair, depression, and a lack of confidence set in, but in this chart, with that beautiful trine to the Sun, these dark moments will be less a problem. In fact, with Saturn on the Ascendant, the trine to Bono's Sun provides a great boost of confidence and the ability to deal with figures of authority as equals regardless of the circumstance.

The other outstanding feature of this horoscope is the Grand Trine between Venus and Mercury conjunct in Taurus, Jupiter in Capricorn, and Pluto in Virgo. This is augmented by a conjunction of the Moon and Neptune, which sextile both Jupiter and Pluto and sit opposite Venus. The opposition between Venus and Neptune is almost exact. This is a very artistic aspect system. It is no wonder that Bono once told an interviewer that the reason he decided to join the band was because he had no other job skills. It was a choice between learning to sing and pumping gas (Wall, 2005). With these aspects, particularly the opposition between Venus conjunct Mercury and Neptune, it would be difficult for any individual to concentrate on any subject outside the arts or, possibly, religion.

Bono's Moon to Neptune conjunction takes place in his 9th House, the house related to education, philosophy, and religion. His Jupiter, trined as it is by Venus and Pluto, is in the spiritual 12th House. These factors combine to make religion and spiritual concern very important, despite the very practical qualities of Bono's Taurus and Capricorn Ascendant. The importance of Saturn in the horoscope indicates that his search for religious truth would center on conventional, socially sanctioned religious organizations, although the Square between his Sun and Uranus shows us that his patience with these institutions would be rather short and that, in the end, he would have to find a more individual expression of his spiritual concerns.

There is also a square between Bono's Pisces Mars and his 12th House Jupiter. This is an aspect of extremes. This tendency to go to extremes will certainly play into the spirituality reflected in the prominence of Neptune, but it will also find expression in other areas of life. On the whole, despite the fact that the aspect is hard, this Jupiter to Mars aspect gives us an antidote for the sometimes depressive and stodgy influences of his strongly placed Saturn. This aspect adds a spirit of adventure to the personality and makes up for the absence of Fire signs in the chart.

THE LIFE

There was little to distinguish the four young men who formed the band that would soon take the name U2 from the multitude of other young teens across the Western world who, at one time or another, tried their hand at making music. None of them had any training beyond avidly listening to pop music on records and on their televisions. What they did have, though, was a phenomenal seriousness about the task they were undertaking. In this they were led by Bono, who took to the stage with an energy and a sense of mission that quickly established the group as a powerhouse in the Dublin music scene. Another thing that separated U2 from other bands was the fact that they often performed original material, with lyrics written by Bono.

Things moved quickly for them. They signed with an agent and were quickly picked up by CBS Records. In 1979, as Uranus opposed Bono's Sun, efforts were made to establish the band in England, but CBS was reluctant to distribute the band's records outside Ireland. In 1980, they moved to Island Records and released their first album, *Boy*. The band performed in Europe and then in New York City. Finally, preparations were made for U2 to tour the United States in support of *Boy*.

The tour began just as Uranus arrived at Bono's Midheaven and in many ways it was phenomenally successful, gaining U2 an appreciative audience in the all-important U.S. market. Unfortunately, the rigors of touring and being away from their homes and loved ones for so many months put a strain on the relationships between the band members. Bono and two of his bandmates, Edge and Mullen, remained devoutly religious, reading their bibles on the tour bus while Adam Clayton refused to join in. There were also conflicts between Bono and the others, resulting in at least one fistfight. By the time the tour was finished, the band called U2 was ready to break up.

At this time **Saturn arrived at its age twenty-one square with Bono's natal Saturn.** Bono's reaction to this influence was typical. In September 1982, one month after the square was completed, he married his high school sweetheart, Alison Stewart. During this same period, he and the other members of the band applied themselves to mending their fragmented allegiances. This couldn't have been an easy process, since three of the men involved, Bono, Mullen, and Edge, had fixed Sun signs, but it was accomplished. The result was a move away from the religious fervor that had gripped Bono and some of his friends, and a move toward more political concerns. This was reflected in the lyrics Bono wrote for the band's next album, *War*, which came out in February 1983.

War and the tour that accompanied it firmly established U2 as a force in popular music. By the end of 1983, they were tagged by *Rolling Stone* magazine as the top rock act of the year. In the midst of all this, **just as Saturn crossed Bono's Midheaven in the summer of 1983**, the young musician was invited by the prime minister of Ireland to join a special committee looking into unemployment in Ireland. This was Bono's first foray into the world of politics and it was not a particularly happy one. Bono was shocked to see that the committee was made up of old men, while the people most impacted by unemployment were men and women his own age. After angrily expressing his disapproval of this state of affairs before the committee, Bono returned to his day job.

Meanwhile, Bono's day job was becoming increasingly profitable. He and the band signed a new contract which made them all multimillionaires. During the next few years, the band would release three more albums, including the wildly successful *The Joshua Tree*. And yet, despite his previous experience, Bono remained intent on giving his life a political relevance. He and the band joined in the Live Aid concert in 1985, and later they performed in benefits for Amnesty International and to help victims of AIDS. Also in 1985, Bono and his wife traveled anonymously to Ethiopia and spent several weeks there helping relief workers.

In 1990, transiting Saturn reached Bono's natal Saturn and his Ascendant. The year before, in May 1989, his first child was born and the rock star felt the need to buy a new home to accommodate his growing family—a typical manifestation of this passage, except that Bono hired a helicopter to help him search out appropriate properties. There were also changes brewing in his other important relationships. Tired of touring and feeling an increasing gap between his own religious beliefs and the role of a rock star, The Edge announced his decision to quit the band. By this time, U2's lead guitarist had become one of the most respected rock musicians in the world—replacing him would not have been easy, but it was certainly possible. Bono refused even to consider this. For him, the four friends who started U2 in the Mullens' kitchen were a unit and the defection of any one of them meant the band would cease to exist. Faced with this ultimatum, The Edge reconsidered and U2 survived to see a new decade.

The 1990s saw no decline in the popularity of U2. The band was busy making albums, touring, doing music for movies and stage production, and, of course, benefit concerts for a variety of causes. Despite these efforts, Bono felt that more needed to be done. The problems of the Third World such as poverty, ignorance, and AIDS continued unabated. The issue took on new clarity for Bono **when Saturn squared its natal place in 1987.** At this time, a friend brought the singer a report showing how the overwhelming debt that Third World countries owed to the industrialized countries was dragging down any hope of economic progress in places like Africa. The few million dollars U2 and other rockers were able to raise with benefit concerts were often dwarfed by the interest payments these countries were forced to pay in order to service their debts. Bono immediately began educating himself on that weighty and extremely complex issue.

In 2000, Bono announced the formation of an organization to advocate debt relief for the Third World. The next year, **a few months**

after Saturn crossed Bono's IC, his father died after a long and painful battle with cancer. Bono was shaken by this passing, but his efforts for debt relief continued unabated. He met with government officials and heads of state all across the Western world, regardless of political and philosophical differences. With typical Earth sign practicality, this Taurus with Capricorn Rising understood that major changes in the structure of political power required the cooperation of the people who wielded that power. Meanwhile, Bono continued to be a rock star, continued making albums and performing concerts all across the world. At these concerts, among the multitude of screaming fans, there would often be a smattering of high-level government officials seated in places of honor or backstage. But it wasn't just his talent and notability as the lead singer for U2 that impressed these world leaders. Many expressed admiration for Bono's knowledge of the issues and the seriousness of his approach.

Despite the intensity and persistence he brought to the task, the changes Bono and his group sought did not come about overnight. Finally, in 2005, the first giant step was made. At the meeting of the eight richest nations of the world, called the G8 Summit, an agreement was forged to cancel $40 billion dollars worth of African debt (Tyrangiel, 2005). This was announced **one month after Saturn completed its crossing of Bono's Descendant**. Bono, the political advocate, scored his greatest victory just as Bono, the rock star, launched the biggest world tour of U2's long career.

SATURN AT WORK

In some ways, Bono's Saturn transits seem to fall precisely in line with what would be expected. At the time of his age twenty-one Saturn square, he married. Then, when Saturn made its first return and crossed his Ascendant, he bought a new house (albeit a very large house) to accommodate his growing family and dealt effectively with a major challenge to his business (the possible defection of The Edge from U2). At the age of forty, with Saturn crossing his IC (a Saturn passage that often brings a realization of one's mortality, especially when it occurs at midlife), he was dealing with the illness and eventual death of a parent.

On the other hand, we see several of Bono's Saturn transits that are not so prosaic or as predictable. There is the painful passage of Saturn across his Descendant and opposite his natal Saturn immediately after the premature death of his mother. This brought a major psychological realignment for Bono, changing the rebellious and capricious boy into a mature and serious young man. Then we have Bono's appointment to a government committee when Saturn transited his Midheaven. In the lives of most performers and artists, such an appointment would have been a lark, a momentary diversion with little impact either on the life of the artist or the political process. But Bono refused to accept this appointment as a lark. He took it seriously and lambasted the politicians for their lack of concern.

Transiting Saturn's square to Bono's natal Saturn at age thirty-seven brought a return to the messy world of politics. At this time, he was forced to confront the fact that, no matter how sterling his intentions, there was just so much that a rock band and benefit concerts could do to change the world. Bono had to make a choice. Would he continue to do what he felt most comfortable doing—singing with his band and giving portions of his ever-growing wealth to good causes—or would he roll up his sleeves and attempt something he had never tried before, something at which he could very easily fail? Bono chose the latter option. He was taking a big risk. There were many who saw him as just another celebrity delving into a political and economic fray about which he knew nothing. They waited for his interest to flag, for the complexities of the issue to overwhelm him, for the singer to become just another plaintive spokesperson for a cause about which few people cared. They waited in vain.

The strength of Saturn in Bono's horoscope is surprising if you consider him as just a rock-and-roll singer. As Michel Gauguelin pointed out many years ago, Saturn is associated with bankers, lawyers, and even politicians. A strongly placed Saturn in the horoscope signifies someone who wants to be taken seriously by the world and who is capable of hard work and determined effort in order to win that esteem. If

Bono's critics had known this about him, perhaps they would have been less surprised at his persistence in the cause of Third World debt relief. Perhaps they would have been less shocked at his willingness to talk to archconservatives like George W. Bush or his former Treasury Secretary, Paul O'Neill. Perhaps they would have understood that Bono would approach the issue with a mixture of political savvy and sober patience. And perhaps they would have understood that a singer in a rock-and-roll band could, in fact, change the world.

SOURCES

Mick Wall, *Bono: In the Name of Love* (London: Seven Oaks, 2005).

Mick Wall, "Bono's Campaign for Africa: After Years of Lobbying the Rock Star Helps Rid the Continent of More Than $40 Billion in Debt," *People Weekly* 63.23 (June 27, 2005): 54.

Josh Tyrangiel, "Constant Charmer, The Inside Story of How the World's Biggest Rock Star Mastered the Political Game and Persuaded the World's Leaders to Take on Global Poverty; And He's Not Done Yet," *Time* (December 26, 2005): 46.

8
JIMMY CARTER

American politician who followed a disappointing single term as president of the United States with a long career as a peacemaker and moralist

THE CHOICE

In 1961, with **Saturn crossing his IC,** Jimmy Carter was embroiled in his first big political battle and, as with most of the political fights in Carter's life, it involved both politics and morality. As chairperson of the Sumter County school board, Carter had come out strong for consolidation of the county's schools. On the surface, his advocacy of this issue was based solely on making the school system more cost efficient, but many whites in his community saw consolidation of the schools as the first step toward integration of the schools. At that time, schools in Sumter County were still strictly segregated by race, and these conservative whites were not going to let a politically ambitious peanut farmer change this fact.

This is not to say that Jimmy Carter had thus far distinguished himself as a crusader for civil rights. Frankly, during his term on the Sumter County school board, Carter had done very little to rectify the grossly deficient state of African-American schools in the community. Although he privately abhorred segregation, Carter was careful not to publicly declare his support for school integration, since doing so in that intensely conservative part of Georgia would have been political suicide. Carter had already sparked the wrath of the racists in his community when he had refused to join a secret and exclusively white organization. Now, even though he articulated his support for consolidation on purely financial grounds, the pressure on Jimmy Carter from this conservative quarter had became more intense and open. Vandals painted a racist slogan on the doors of his warehouse and members of the community, even his relatives, refused to speak to him.

Carter persisted, however, confident that as vocal as the racist faction was, they did not express the opinion of the entire population. When the matter was put to a vote, he was almost proven correct. The school consolidation measure was defeated, but by only eighty votes. This was Jimmy Carter's first political defeat, and it was also his first moral victory.

THE HOROSCOPE

Jimmy Carter is another one of those people for whom every Saturn passage carried a double punch. His natal Saturn is just a few degrees below his Ascendant and close to a 90-degree aspect to his Midheaven, meaning that every time Saturn crosses one of his angles, it makes an important aspect to natal Saturn a couple of months later. It also means that Carter's personality is dominated by the qualities of Saturn. Having Saturn so significantly placed in the horoscope is the mark of a serious person, a practical and self-motivated person with a huge capacity for hard work and self-discipline. It describes a goal-centered personality, somewhat judgmental and at times harsh, with a tendency toward periods of depression and withdrawal.

The fact that his Sun and Ascendant are both in Libra certainly helps to sweeten the hard-driving qualities of Saturn on the Ascendant, or at least cover them over with a cheery smile. Carter's early life can be characterized as a constant battle between the seriousness of Saturn and the sociability of Libra. As a student, both in high school and in the naval college at Annapolis, Carter worked hard and generally excelled, but his studious habits tended to isolate him from his

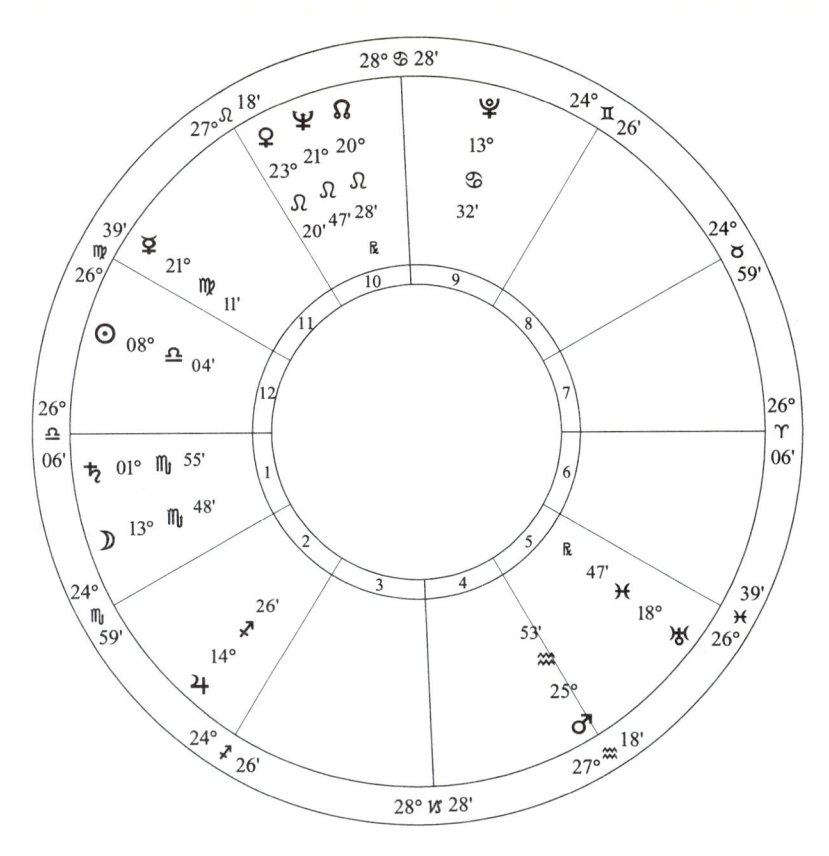

Jimmy Carter

October 1, 1924, 7:00 AM CST
Plains, GA, 32N02 84W23

peers, as did his deep religious convictions and high moral standards. Later in life, many considered Carter cold and calculating, a man whose only concern was proving himself the best at whatever activity he took up, even those, like golf, that he intensely disliked.

At the same time, Carter joined and actively worked in just about every social group open to him, from his church to business and professional organizations. He also developed significant friendships with people in the community who shared his progressive ideas. Though people who observed him from afar might have considered him standoffish, Carter's ability to communicate one-on-one was phenomenal. Later, during his presidential campaign, this Libran, person-to-person charm would become the hallmark of his political style.

There is a whole lot going on in Jimmy Carter's horoscope besides Libra and Saturn. It is, in fact, a spectacularly complex horoscope. Pluto trine his Moon in Scorpio provides for a talent for secrecy and even skullduggery when the need arises, and the opposition between Mercury and Uranus indicates a precise, if somewhat abstracted, way of thinking, along with an affinity for technology and innovation.

But perhaps the most interesting aspect in the horoscope is the opposition of Mars in Aquarius to his conjunction of Venus and Neptune in Leo. There is a great deal of sexual tension represented in this aspect, though little of this would be apparent considering the restrictive edifice of Saturn on the Ascendant. (Carter's interview in *Playboy*, in which he acknowledged "lusting in his heart," is a fitting summation of how these two factors worked against one another.) It is the influence of Neptune in this aspect that is most significant. During his years as a politician, Carter always presented himself as a paragon of uncompromising honesty, and yet closer examination of the statements he made during this time and the methods he used show a disturbing tendency to stretch the truth and tell people what they wanted or needed to hear at that moment. This is a manifestation of both the ends-justifies-the-means ruthlessness of his Moon to Pluto trine and the tendency of Neptune to dissolve boundaries and to obscure and romanticize the factual. The conflict between these tendencies and the need for straightforward honesty provided by Saturn are central to the function of this horoscope.

THE LIFE

By the time of his school consolidation fight, Carter's double doses of Saturn had already played a significant role in his life. **When Saturn crossed his Midheaven and squared his natal Saturn in 1945,** he had graduated, after only three years, from Annapolis and married a shy young woman from Plains named Rosalynn Smith. Just after **Saturn passed over his Ascendant and reached his natal Saturn in November 1953,** Carter's father died and the ambitious young naval officer was forced to give up his promising career in the military and return to Plains to run the family business. So there can be little doubt that the Saturn aspects that occurred in 1961 also changed Carter's direction in life, and it should come as no surprise that a year later, seemingly at the last minute, Jimmy Carter decided to run for the state senate. After a tough campaign, during which Carter uncovered a plot on the part of his opponent to stuff the ballot boxes, Jimmy Carter became perhaps the hardest working state senator in the history of Georgia. Again his strict attention to the details of his new position made it difficult for him to form alliances within state government, but this didn't stop Carter from running for governor in 1966.

His opponent was Lester Maddox, a restaurant owner and local radio personality who had gained national fame when he refused to allow African-Americans to eat at his restaurant. Although Maddox maintained that he was not a racist and was only opposed to federal intervention into the affairs of honest businessmen, he immediately became the darling of conservative segregationists in the state. Entering the race, Carter felt certain that his experience in state government and his rational approach to the state's problems would easily outshine Maddox's gift for self-promotion. The voting public proved him wrong.

In his later accounts of his life, Carter considered this political defeat a turning point. It led him to a serious reappraisal of his life and a new, born-again commitment to his religious beliefs. Carter left Georgia for a time and worked as a missionary. He found the experience exhilarating. And yet, he continued to talk about running for governor again in 1970 and he gathered around him a core of workers with whom he studied and abstracted the voting histories and political demographics of every county in Georgia. Carter's combined Saturn aspects, **this time the conjunction of Saturn with his Descendant and the opposition of Saturn to its natal place, occurred between August 1968 and May 1969.** Although it is probably true that Jimmy Carter became a born-again Christian during this period, it is obvious that he was determined to make himself a born-again politician as well.

The key to Carter's 1970 campaign was the Democratic primary, where he was matched against a liberal lawyer from Atlanta. In a carefully calculated and, some might say, cynical ploy, Carter conveniently forgot about his college education, his high-level training aboard the nation's first nuclear submarines, and his opposition to segregation, and portrayed himself as a simple country boy trying his luck against the rich folks in the big city. He was careful not to bring up issues of race, and when they were brought up he was quick to portray his opponent as the true "race-mixer." He also made a variety of accusations about his opponent's finances and business practices. These accusations all proved to be false, but by the time this was accomplished Carter had secured the nomination.

It was only after Jimmy Carter was elected governor, after easily defeating the Republican candidate, that he revealed his true colors to the public. In his inaugural speech, he made it clear that he would work toward securing civil rights for African-Americans in Georgia. How those who had voted for the simple farm boy felt about this was not recorded, but the national press was definitely intrigued by this progressive young Southern governor. Carter made the cover of *TIME* Magazine and gained his first taste of national exposure. He was determined it would not be his last.

It seems that even as he took the office of governor of Georgia, Carter was already looking ahead to an even higher office. Uranus had crossed his natal Sun during his primary victory, and his secondary progressed Jupiter was trine his natal Venus. His confidence was high, some might say euphoric, and he was thoroughly enjoying his role as governor. It was only natural, given his ambitious, Saturn-driven nature, that he would start making plans to run for president.

Carter began his run for the Democratic presidential nomination the same way he began his successful run for governor. He started early, worked hard, and made as much use of his one-on-one political charm as was physically possible. Still, Carter faced an uphill fight. After the Watergate affair, there was a virtual flood of candidates vying for the Democratic nomination. Carter was just one of a large field of politicians. Carter's careful, labor-intensive political methods and his emphatically moderate message seemed ill-suited to make him stand out in the pack.

Then Saturn came to his rescue. **Saturn made its first contact with Carter's MC** in September 1975, at the time when Carter was campaigning in Iowa, preparing for that state's caucuses. An article in the *New York Times* published in October noted that Carter's grassroots organization was far superior to that of all the other Democratic candidates. This gave Carter's campaign credibility that it desperately needed. **When Saturn squared his natal Saturn,** Carter won the Iowa caucuses. **By the time Saturn crossed back and forth across his Midheaven again and made its final aspect with its natal place in June 1976, he had won enough delegates to assure his nomination.**

After Watergate and the resignation of President Nixon, with the unimpressive and politically tainted Gerald Ford as his opponent, Carter's path to the White House should have been assured. And yet, the ambitious Southern governor, with his infectious smile and soft Georgia drawl, made a number of missteps. He proved to be the perfect Libran candidate, arguing first one side of contentious issues like abortion and civil rights and then the other. It was the kind of duplicity that had worked well for him during his 1970 campaign for governor, but on the big stage of a presidential campaign with the media reporting his every word, it became a severe liability. Carter's flip-flops and apparent lack of a political agenda caused many voters to wonder, but in the end he was elected president.

Carter's problems did not end with his inauguration. Though many positive things were accomplished during his term in office, such as the SALT II treaty, the Panama Canal treaty, and the historic Camp David accord, which rewrote the history of the Arab/Israeli conflict, most historians consider the Carter presidency a study in how not to succeed as president. Carter himself acknowledged that he tried to "manage" the country, just as he had so successfully managed his businesses and the state of Georgia, when he should have been "leading" (Morris, 1996). Management, even the most sincere and careful management, was not what the American people needed in the face of runaway inflation, rising oil prices, and the hostage crisis in Iran. They quickly tired of Carter's calls to conserve gasoline and turn down the thermostat. They didn't want to be told they were in a "malaise," as truthful as that statement may have been (Morris, 1996). Nor were they happy showing "restraint" when religious extremists took over the American embassy in Iran. Carter brought a nose-to-the-grindstone, morally upright, Saturn kind of an administration to a country that was looking for Aquarian vision, or at least a little Aries belligerence. Thus it was not a surprise when, in 1980, incumbent president Jimmy Carter lost the election to an Aquarian actor with a bellicose, cowboy attitude.

Immediately after the election and for the next several months, Saturn was aligned with Carter's Sun. This was a difficult time for the ex-president. Not only did he have to absorb his crushing defeat by Ronald Reagan, but he found that his businesses in Plains had suffered greatly during his absence and he was forced to sell his peanut warehouse to pay debts. Also, Carter found himself marginalized in the political world both by liberal Democrats, who remained unhappy with his centrist message, and conservative Republicans who regarded him as a failure.

By the time Saturn reached his Ascendant and its second conjunction with his natal Saturn, Carter was starting to fight back. He had resolved that the monument to his presidency was to be more than a library filled with his papers. He envisioned something he called the Carter Center, which would be a philanthropic organization that could help the poorest people in the world, work for fair elections in young democracies, and arbitrate peaceful resolution of international disputes. **By 1983, when Saturn made its final contact with his natal Saturn**, enough funding had been secured to put the project into motion.

Over the next two decades, the Carter Center would engage in important charitable work all across the world, fighting disease and poverty. With the backing of the Carter Center, Jimmy Carter would become an itinerant peacemaker, taking the negotiating finesse he had proven during his presidency to a variety of hot spots, often with dramatic results. On the domestic front, the ex-president's volunteer work with Habitat for Humanity has helped popularize that charitable organization. Carter has also become a prolific author, writing memoirs and books on important issues like the situation in the Middle East. More than any other former president of our time, he has maintained his public voice and public influence, and it is the opinion of many that he has proven himself to be a more effective leader as an ex-president than he ever was as a president.

SATURN AT WORK

After his crushing 1966 defeat to Lester Maddox, Carter's sister, Ruth Carter Stapleton, asked him if he was willing to give up politics for the sake of his faith (Mazlish and Diamond 1979). It was a question for which Carter had no immediate answer. When Saturn crossed his Descendant in 1967 and opposed his natal Saturn, he was offered this same choice. Was his destiny going to be driven by his religious faith or by his political ambitions? Carter chose both. As a politician he would do whatever was required to win elections. As a Christian he would profess and attempt to hold himself to a higher moral standard.

The fallacy in this double choice is obvious and yet, for a while, Carter seemed to be making it work. He was able to find room in his complex personality for both the ruthless competitor and the open-hearted Christian. While others might have seen contradictions between his methods and his message, Carter remained oblivious. He was certain that it was possible to be both an effective politician and a staunch moralist.

In 1976, Jimmy Carter achieved the highest goal to which any American politician could aspire, but it came at a price. In a manner of speaking, in giving Carter exactly what he wanted from life, Saturn was also exposing the fallacies of his previous choices. As president, Carter found that he could not just drop his role as effective politician and assume the mantle of a moral leader, and his attempts to do so only convinced many Americans that he was untrustworthy while others viewed him as weak.

It was only after Carter was voted out of office and his political ambitions were finally dashed that he was able to resolve the fallacy of his disastrous double choice. At this point, he was able to put aside his role as a politician and devote himself to promoting the values of justice and peace that are so crucial to his Christian faith. As a moralist, and moralist only, Jimmy Carter has thrived. He has been able to actualize the best qualities represented in his horoscope, from his peace-making Libra Sun and his practical, tradition-loving Saturn. He has become our voice of reason in a time when every other voice seems shrill and tainted by partisanship.

SOURCES

Bruce Mazlish and Edwin Diamond, *Jimmy Carter: A Character Portrait* (New York: Simon & Schuster, 1979).

Kenneth E. Morris, *Jimmy Carter: American Moralist* (Athens, GA: University of Georgia Press, 1996).

9

MICHAEL J. FOX

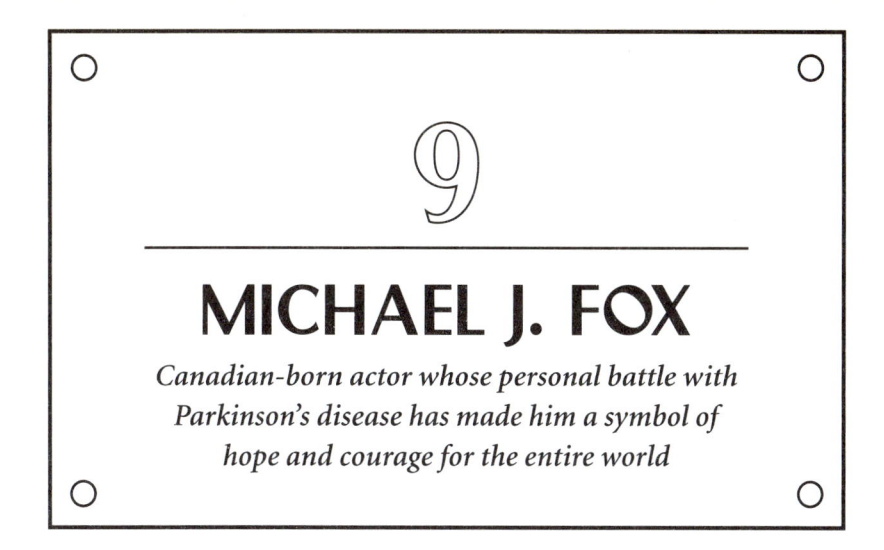

Canadian-born actor whose personal battle with Parkinson's disease has made him a symbol of hope and courage for the entire world

THE CHOICE

In November 1998, a man prepared for the end of his career. It was not a matter of retirement. The man in question was only thirty-seven. Nor was he unhappy with his career. He was an actor and he loved his work. His ability to slip in and out of roles and make people laugh and cry was a key element to his identity and had been since he was in junior high school—but now he was making a decision that would, from his point of view, irreparably damage his rapport with his audience and, in all likelihood, end his thriving career. The man was Michael J. Fox, and he was about to reveal to the public that he suffered from a serious degenerative illness called Parkinson's disease.

Fox had been avoiding this decision for seven years, since his first symptoms and the devastating diagnosis. He had done so partly because of his career, but also because of his own reluctance to admit to himself that he was a sick man. He had fought off his symptoms with medication and his own will. He kept on performing when the constant tremors and weakness in his limbs made it nearly impossible for him to move. After his diagnosis, Fox had gone on making movies and he had become the star of a popular TV sitcom, *Spin City*. The personal effort Fox put into these achievements was a painful contrast from the fresh, uncomplicated persona that had become his trademark, and that effort became more painful and exhausting with each passing day. Meanwhile, the news media began asking questions about Fox's frequent absences from rehearsals and his many "nervous" ticks. Finally, as **Saturn made its separating square to his natal Saturn**, Michael J. Fox came to understand that his attempts to conceal his illness were becoming as much an impediment to his work as the illness itself. He made his confession and prepared for the worst.

THE HOROSCOPE

Michael J. Fox's horoscope is dominated by three conjunctions. The most dramatic of these is the conjunction of Mars and Uranus in Leo on Fox's Descendant. This is an extremely dynamic aspect, providing for extraordinary daring, extreme expenditure of physical energy, and amazing instances of both good and bad luck. It is the kind of aspect one might associate with a sports hero (Fox's earliest ambition was to be a hockey star) or an inveterate speedster (the first major purchase Fox made after he landed his role on *Family Ties* was a sports car). What this aspect definitely does not describe is a personality content to sit and wait. For better or worse, it is the aspect of a fighter, an activist, a highly independent individual who thrives on competition.

It is significant that this conjunction forms a close sextile to Fox's Sun in Gemini, which is very near his IC. This connection ties all of the previously mentioned qualities to the core of Fox's ego. It also emphasizes the fact that Mars and Uranus are in Leo, the sign ruled by the Sun. The patient, dignified qualities of this sign help soften some of the extremism and restlessness of Mars and Uranus, while countering the shrill contentiousness of this conjunction with a high degree of self-confidence and a touch of charisma.

The second crucial conjunction in this horoscope involves the Moon and Venus within a degree of each other in the placid sign of Taurus. This is an aspect of charm and grace, inherently likable, with a good dose of earthy fun. Self-indulgence and blind materialism is often a problem with

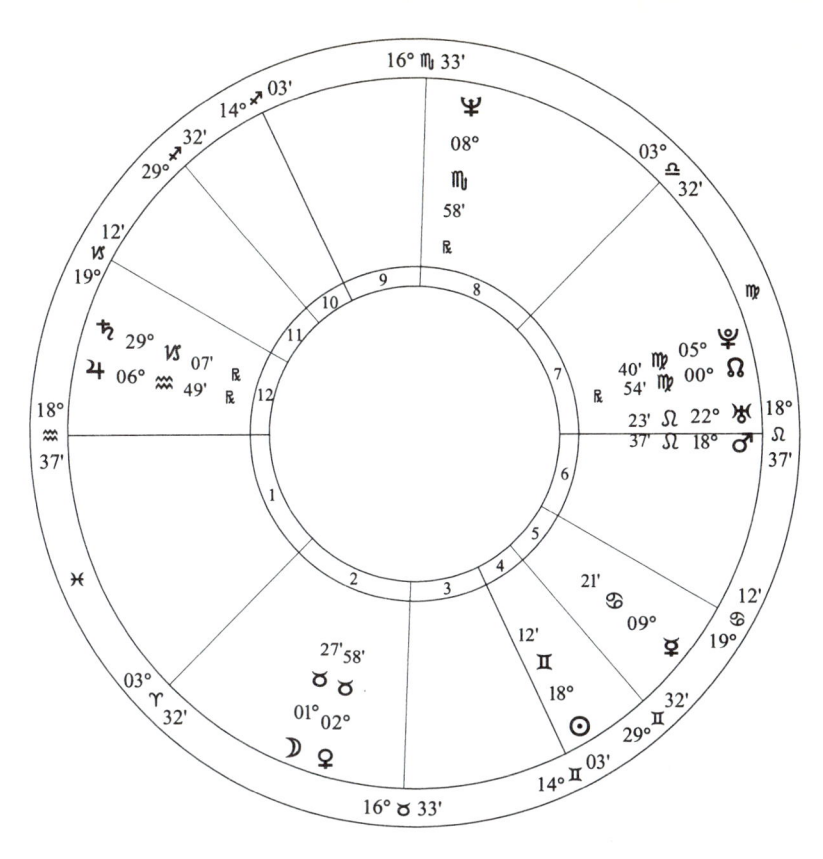

Michael J. Fox
June 9, 1961, 12:15 AM MST
Edmonton, Alberta, Canada, 53N33 113W28

an aspect of this sort, but there is such gentleness, such an appreciation of beauty, such a knack for artistry and love, that these faults are easily overlooked. The trine between this Moon to Venus conjunction and Fox's Pluto in his 7th House indicates a talent for using this personal charm in a very conscious and measured way to control relationships and smooth over conflicts (particularly conflicts brought on by the wild and often inconsiderate tendencies of his Mars to Uranus conjunction). This Moon to Venus conjunction also works very well with Fox's Gemini Sun. The "easy to like" qualities of this aspect add an irresistible sweetness to the natural wit and playfulness of a Gemini Sun sign.

The third conjunction in Fox's horoscope is a rather wide conjunction of Saturn and Jupiter in his 12th House. What makes this conjunction so important is the fact that both Saturn and Jupiter form a square to Fox's Moon to Venus conjunction. In fact, if we include Neptune, which is positioned directly across from the Moon and Venus in Scorpio, we have a somewhat spread-out T-square. This setup indicates that, despite the charm it provides, Fox's Moon to Venus conjunction is also the center of a good deal of trouble within the chart. In particular, the square between the Moon and Saturn, which is the closest single aspect in the system, is famously problematic. It predicts a tendency toward depression and intense self-doubt. With this aspect, there is always the danger of self-destructive behavior, particularly when the person gives in to his or her pessimism and loses hope for the future. The presence of Jupiter in this equation helps to curtail some of the depressive qualities of this aspect, but there will certainly be moments of self-doubt and instances of self-degradation. For Fox, these moments were evident in his dependency on alcohol and his unwillingness to squarely face the facts of his illness for many years.

It should also be noted that Fox's horoscope is one of those that belies the influence of the Sun sign. Fox is a Gemini Sun Sign, yet the Sun is the only body in his chart in Gemini. More importantly, aside from his Pluto in Virgo, he has no other placements in mutable signs. Instead, fixed signs (Aquarius rising, the Moon and Venus in Taurus, Mars in Leo) dominate the chart. This gives us a personality that is much more determined, strong-willed, and stubborn than the typical Gemini Sun.

THE LIFE

Michael J. Fox grew up in the small town of Burnaby, British Columbia. His father was in the Canadian military and during his earliest years the family had moved frequently but, by time Michael was ten, his father had retired and Burnaby became their permanent home. Here, Fox's childhood was thoroughly normal. He was an active child with a keen interest in sports. In this area he often excelled, despite his small frame, because of his skill and his aggressive, head-first enthusiasm. The only painful event he recalled from this period was the sudden death of his grandmother, which occurred just as Saturn crossed his natal Sun.

By the time Fox entered middle school, his consuming passion was music. He took up the guitar and formed a rock band. The band performed in some local venues, but made little money. He began hanging out with other kids who shared his taste for loud, raucous music and playing the rebel. Meanwhile, his practical parents had to wonder what would ever become of their flighty son.

Fox found another interest in middle school. It was his drama class. It seemed that he was a natural on stage, that acting and performing in front of an audience was his inherent gift. His teacher was so impressed with Fox's ability that in 1977, shortly after the boy's sixteenth birthday and **just as Saturn crossed his Descendant**, he urged Michael to audition for a part in a Canadian television show called *Leo and Me*. It was a typical "cattle call" situation with hundreds of young men trying out for the part. Fox strolled into the studio and won it with seemingly little effort.

Suddenly Michael J. Fox was a TV star, at least in Canada, and he was making as much money in a day as he could make all summer working a regular job. He returned to high school that fall, but his real interest was in finding new acting jobs. The more he succeeded in this effort, the more Fox became convinced that school was a waste of time. Neptune was moving between a conjunction with his MC and an opposition to his Sun at this time; a dangerous time to make career decisions, and Fox was about to make a momentous one. At the end of the semester he dropped out of high school. The next year, still under this Neptune aspect, Fox moved to Los Angeles.

At first, everything seemed to be going Fox's way. He quickly found an agent and a job in a Disney production but, as often happens with decisions made under the influence of Neptune, this good fortune was short-lived. Soon Fox was struggling. Through 1980 and 1981 he found little work and was reduced to taking calls from his agent on a pay phone because he could no longer pay his phone bill.

Then, in 1982, there was a glimmer of hope. He got a part on a new TV sitcom called *Family Ties*. In March 1982, NBC agreed to pick up the show, but Brandon Tartikoff, then the head of NBC, felt Fox was too short to play the part of the family's teenage son. He wanted the part of Alex Keaton recast. Fortunately, the producer of the show remained adamant in his support of Fox. Fox kept the part and, when the show was aired that fall, it became an immediate hit. More importantly, it quickly developed that everyone's favorite character on the show was Michael J. Fox. **By the time Saturn began its age twenty-one square to his natal Saturn in November 1982**, Fox was an American television sensation.

The quality Fox brought to his character, intended to be an abrasive and utterly materialistic foil to his hippie parents, was a gentle humanity — a combination of youthful bravado, charm, and a hint of insecurity. It was a fairly true reflection of Fox's off-screen personality. Away from the cameras, Michael Fox was an emphatically regular guy. He liked fast cars, sports, hanging out with his buddies, and drinking beer. His fondness for alcohol did not present a problem for Fox at this point of his life. With so many young celebrities falling to drug addiction, getting wasted on beer seemed relatively innocuous.

Besides, at this point in his life, Michael J. Fox had a lot of things to celebrate. Uranus was crossing first his Midheaven and then moving opposite his Sun. With Uranus so strong in his natal chart, these transits naturally brought dramatic events. In January 1985, Fox was offered the lead in a Stephen Speilberg film that was to be titled *Back to the Future*. Fox had already made one movie, a teen comedy called *Teen Wolf*, but the opportunity to work with a director as important and talented as Speilberg was an offer Fox could hardly refuse. For the next several months, Fox worked two highly demanding jobs, first rehearsing and performing his part on *Family Ties*, and then racing to another studio to work on *Back to the Future*. It was a grueling schedule, but the payoff was tremendous. When *Back to the Future* was released that summer, it was a blockbuster hit and Michael Fox was launched to a level of fame he could hardly have imagined growing up in Burnsby.

Now that he was a mega-star, Fox could have easily withdrawn from *Family Ties*, but he loved doing the show. This love was rewarded the next year when he won an Emmy for his portrayal of Alex Keaton. That same year Tracy Pollan joined the cast, playing Alex's girlfriend. At first, Pollan was not impressed with Fox. His shiny new celebrity and his penchant for fancy cars and nightly parties struck her as crass and self-destructive. Early in 1987, however, the cast traveled to London to do a television movie. There, Pollan and Fox began what would be a whirlwind courtship. By that summer the couple was shopping for houses together. By October they announced their engagement. **Saturn crossed Fox's MC in August 1987.**

At this point, the life of Michael J. Fox seemed to level off at a very comfortable cruising altitude. He was happily married (on July 16, 1988), he had a son (born in May 1989), and he made movies. None of these movies were as tremendously successful as *Back to the Future*. Some were good and some were thoroughly forgettable. Still, Fox remained a bankable Hollywood star and the offers continued to come his way.

Unfortunately, people with horoscopes dominated by Uranus cannot expect such periods of peace and comfort to last long. For these people, sudden ascents are typically followed by sudden descents. For Fox, this descent began in January 1990 with the death of his father. Transiting Pluto was square his natal Mars (and his Descendant) at the same time that secondary progressed Mars moved slowly across his natal Pluto. These are aspects of transformation, often painful transformation. The transformation continued for Fox later that year when he experienced his first tremors, the early symptom of Parkinson's disease.

At first these physical symptoms were relatively mild. **Early in 1991, with Saturn returning to its natal place,** Fox resolved to take a rest, cut back on his drinking, and get a little more exercise, but nothing he did seemed to stop the tremors. By the summer, evidence of his physical deterioration was increasing and his wife was becoming alarmed. Fox began seeing doctors. **Meanwhile, transiting Saturn was moving retrograde, back toward its natal place. It stopped just one degree shy of that position in October 1991.** That month, Fox was finally persuaded to see a neurologist who diagnosed his problem as Parkinson's disease.

Fox claims his first reaction to the diagnosis was rage, followed by denial. He took the pills his doctor prescribed and he kept his appointments, shuffling in and out back doors to avoid being seen, but he refused to accept his illness as an integral part of his life. He buried himself in his work and when that was not enough, he turned to alcohol. His beer binges had previously been a source of entertainment. Now they became a means of escape. Fox was still mindful that he was a family man. He tried to limit his excessive drinking to periods when he was away from his wife and son. Predictably, however, in the summer of 1992, one of his carefully scheduled indulgences ran too long and his son found Fox passed out on the floor of their home. **Saturn was moving across his Ascendant at this time**, adding the sting of personal failure and judgment to Fox's obvious embarrassment. The actor immediately resolved to quit drinking entirely.

Fox's new sobriety in no way changed his attitude toward his Parkinson's disease. He was still determined to keep his illness a secret and work as hard as was physically possible. During the next few years, Fox made a series of unsuccessful films. Finally, in 1996 he told his agent that he wanted to return to television. His agent balked, thinking that this would be a step backward for his client, but Fox persisted until he gained the lead role in a sitcom called *Spin City*. The series became a hit and once again, Fox's career seemed to be on the rise.

In the meantime, Fox's symptoms continued to worsen. In March 1998, he had brain surgery to lessen the tremors on his left side, but this only increased the tremors on the right side of his body. His work was impacted. The grueling day-to-day schedule of rehearsals and shooting necessary to produce a weekly television show, a challenge that he had accepted with gladness in his youth, now became impossible for him. **When Saturn squared its natal place** and Fox made his decision to reveal his condition, it was, for him, a final surrender. However, it quickly became evident to Fox that his surrender was, in fact, a victory. Support for the actor, both from his fans and from other victims of Parkinson's disease, gave Fox a new notoriety. Even as he withdrew from his role in *Spin City* and prepared for the end of his acting career (though he went on to prosper as the voice of animal and animated characters in several popular movies), Michael J. Fox was launched into a new career.

The form this new career would take became very evident for Fox **in April 2002, a month before Saturn crossed his IC**. His recently published autobiography, *Lucky Man: A Memoir*, had just become a number one bestseller and he was called upon, along with boxing champion Muhammad Ali, to testify before Congress in support for increased funding for research into Parkinson's disease. Fox was already prepared to take on the role as an advocate for Parkinson's patients. The profits from his autobiography went to the Michael J. Fox Foundation, which Fox had formed in 2002. In August 2002, the foundation offered a $4 million dollar grant to scientists looking for a cure for the disease (Larkin, 2002).

Fox's new role was further defined when **Saturn made its opposition to natal Saturn in July 2005**. At this time, Fox was asked to testify before Congress again, but now he was asking the House of Representatives to rescind restrictions imposed by the administration of President George W. Bush on stem-cell research. His testimony placed him in direct opposition to the president and the conservatives who felt using human stem cells in research was immoral (Monro, 2002). Fox continued to speak out on this issue and he supported candidates who favored his position in the congressional elections held in November 2006. Shortly before those elections and **shortly after Saturn crossed Fox's Descendant**, conservative radio commentator Rush Limbaugh parodied Fox's jerky speech on the air and accused the activist of pretending to be more afflicted than he really was. Limbaugh's outrageously insensitive remarks backfired and many rose to defend Fox. After Democrats who supported stem-cell research won majorities in the House and Senate, some even said that it was Limbaugh's remarks and Fox's likeability that helped turn the tide (Yuan, 2006).

SATURN AT WORK

Growing up is never easy. For someone like Michael J. Fox, who had experienced phenomenal success during his early twenties, mostly while playing characters ten years younger, it would have been a difficult transition even under the best of circumstances. The choice presented to him during his first Saturn return, the major grown-up Saturn passage, came in circumstances that were far from the best. Faced with a dire diagnosis that irreparably changed his life and career, Fox could hardly be blamed for delaying a decision, for gamely and hopelessly pretending that it had never happened. These evasive tactics worked for several years, until Saturn made a separating square to its natal place—then it was time for Fox to admit that his run of exceptional good luck had come to an end, and that a painful transformation was in the offing.

It should also be noted that the passage of Saturn over his Midheaven did not coincide with events directly related to Fox's career. Instead, this was the time during which he and his wife-to-be fell in love. The importance of this relationship to Fox's development can not be overstated, a point Fox frequently makes in his autobiography and in interviews. Tracy Pollan became the tough, yet beloved, female figure so aptly configured in Fox's horoscope through the square between his Moon to Venus conjunction and Saturn and Jupiter. Supported by Pollan, Fox was able to find his way to a new career track that came to overshadow both his identity as an actor and his efforts as an advocate for Parkinson's research. That new role, discovered as Saturn crossed his Midheaven, was as a husband and a father, and his ability to identify himself with this role not only has helped him deal with his illness, it has become one of the chief reasons that Fox, in his bestselling autobiography, referred to himself as a "lucky man."

SOURCES

Daisy Maryles, "'Lucky Man,' Says He," *Publishers Weekly* 249 (April 15, 2002).

Neil Munro, "Cloning Begets Diverse Factions," *National Journal*, 34.17 (April 27, 2002).

Michael Larkin, "Parkinson's Disease Research Grant Available," *The Lancet*, 360.9332 (August 17, 2002).

Michael J. Fox, *Lucky Man: A Memoir* (New York: Hyperion, 2002).

Jada Yuan, "Bullying Rush OK With Fox: Helps Stems," *New York*, 39.42 (November 27, 2006).

10

RALPH NADER

Consumer advocate who rose to fame as the champion of automobile safety and for his opposition to corporate influence on American government

THE CHOICE

In 1961 there was a terrible traffic accident and a young man was badly injured. It is an event that might seem tragically prosaic until you understand that the young man in question was a friend of a recent graduate of the Harvard School of Law named Ralph Nader. Previous to this event, the subject of automobile safety had been a concern of Nader's, but largely an academic concern. He had written a paper on it in law school, written articles on the subject for magazines, and even testified before state legislators. But after 1961, his interest became a passion. Another buddy from law school, who had landed a job working for the Illinois legislature, made the mistake in 1961 of telling Ralph that his bosses were considering, very tentatively, a bill to require seat belts in cars. Nader responded with a series of fiery letters preaching the importance of the issue and quoting the numbers of dead and injured that could be saved. **Saturn had just crossed Ralph Nader's Ascendant** that year, and what had once been a school project now became the ultimate direction of his life.

Prior to 1961, many might have wondered exactly what young Ralph Nader was going to do with his life. After graduating *magna cum laude* from Princeton (**when Saturn passed over his Midheaven**), he had easily gained admittance to Harvard law school where, despite the fact that he felt Harvard was too elitist and oriented toward maintaining the status quo, he advanced to edit the *Harvard Review*. His friends were somewhat surprised when, after graduation, Ralph took a position at a small law firm in Hartford, Connecticut, near his family home. Ralph's main passion at this point in his life seemed to be travel. By the time he graduated from Harvard he had traveled all across the United States and to the Middle East (his parents had come to the United States from Lebanon). After graduation, he took off for Cuba with a buddy, and in 1961 he visited Chile, Sweden, and the USSR. His friends were used to getting phone calls from Ralph, telling them that they had to drop everything and fly off with him to some distant destination. The problem was that more and more of these friends were settling down with important jobs, wives, and mortgages. Nader, who remained single and relatively free of responsibilities, seemed bound to become a brilliant but hopelessly eccentric gadfly.

THE HOROSCOPE

If they had had an understanding of Ralph Nader's horoscope, his friends would have never doubted the young man's ability to do something important. Sure, he had a Pisces Sun sign, and sometimes appeared a bit muddled. The deep emotionality of Pisces is reflected in the close ties Nader maintained with his family throughout his life and the fact that he chose the security of taking a small-time job near home over the challenge of joining a top-level law firm in a major city. But this emotional mush is aptly covered by a cool and idealistic Aquarius Ascendant. Moreover, with Saturn and Venus in the 1st House, there is a lot of drive and self-discipline in the chart. There is even just a touch of narcissism with Venus in the mix. These tendencies are furthered by the Moon's angular placement in Leo. This is a proud, strong-willed personality in which the vision and passion of

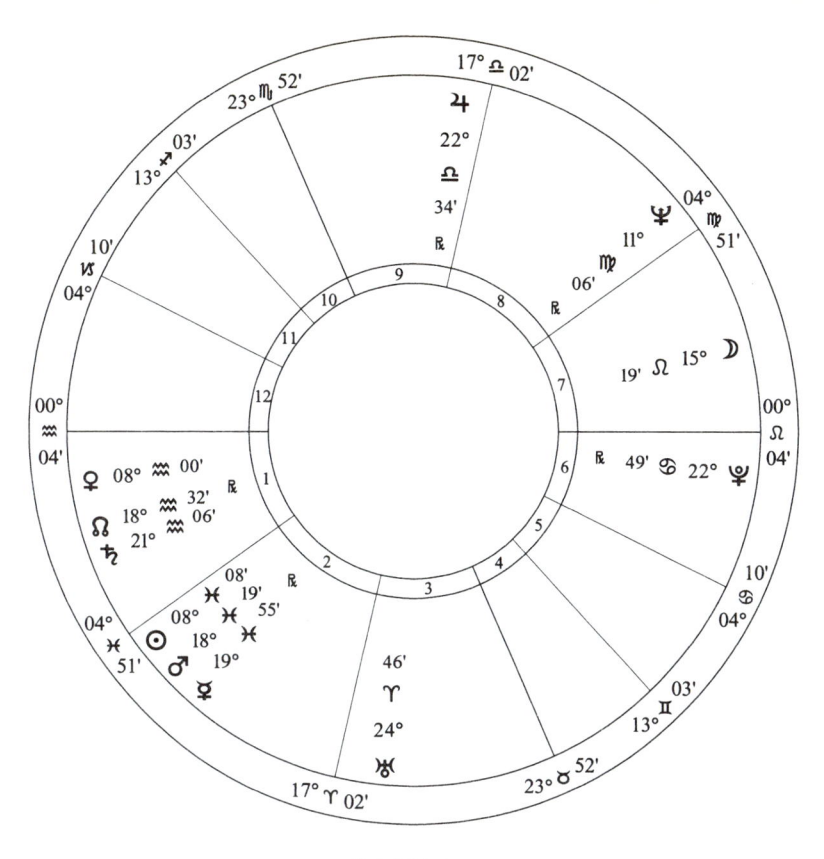

Ralph Nader

February 27, 1934, 4:52 AM EST
Winsted, CT, 41N55 73W04

Pisces will be mingled with the all-or-nothing idealism of Aquarius and the fiery egotism of Leo.

The most dynamic aspect in the chart is a close T-square between Jupiter, Uranus, and Pluto. Saturn is also involved in this system, making a trine to Jupiter, a sextile to Uranus, and a quincunx to Pluto. This is something of a generational aspect between three slow-moving planets. It would be found in the horoscopes of anyone born during the first few months of 1934, but in Nader's horoscope this impersonal aspect makes a very personal contact with his natal Sun. His Sun is within a degree of an exact sesquiquadrate (135-degree aspect) to both Jupiter and Pluto. The sesquiquadrate is generally not thought of as an important aspect. In fact, it probably shouldn't even be considered outside of an orb of 60 minutes. In this case, however, it links the ego with a very powerful aspect system. Here we see the ego reacting to both the expansive, benevolent influence of Jupiter and the fatalistic restrictions of Pluto. It is an aspect that implies a toughness and resiliency within the ego as well as a strong sense of personal worth. Since the sesquiquadrate is typically considered a negative aspect, there is the potential that this expansive sense of personal worth can become exaggerated and unrealistic and the toughness can deteriorate into an addiction to power.

Despite their negative implications, these sesquiquadrate aspects add a great deal of focus to the personality and a capacity for leadership. Taken in concert with the conjunction of Mercury and Mars, they give us the horoscope of a fighter, a person who uses words and idea as weapons. The most negative aspect in the horoscope is the opposition between the Sun and Neptune. This aspect is negative because it reinforces some of the worst qualities of Nader's Pisces Sun. It increases a tendency for self-deception and unrealistic thinking, as well as making it more likely that Pisces emotionalism will often interfere with his Aquarian logic.

THE LIFE

In late 1963, when Saturn reached a conjunction with his natal Saturn, Ralph Nader quit his job in Hartford and hitchhiked to Washington to work part-time for the Department of Labor. He was determined to do something about automobile safety at the national level, and he used his position to amass a gigantic hoard of data on the subject. It just so happened that Congressman Abraham Ribicoff was thinking along the same lines. He was about to begin hearings in the Senate on the subject, and in 1964, as Uranus opposed his natal Sun, Nader was interviewed by one of Ribicoff's aides. The man was so impressed by the wealth of knowledge Nader possessed that he encouraged his boss to hire Nader to help with the research. At the same time, a small publishing house asked him to write a book on auto safety or the lack thereof. After missing two deadlines, Nader finished *Unsafe at Any Speed* in a blaze of speed and it was published the next year. Meanwhile, Ribicoff's hearings were getting underway and, as the author of a book on the subject, Nader was called as an expert witness. About this time, the new author became aware that he was being followed. Strangers were quizzing his friends about his habits and personal life, and he was receiving vaguely threatening phone calls. For Nader, the breaking point came when strange women began approaching him in public and inviting him to come to their rooms. Nader went to the press. Sensing a juicy story, reporters quickly determined that a private detective had been hired to investigate Nader, and the detective's client turned out to be none other than the head of General Motors.

When Nader came to testify for a second time before Ribicoff's subcommittee, the matter of concern was not automobile safety; it was whether or not one of the subjects of the investigation had tried to intimidate and impugn one of its expert witnesses. The gallery was full and the press hung on every word as the CEO of General Motors made his cool—but none too convincing—denials in the face of heated questioning from the enraged senators. Then Nader (who had arrived late to the hearings) was called to testify. His outrage and sense of absolute righteousness captivated the audience and, via the press, the entire nation. Here was a little guy taking on one of the largest corporations in the world, a man whose only concern (borne out by his enemy's own investigation) was saving lives and finding justice, and he was winning. A few months later, while the automobile lobby was back in Detroit licking its wounds, Congress passed a sweeping bill mandating the manufacture of safer automobiles.

After his testimony before the Senate, sales of *Unsafe at Any Speed* skyrocketed, and Ralph Nader became something of a folk hero. He did not rest on his laurels. Immediately after the auto safety bill was passed, Nader began working for tougher standards for meat processors, and again he won an impressive victory against entrenched corporate interests. In 1968, he brought six young lawyers to Washington, the first band of the so-called "Nader's Raiders." They uncovered egregious corruption in the Federal Trade Commission, forcing a major reorganization of that agency. The next year, the number of Nader's Raiders was greatly expanded, as was the number of causes and investigations. Meanwhile Nader maintained the same frugal lifestyle that had sustained him during his lean first months in Washington. He lived in a rooming house, did not own or drive a car, kept his own personal expenses at a subsistence level, and remained entirely devoted to his work.

The years 1970 and 1971, the period when **Saturn reached his IC**, are generally considered the peak of Nader's influence in Washington and his nationwide popularity. It was during this period that Nader came up with the idea of Personal Injury Research Groups (PIRGs). The basic notion was to have offices permanently staffed with attorneys whose only mission was consumer protection. These groups were set up near college campuses all across the country, and the participation of students in researching and preparing cases was encouraged. PIRGs became sort of a franchise of Nader's ideas about public safety and consumer rights. He also started a fundraising organization called Public Citizen, and an organization devoted to investigating abuses in the medical field called the Health Research Group. He was a frequent guest on television talk shows, and much in demand as a speaker at colleges and other venues. Then, in 1971, he was approached by a group of disgruntled Democrats to run for president on a third party ticket. Nader turned down the offer.

During this same period, however, Nader was beginning the trend that would eventually lead to his downfall. Despite his many years in Washington, Nader had never become a politician. The notion of political realism, compromise, and incremental change seemed to him, with his passion for saving lives and protecting the innocent from injury, sinful. Also, Nader's early victories had been complete and sweeping because the problems he addressed were so obvious, and caused public outcry when they were revealed. By 1970, his work had progressed to issues like air quality and occupational safety, which simply did not capture public attention the way car crashes and bad meat did. When Nader saw congressmen and senators accepting, even celebrating, watered-down, compromised laws and standards regarding these issues, he spoke out with righteous outrage. Unfortunately, among the people he savaged during this period were liberal members of Congress who had once been his closest allies, including his old friend, Abraham Ribicoff.

A few months after Saturn passed over Nader's IC, the activist called upon his Raiders to begin a comprehensive investigation of Congress. Every member was to be interviewed and studied and a report was to be written on the voting patterns and connections to corporate interests of each. It was a daunting task, even for Nader's fervent minions—particularly because many of the more liberal senators and representatives took the raid as personal betrayal. In the end, the effort failed to produce any results except the alienation of most of Nader's friends in Congress. Later, when Nader was fighting to broaden the Freedom of Information Act, he found, apparently to his surprise, that his old friends were no longer willing to listen to him or to put their reputations on the line because of his sense of righteousness. The bill to expand the Freedom of Information Act died.

In June 1976, when **Saturn made its last contact with Nader's Descendant**, it looked like help was on the way. Jimmy Carter had sewn up the Democratic nomination and appeared to be poised to take the White House. Nader met several times with Carter during this period, and even umpired a softball game between Carter's staff and reporters in Plains. He felt he would finally have an influence at the highest level of government. But Carter was essentially a centrist Libra, adept at convincing both liberals and conservatives he was on their side. Once Carter won the election and started announcing the members of his cabinet, Nader came to realize his influence was never going to reach he level he had hoped for.

In January 1977, Nader appeared as the guest host of the popular comedy show, *Saturday Night Live,* and managed to have a great deal of fun with his stiff and ascetic public persona. In reality, his time as a major player on the Washington scene was coming to a close. The mood of the country was changing. "Business friendly" was replacing "consumer friendly" as a watchword, and the call for deregulation was drowning out Nader's persistent cries for more and stricter regulation. If the Carter administration proved to be frustrating for Nader, the Reagan administration was political death. After 1980, Nader found himself completely shut out in Washington, and many of the policies he had fought so hard to get through Congress and see implemented were rolled back.

Nader's career obviously did not end with Ronald Reagan. He continued to work on grassroots efforts toward consumer activism. A fighter by instinct, no battle could either be too big or too little for his appetite. Then, when **Saturn made another contact with his Ascendant** in 1992, Nader made his first run for president. It was a half-hearted effort in New Hampshire in which he urged New Hampshire Democrats to write in "none of the above" on their ballots. In 1996, with Saturn conjunct his Sun, he ran on the Green Party ticket, but since he was never actually a member of the Green Party, his campaign was never completely energized. Finally, in February 2000, Nader announced a full-tilt third party bid for the presidency.

This run was highly controversial. It was feared that Nader would take votes away from the Democratic candidate and throw the election to the Republicans. Nader was undeterred by these fears. **Saturn was conjuncting his IC** and once again, as he had back in 1971, Nader seemed to feel the weight of time. From his point of view, the influence of giant corporations and big money had totally corrupted both parties and obliterated the vision he once had for the nation. Party politics could not be a concern. Thus, when the election was held and the votes Nader cost Democrat Al Gore in Florida appeared to allow George W. Bush to carry the state and the nation, Nader remained unrepentant. Perhaps he was making the same mistake, showing the same emotional blindness to rational compromise, the same egotism that had started his downfall in 1971. Or perhaps he simply understands that, without these hopeless, quixotic runs for president, the ideas he cares most about might be lost forever.

SATURN AT WORK

In some ways, Ralph Nader's Saturn transits do not follow the typical pattern. He did not begin his ascent to nationwide recognition until some years after his Saturn return. In fact, while under this aspect, Nader was still working part-time in the Department of Labor, gathering information about automotive safety and generally putting people off with his eccentricity and his suspicious attitude toward the Washington establishment. And yet, it was during this period of obscurity that Nader assumed the role and began the mission that would define his adulthood. He came to Washington with the understanding that his job was to bring the facts about the issue to the attention of people with the power to make changes. All he needed to do was find the right ally within the halls of government. By the time Ribicoff took up the cause of automobile safety, Nader was ready to make full use of the opportunity afforded him.

It is easy to say that Nader let his Piscean emotional energy get away from him when Saturn reached his IC, and he began his investigation of members of Congress. In hindsight, it appears that he was making a huge mistake by pointing out the potential for corruption he saw in the offices of some of his closest allies. And yet, considering how the political winds would change in the next few years, it could also be said that Nader was desperately trying to do as much for the cause of good government as he possibly could within a very narrow window of opportunity.

Oddly enough, Ralph Nader's Descendant is only a couple of degrees ahead of Jimmy Carter's Midheaven so that, in May and June of

1976, both men witnessed a dramatic change in their destinies. For Jimmy Carter it was sewing up the Democratic nomination for President of the United States. For Ralph Nader, it was the same thing. Even though Nader at first thought he could work with Carter (a product of his Pisces willingness to believe and Carter's Libran charm) the fact was that, in terms of his attitude toward the relationship between government and business, Carter was a conservative. It was with the election of Carter that Nader's window of opportunity was closed. The election of ultra-conservative Ronald Reagan four years later was just the final click of the lock.

SOURCES

Robert F. Buckhorn, *Nader: The People's Lawyer* (Englewood Cliffs, NJ: Prentice-Hall, Inc., 1972).

Justin Martin, *Nader: Crusader, Spoiler, Icon* (Cambridge, MA: Perseus Publishing, 2002).

11

GLORIA STEINEM

American writer and magazine editor who has become one of the intellectual leaders of the feminist movement in the United States

THE CHOICE

In February 1963, a pretty young writer named Gloria Steinem slipped into a bizarre apparatus called a "bunny" costume and prepared for her first day at work in the new Playboy Club in Manhattan. She was not the typical Playboy Bunny. She had taken the job at the behest of the editors of *Show* magazine in order to gather information for an article. The idea for the article had come up in an editor's meeting. Steinem had not immediately volunteered for the assignment but, in the end, she had been deemed the only female writer available who was young enough and good-looking enough to work her way inside one of the legendary Hugh Hefner pleasure palaces. By this time, Steinem had been writing feature articles for major magazines in New York City for five years. She wrote whatever was demanded of her—satire, topical articles, and fluff—and she did it well. "A Bunny's Tale" was just supposed to be another of those assignments. The problem was that **Saturn would be crossing her IC in just another two months**, and the things that Gloria Steinem would learn researching this article would eventually change her life.

The purpose of the article was straightforward. Steinem was there to test the claims made by Hugh Hefner and his Playboy organization that the Bunnies in his clubs were highly paid and well-treated: that they were happy, well-educated women who lived glamorous lives full of fun and travel. It took Steinem hardly any time to debunk these claims. Her report revealed that the only difference between a Playboy Bunny and any roadhouse waitress was the fact that the Playboy Bunny was expected to work the long hours for low pay while wearing five-inch heels and a corset that fit like a bear trap. Of course, this was hardly surprising. What is remarkable about the article is the difference between the role played by men and women in the piece. Steinem wrote about the women with a degree of sympathy. After all, they were just trying to make a living. The men, however, breeze through the article like medieval lords — haughty, crude, and certain of their higher status. These men, both customers and male managers, treated the women as if they were pieces of property, extraneous adornments to be fondled, poked, and propositioned without restraint.

At the time she wrote "A Bunny's Tale," Gloria Steinem was not a feminist. Feminism as a movement in the United States was just getting started. The immediate result of the article for Steinem was that it made her famous, so much so that **in February 1964, when Saturn reached her natal Saturn**, she became the subject of a feature article published in *Glamour* magazine. The Bunny article also caused her to be named in a spurious lawsuit filed by a Playboy Club manager and it labeled her as a writer of light, "feminine interest" pieces, preventing her from writing about the serious, political subjects she longed to cover. Still, as time passed and her view of the relationship between men and women matured, Steinem came to look at her Bunny article with different eyes. It was no accident that her first book on feminism, *Outrageous Acts and Everyday Rebellions*, which was published twenty years later, begins with a reprinting of "A Bunny's Tale." The article represented the beginning of her conversion to the feminist cause.

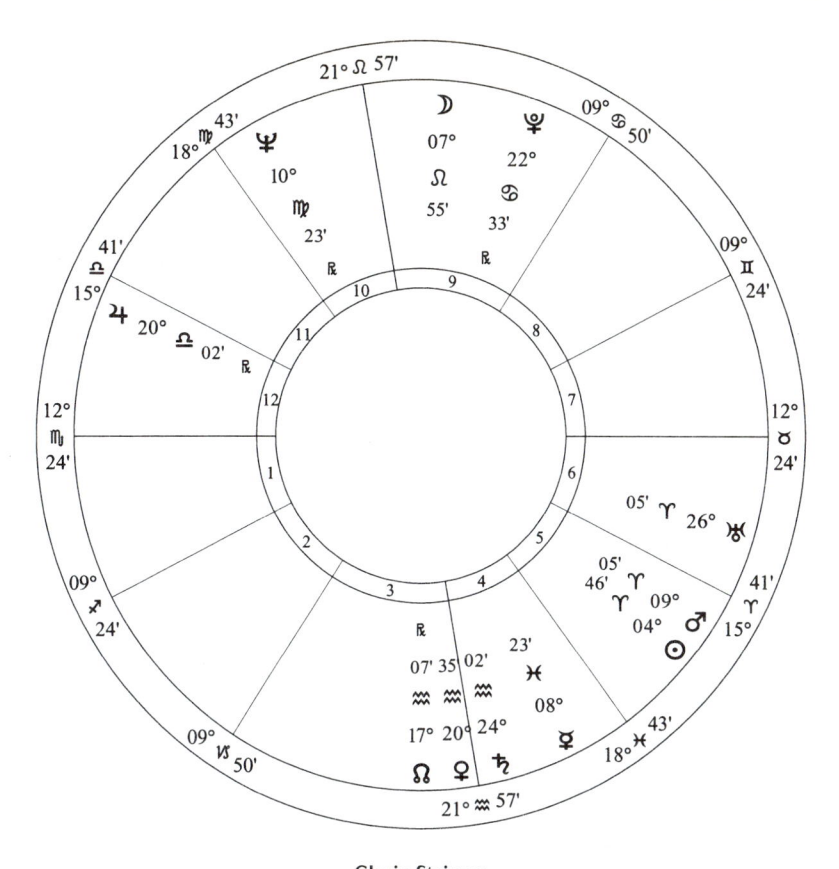

Gloria Steinem

March 25, 1934, 10:00 PM EST

Toledo, OH, 41N39 83W33

THE HOROSCOPE

The first thing we notice about Gloria Steinem's horoscope is that her Sun in Aries is conjunct with Mars and that she has Scorpio rising. Her Leo Moon is trine to both the Sun and Mars. This configuration describes a fighter, a crusader, a person who needs the high-energy give and take of battle. It is no wonder that Steinem became such a controversial figure, attracting the ire of both anti-feminists who saw her as a threat to traditional family values, and old-guard feminists who saw her as a glamorous interloper. The dynamic combination of her Aries Sun and her Leo Moon, both activated by Mars, makes Steinem a natural leader and a person with no compunction about breaking through the comfort zones of the people around her. Meanwhile, her Scorpio Ascendant is no less aggressive and no less relentless in combat, but it hides the furious energy of her Aries Sun and Leo Moon behind an inscrutable mask of indomitable reserve. In a straight-up fight, this is not someone to be taken lightly.

Given the combative nature of so many indicators in this horoscope, it is remarkable that the most strongly placed planet in the chart is peace-loving Venus. Venus is in Aquarius, almost directly on Steinem's IC. It conjuncts Saturn and is in an almost exact trine with Jupiter. The trine between Venus and Jupiter provides for both beauty and a pronounced femininity, while the conjunction with Saturn strengthens the reserve and tendency to restrain feelings already seen with her Scorpio Ascendant. The emotional effluence one might expect with a Leo Moon and a strongly placed Venus trine Jupiter is largely curtailed and the natural coolness of Aquarius comes to the fore. According to astrological tradition, the conjunction of Venus and Saturn stifles real love and either prevents or delays marriage. Though Steinem has enjoyed several long-term relationships with men during her busy life, she did not marry until she was sixty-six.

Given the emotional restraint and coolness we see with Steinem's Venus, it is interesting that her Mercury, placed in Pisces and opposed by Neptune, describes a thinking process that is thoroughly emotional. With this placement, intuition and feelings often dominate ideas and reasoning is never precise. Even her supporters note that in her speeches and autobiographic writings, Steinem sometimes rearranges facts or at least provides a very subjective rendering of them but, in the art of polemic, overstatement and selective logic can become assets.

The opposition of Neptune to Mercury has to be considered along with the nearly exact quincunx between Mercury and the Moon. In his venerable text, *The Astrological Aspects* (published in 1930), CEO Carter noted that people with this sort of aspect between Mercury and the Moon are oversensitive to the troubles of other people and are apt to become "champions of the weak." Taken together, these Mercury aspects describe a situation in which sympathy drives judgment, and good sense, particularly in regard to one's own well-being, is often overridden by subjective feelings.

THE LIFE

It is hard to imagine two people more mismatched than Gloria Steinem's parents. Her father was an irresponsible spendthrift who loved to travel and whose optimism was as ever-expanding as his substantial waistline. Her mother, on the other hand, was a compulsive worrier, prone to bouts of depression that became increasingly debilitating after Gloria was born. By the time **Saturn crossed Steinem's Descendant in 1940 and 1941**, they were separated and, with her much older sister already living on her own in another city, six-year-old Gloria became her mother's prime caretaker.

Mother and daughter moved back to her parents' hometown of Toledo, where Steinem's mother had inherited a rundown house that had been broken up into apartments. Living off the rent from the other two apartments and occasional charity from their more well-to-do relatives, the two barely survived, and Gloria saw her mother's behavior grow more and more bizarre. A particularly low point came **in 1947, as Saturn crossed Steinem's MC** and **made its adolescent opposition to her natal Saturn**. The old house became suddenly infested with rats to the point that Steinem had to inspect her bed every night to make sure no rat was hiding beneath the covers. **Saturn repeated this passage in July**

1948 and two months later Steinem began high school. There Gloria was a good student, popular, and active in school affairs. The troubles and daunting responsibilities of her home life remained a separate, secret existence.

In 1951, Pluto, the planet of transformations, crossed Steinem's Midheaven and her bleak circumstance was suddenly exposed to the light. Her father agreed to take over care of her mother for a year so that Steinem could finish her last year of high school in Washington, D.C. (where her older sister lived), and prepare herself for college. Enough money was found for Gloria to attend one of the more prestigious women's colleges in the country, Smith College. At Smith, Steinem truly blossomed. Her good looks and wit made her popular with other students, while her intelligence and serious manner made her a favorite with her instructors. During her junior year, she won the privilege to study abroad in Switzerland for a year. **Saturn crossed her Ascendant and then squared her natal Saturn three times that year. During the last of these squares, in October 1954**, Steinem, now back at Smith, began her first serious love affair.

For a young woman coming of age in the 1950s, there were few options beyond marriage. The natural progression of falling in love and then getting married and having a family was all but inviolable. Steinem certainly felt this and, for a while, she seemed determined to ride it out. Certainly her new beau, Blair Chotzinoff, was husband material. He was a handsome, exciting young man from a cultured and musically gifted family who had spent a few years knocking around and was now ready to settle down. During this period, transiting Uranus was conjunct with Steinem's Moon, while her secondary progressed Sun and Mars were crossing her natal Uranus. She was ready to give herself over to a whirlwind romance. In the spring of 1956, the couple was engaged, but in the months that followed the unstable influence of Uranus began to turn. By August of that year, Steinem had broken off the engagement and was applying for a fellowship to study in India. This rocky Uranian journey took another unexpected turn in January 1957, when Steinem realized she was pregnant and had an abortion.

Steinem enjoyed her year in India. Though she was ostensibly there to study the Indian Communist Party, she spent a good deal of time traveling around the country and helping the poor, just the sort of work to which she had always felt drawn. But once she arrived back in the United States, Steinem found that her Indian experiences and her exclusive Smith College education were not enough to get her a job. For a while she worked as an organizer for the National Student Association. She also took freelance jobs as a writer. At the same time, she was dating men involved in publishing and writing, and as these men advanced in their careers, so did Steinem. By the time "A Bunny's Tale" was making her famous, Steinem was involved with Ted Sorenson, a speech writer and close adviser to President John Kennedy. She moved from this relationship to an affair with the noted stage and film director, Mike Nichols. Though Steinem worked hard to make her mark as a writer, many thought that her greatest asset was her sex appeal and her ability to mingle freely with the rich, famous, and powerful.

Steinem still longed to use her writing for causes that were more significant and political. She got her chance when an ex-lover started his own magazine, called *New York*, and hired Steinem to write a regular column on the politics of the day. This was in 1968. The same year, Steinem met farm worker activist Cesar Chavez and she became active in the cause of oppressed immigrant workers. She worked in George McGovern's campaign for president and she witnessed firsthand the police riot that occurred in Chicago during the Democratic convention. Yet, it wasn't until Uranus conjoined with her natal Sun in 1969 that Steinem found the cause that would become the focus of her political activity. She became a feminist.

In May 1970, just as **Saturn made contact with her Descendant**, Gloria Steinem testified before a Senate subcommittee in support of an early version of the Equal Rights Amendment. Her conversion to the feminist cause had been slow in coming, but now it was complete. At the same time, Steinem was traveling around the country with the flamboyant lawyer and activist, Florynce Kennedy, speaking out on feminist causes. A few months later, when *Newsweek* magazine published an article on feminism, they put Steinem on the cover. Other publications brought out similar articles, always with the words and images of Gloria Steinem prominently featured. The next year, when Steinem spoke at the commencement for her alma mater and **Saturn squared her natal Saturn,** she did so as a recognized leader of the feminist movement.

Not everyone was happy with Gloria Steinem's sudden rise to prominence. Certainly many men and conservatives in general objected to her, but some of the most vociferous opposition came from within the feminist movement. After all, wasn't this the same Gloria Steinem who, just a couple of years ago, had been seen at all the best parties in Manhattan? Wasn't she the author of "A Bunny's Tale," *The Beach Book* (the cover of which doubled as tanning reflector), and hundreds of other light, feminine-interest articles? What business did she have sharing the stage with such grizzled veterans of the war for women's rights as Betty Friedan, Bella Abzug, and Shirley Chisholm? It didn't help that Steinem was often singled out by even the most hostile critics of the movement as the pretty feminist, the one who still looked good in a miniskirt.

Steinem paid little attention to the divisive complaints. Her goal was to give feminism a unified voice and, with her secondary progressed Sun rising toward her Descendant, she was soon well on her way to doing this. In December 1971, *Ms.* magazine appeared as an insert in *New York* magazine. In July of the next year, it came out as an independent publication. Along with her labors with *Ms.*, Steinem continued to advance the feminist cause in the political arena. She remained constantly active in Democratic politics before and after the 1976 election and the National Women's Conference, which was held in 1977. Here, **just three months after Saturn completed its passage over her Midheaven,** Steinem battled conservative delegates who had come to the conference with the expressed intention of disrupting it while she and other leaders tried to hammer out a coherent feminist agenda.

Even as she was engaged in these battles, however, Steinem was dreaming of taking a year off in order to return to writing. In December 1977, **around the time that Saturn opposed her natal Saturn,** she took up a Wilson Center Fellowship which promised her a stipend and a cozy office in Washington D.C., in which she would have nothing to do except write. The promise was not completely fulfilled. The demands of her magazine and various other organizations and causes to which she felt obligated continued to call Steinem away from her writing. The book she had hoped to produce during this relatively quiet interlude had to wait another six years, until **Saturn neared her Ascendant in 1983**, and it was published as *Outrageous Acts and Everyday Rebellions*.

It was during **this last Saturn passage** in May 1984 that Steinem's friends and supporters held a combination fiftieth birthday party and giant *Ms.* fundraiser in her honor. Shortly before the event, Steinem began seeing a multimillionaire named Mortimer Zuckerman. Zuckerman went on to alienate many of Steinem's feminist friends with his overbearing manner and open talk of marriage and children. Steinem's passivity in the relationship surprised many, but it did not last. The couple broke up in 1988 (as Pluto crossed Steinem's Ascendant), and Zuckerman went on to marry and have a child with another woman.

Steinem later claimed that one reason she stayed with Zuckerman despite their political differences was the fact that she thought his money could help the magazine. The fact was that *Ms.* was chronically short of cash. In 1979, the magazine was made part of the nonprofit Ms. Foundation to cut down on postage costs. This proved to be only a temporary solution and, in 1987, Steinem and her partners sold *Ms.* to an Australian group. Meanwhile, Steinem became better known as an author of books. She published *Marilyn*, a book on Marilyn Monroe, in 1986; *Revolution from Within: A Book of Self-Esteem* in January 1992; and *Moving Beyond Words* in 1994. At the same time, Steinem seemed to be accepting life at a less frenetic pace and giving more attention to her home in Manhattan and her "adopted family" of close friends and assistants. Steinem still maintained her ability to shock, however. In 1999, Steinem and a group of female investors bought *Ms.* magazine after it had been discontinued (Harvey, 1999). At around the same time, as **Saturn crossed her Descendant**, Steinem met former pilot and environmentalist David Bale. In September 2000, **shortly after Saturn**

completed a square to her natal Saturn, the sixty-six-year-old Steinem married the sixty-one-year-old Bale (*People Weekly*, 2000).

SATURN AT WORK

In 1940, six-year-old Gloria Steinem faced a choice that very few people ever have to consider during their earliest Saturn crossing: would she become a caretaker for her deranged mother or not? She could have run away. She could have turned the matter over to other relatives, or even the state. She could have held out for a normal life, but she didn't. She rose to the challenge with all the strength of her Aries Sun and Leo Moon, and she responded to her inborn sympathy for the weak. She lived through the experience by treating it as if it were normal, and in this way she was able to carry on and keep her pain and insecurities a secret from her schoolmates.

When Saturn squared her natal Saturn in 1955, her age twenty-one square, she faced another choice. Once again a normal life called out to her, this time in the form of an eligible young man who might have become a very good husband for her. As Saturn made its last contact, it seemed she was ready to take the normal route of marriage and family. Or was she just looking for someone new to take care of? In either case, a rash of Uranus aspects upset her plans and she was off to India to put herself at the disposal of the poor and needy there.

Once she returned to the United States, Steinem searched for work that was meaningful. Her work with the NSA did not satisfy this requirement, and certainly the articles she was writing on fashion and celebrities didn't either. It wasn't until her "Bunny" article that she got a glimpse at a group that needed her help, a group with which she could easily identify—working women.

It would take a while for this realization to sink in. After all, making a living as a freelance writer is demanding, and Steinem was also having a good deal of fun, seeing a variety of men, and moving toward the center of the Manhattan social scene. Later on, many of these lovers, friends, and social contacts would be called upon to donate money and influence in the service of her cause.

So it wasn't during the turmoil of 1968 and 1969, when Steinem's conversion to feminism became complete, that Saturn came to call. It was in 1970, when she suddenly emerged as the voice and the image of the second wave of feminism. Her detractors might have balked at her short skirts and her sexy figure, but they could not fault her devotion to the cause. Gloria Steinem had found the group that most needed her to be their champion. Her past, her skill as a journalist, her ability to hobnob with the rich and famous, and her array of social contacts would become her weapons and she would wield these weapons with the zeal of a righteous prophet.

SOURCES

Gloria Steinem, *Outrageous Acts and Everyday Rebellions* (New York: Holt, Rinehart and Winston, 1983).

Carolyn G. Heilbrun, *The Education of a Woman: The Life of Gloria Steinem* (New York: Dial Press, 1995).

Sydney Ladensohn Stern, *Gloria Steinem: Her Passion, Politics, and Mystique* (Secaucus, NJ: Carol Publishing Group, 1997).

Mary Harvey, "Women Investors Take Back *Ms.*," *Folio: The Magazine for Magazine Management*, 28.1 (January 1999): 12.

Sydney Ladensohn Stern, "After Insisting She Wasn't the Marrying Kind Feminism's Golden Girl Finally Took the Plunge," *People Weekly*, 54.27 (December 25, 2000): 68.

Evelyn Crowley, "Gloria Excelsis: Flashback Gloria Steinem," *W* 35.6 (June 2006), 32.

12

CARL GUSTAV JUNG

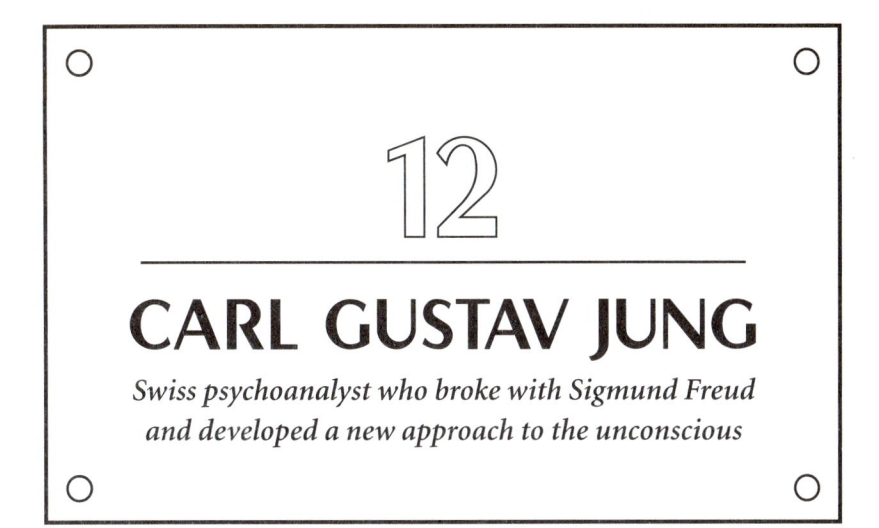

Swiss psychoanalyst who broke with Sigmund Freud and developed a new approach to the unconscious

THE CHOICE

Eleven-year-old Carl Gustav Jung hated his new school. In the rural primary school near his father's parsonage, he had always excelled, but now he was being forced to attend a school in the city of Basel where the other students considered him an oversized country rube and the faculty had concluded he was both a dunce and a pugnacious troublemaker. The climax to all this came when one of Carl's schoolmates shoved the future psychologist to the ground and Carl suffered a hard blow to the head. The next day, when Jung went to school, he fainted and had to be sent home. These symptoms persisted and finally the child had to be withdrawn from school altogether.

Of course, Carl was hardly distraught at these developments. To him it seemed that the adults were finally seeing things his way and giving him the freedom he craved. Still his symptoms remained very real and even reading a school book at home was enough to make him dizzy. Carl's parents desperately sought a medical solution for their eldest child's malady. One doctor offered epilepsy. Others just shook their heads. The prognosis was not good. Then, when **Saturn made**

its first contact with his Descendant, Jung chanced to hear his father lamenting that his poor, crippled son might never be able to earn a living. The shock of hearing himself referred to as a cripple and a potential lifelong dependent caused the youngster to take matters into his own hands. He forced himself to study, fighting back the dizziness he felt, until he was finally able to return to school where, eventually, he became both an outstanding scholar and popular with the other students.

Many years later Jung would recognize that the condition that kept him out of school for so long and had befuddled the doctors of the time was a neurosis—a mental stumbling block that had expressed itself through very real physical manifestations. So this event from his childhood became Carl Jung's first encounter, as up close and personal as it could get, with the human condition that would become his life's work. He had been introduced to the power of the mind, and he would never forget how that power had controlled him.

THE HOROSCOPE

Jung's horoscope can readily be divided into two distinct parts. The first begins with a close square between Jung's Moon in Taurus and his Uranus, which is right on the Descendant. This is an incredibly dynamic aspect that combines a conservative indicator (the Moon in Taurus) with one that is flat-out revolutionary (the square to a very strongly placed Uranus). Obviously, originality is the keynote of this personality, even though it is offset by a degree of self-indulgence and inflexibility. This aspect actually mimics the situation of the Ascendant, which is placed in revolutionary Aquarius, with staunchly conservative Saturn just a few degrees away. Both of these placements reflect a need to be a unique, even revolutionary personality, but within the confines and comforts of a conventional career.

The second trend in Jung's horoscope centers on the extremely close square between his Sun and Neptune. Here the boundaries of the ego become blurred, and there is a strong tendency toward mysticism and visionary experiences. During his youth, Jung often felt the presence of a secondary personality lurking behind his everyday self. It was the

Carl Gustav Jung 119

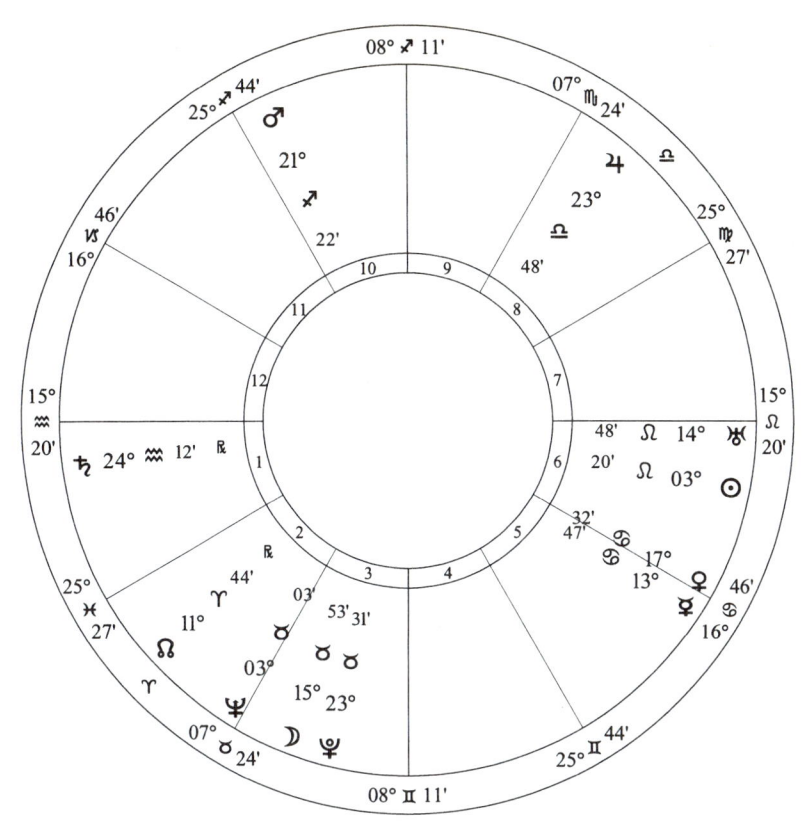

Carl Gustav Jung
July 26, 1875, 7:32 PM GMT
Kesswil, Switzerland, 47N36 09E20

personality of an eighteenth-century man of great importance, an older gentleman who expected to be treated with a deference and respect that the youthful Jung seldom inspired. It is easy to see that this secondary personality was an expression of Neptune's imaginary power. This aspect also provides the potential for a highly spiritual attitude and it strengthens the tendency toward service and healing already provided for by the placement of Jung's Sun in the 6th House. On the negative side, there is always the potential for self-deception, insincerity, and even dishonesty with strong Neptune aspects.

Fortunately for Jung, there are aspects elsewhere in his chart that certainly helped him blend these two strong and divergent trends. Both Venus and Mercury sextile the Moon and his Sagittarius Mars is sextile to both Saturn and Jupiter. These aspects provide for an infinite capacity to charm and an intellectual deftness that can smooth the rough edges that naturally come from his Moon to Uranus square. Meanwhile his Mars aspects, along with aptly describing his imposing and extremely hearty physique, provided Jung with the ability to balance the discipline of science (via Saturn) with new ideas about the mind that bordered on religion (Jupiter). More importantly, though, Jung's Uranus personality and his Neptune personality function to counterbalance each other. The lightning-bolt clarity and brash honesty of Uranus is the perfect cure for the fuzzy, delusional qualities of Neptune square Sun, while the openness and breadth of vision that come with that aspect effectively counters and softens the arrogance and revolutionary intensity of his Uranus to Moon aspect.

THE LIFE

Jung's next encounter with transiting Saturn came when he sat down with his mother, younger sister, and two young female cousins to conduct a séance. This occurred at the same time that **Saturn squared his natal Saturn on its way to a conjunction with his Midheaven**. It was not the first séance Jung had conducted with these women. The meeting had begun two years earlier, but family duties had interfered. The star of the proceeding, Jung's teenage cousin, Helene, had been called away to complete her religious instruction. In the meantime,

Jung faced his own family crisis. His father died (as Jung's secondary progressed Sun opposed his natal Saturn), and the young student had to become the head of the household, providing for the continued financial security of his mother and sister (arranged for mostly through the generosity of his mother's family), while assuring that he would have the means to stay in medical school. It was only after all these things had been accomplished that the séances could begin anew.

In these meetings, Jung had been fascinated by the ease with which Helly (Helene's nickname) could go into a trance, and the authority and conviction with which she could speak of situations and events of which she had no knowledge, in voices and dialects that were totally unnatural for her. To the budding psychologist, it was once again ample proof of the power of the mind over the body. But, more importantly, Helly's trances and her conversations with the dead gave hints of an even greater power, a concept of human consciousness that reached outside the individual intellect and toward a larger, collective reality or, as Jung would come to call it, a collective consciousness.

Helly, of course, had no conception of laying the groundwork for a new theory of psychology. In fact, as the séances continued and **Saturn crossed his Midheaven**, it became increasingly and painfully apparent to Jung that the main concern of his adolescent cousin was pleasing him. As she got older, Helly's mediumistic talents began to fade. On one occasion Jung brought some of his friends from medical school home to observe her and the poor girl was caught resorting to cheap parlor tricks in order to impress her audience. The séances continued after this debacle, with other females trying to duplicate Helly's glory, but with far less satisfying results. The spirits were apparently seeking new avenues of expression. **In the midst of Jung's Saturn transit to his Midheaven,** a heavy table in his mother's kitchen sudden cracked for no reason, and a carving knife that had been in the family for generations mysteriously exploded into four pieces. For Jung, these events were ample proof that not only could the mind find access to levels of knowledge and understanding far beyond the personal, but that there was also a power within that realm that went far beyond human reason.

At about the same time that Jung was finishing up the séances he was also making the momentous decision to direct his studies in medical school toward the very new and uncertain field of psychology. It is apparent that, when he made this decision, Jung was already thinking of his experiences with Helly as the fodder of his doctoral thesis. The idea may have been percolating in his mind since the very beginning. He not only paid keen attention to these proceedings; he was often guiding and encouraging his youthful medium. He had read deeply the accounts of spiritualists and spiritually inspired visionaries like Emanuel Swedenborg. Without a word of warning to his subject, Jung proceeded to write his thesis on the psychological implications of Helly's performances as a medium.

Jung wrote about his cousin as a scientist. The dead people who spoke through Helly were called "complexes," divergent pieces of her own personality or consciousness that had been split off from the main stem. In his thesis, Helly ceased to be his relative and became instead a subject or, even worse, a patient. The implication was obvious. The Helly of Jung's thesis was insane, and her mediumistic abilities were the product of her mental aberration.

When Jung wrote his thesis, he naturally took steps to conceal the names of participants, but, to the people who knew Helly and Jung's family, these efforts were transparent at best. Helene's reaction to Jung's thesis was never recorded. Members of her family, the same family that had been Jung's financial salvation when his father died, were quick to declare that the publication had ruined her life. After Jung's thesis was published, Helly and her family were ostracized. The conservative residents of Basel wanted nothing to do with the family of a madwoman. Helene finally left Basel after her only suitor suddenly withdrew his proposal of marriage. She moved to France where she established a successful dressmaking shop. She died in Paris of tuberculosis at the age of thirty.

The period between Saturn's crossing of his Midheaven and its contact with his Ascendant was a very fruitful one for Jung. He moved from Basel to the University of Zurich, where he received a degree in psychology and got his first job as a doctor at the mental hospital at Burgholzhi. He also became secretly engaged to a bright young woman named Emma Rauchenbach, whose family was quite wealthy. By 1902, when his dissertation was published (much to the consternation of Helly and her family), Jung felt he was on the verge of great things. He quit his boring job at the mental hospital and took off to study in Paris, where he hoped he would find advancement worthy of his ambition.

Unfortunately for Jung, although Paris offered exciting educational opportunities, it did not serve as a springboard for his career. He and Emma were married in 1903, but the prospect of living on his wife's money had no appeal for the proud young professional. So Jung was forced to return, hat in hand, to Burgholzhi. In October 1904, **as Saturn crossed his Ascendant**, he was finally given back his old job.

Despite this setback, Jung continued to push toward the top of his profession. If he couldn't be a star in Paris, then he would certainly be one in Zurich. In 1905, a few months after **Saturn made it first return to its natal place**, he was promoted to chief assistant. Among other things, this new position gave Jung the opportunity to give lectures at the university that were open to the public. Jung was a tall, striking young man with a big voice and tons of charisma. His lectures quickly became standing-room-only affairs, with young women making up a large part of the audience.

The next year Jung published a book concerning his research on hysteria. The book became controversial because Jung frequently cited Sigmund Freud, and his findings tended to support many of Freud's theories. At this time, Freud was still looked upon as a pariah by the scientific community. His theories on human sexuality were considered at best unscientific and at worst perverted. Jung understood the chance he was taking by championing Freud's work. He still maintained many reservations about Freud's notion that sex was the primary force in all human behavior. But Jung was nothing if not courageous, and he felt certain that Sigmund Freud's idea had merit.

Soon Carl Jung was corresponding regularly with the master. He advanced quickly within Sigmund Freud's psychoanalytic group, although this had less to do with his brilliance than his ethnicity. Almost all of

Freud's early converts to the psychoanalytic cause were Jews. Freud understood that, given the anti-Semitism of Europe at the time, his movement would never gain mainstream support as long as it was seen as a Jewish phenomenon. Jung was not only a gentile; he was, with his rugged build and neatly clipped mustache, the very picture of an Aryan hero. Early in their relationship, Freud began treating Jung as his heir apparent as leader to the psychoanalytic movement.

The problem with this was that Jung had never gotten over his doubts about the primacy of sex. To Freud, this was the central tenant of his ideas and he preached it constantly, but Jung felt that any theory of psychology also had to include religious and spiritual motivations. For a while Jung went along quietly with Freud's notions, awed by the intellectual courage of the older man and enjoying his rise in prestige and power within Freud's organization. He became editor of the psychoanalytic journal and president of the International Psychoanalytic Society. Then, in 1912, **as transiting Saturn squared his natal Saturn,** Jung began advancing his own ideas about the relationship of religious imagery and psychology in a book that later came to be called *Symbols of Transformation*. Sigmund Freud viewed this turn in Jung's thinking as an act of betrayal and he immediately began marshalling his more loyal supporters against the Swiss renegade.

The showdown came at a conference of the International Psychoanalytic Society in 1913, when **Saturn arrived at Jung's IC**. Jung's "Zurich faction" was effectively isolated and expelled by the hard core Freudians. Jung and his supporters went on to form their own group and Jung became the leader of his own school of psychoanalysis. He also began a phase of intense self-examination that he later termed a confrontation with his "unconscious." Others, mainly his enemies among the psychoanalytic community, called it a period of outright psychosis during which he became obsessed by fantasies, dreams, and childish pastimes. Whether it was a period of discovery or madness, the phase lasted until **Saturn crossed his Descendant** again in 1917. Then Jung emerged as one of the most influential thinkers of the twentieth century.

SATURN AT WORK

Saturn's crossing of Jung's Descendant in 1888, its later age twenty-one square, and its crossing of his Midheaven in 1898 all involved an encounter between the future psychologist and the undeniable power of the mind. He learned both the capacity of his own mind to induce physical illness and the power of his cousin's mind to attain states of altered consciousness. At the same time, his experience with a broken knife led him away from a purely materialistic view of the world. Quite naturally, these early Saturn transits were crucial in guiding Jung's decision to make psychology his career.

Jung's 1898 passage also presented him with a very delicate moral choice. By choosing to make his observations of his cousin Helly the subject for his thesis, Jung put her reputation and the reputation of her family in jeopardy. Some might regard this choice as selfish and egotistic but it was, at the most basic level, a continuation of the exploration of the human psyche to which Jung had already committed himself. To put aside this research in deference to Helly's privacy would have been not just a disservice to Jung's professional ambitions. It would have been a disservice to science. And, with his strongly placed and aspected Uranus, Jung's loyalty to the larger community and the overarching ideal would always outweigh personal issues.

The period between Saturn's crossing of Jung's MC and its passage across his Ascendant was extraordinarily active. He finished his schooling, got his first job, married one of the richest girls in Switzerland, and published his thesis. There seemed to be little doubt that this brilliant and ambitious young man would succeed. What Saturn did when it crossed Jung's Ascendant was show this wonder boy his limitations. He was not yet ready to take on the world. He needed to stay in Zurich at the Burgholzhi mental hospital and let his career develop in a slower and more enduring fashion. Jung was not happy about his return to Burgholzhi. He referred to the hospital as his "millstone" (Bair, 2003). But it was his experiences with patients there that directed him to ideas of Sigmund Freud, and Zurich remained Jung's home and base of operations throughout his long career.

When Saturn crossed Jung's IC in 1913, it seemed that he was facing another setback. His expulsion from Freud's circle was a traumatic development for Jung but, considering the extent of his ambitions, it was inevitable. Once again, this setback directed Jung toward a new and more fruitful goal: the development of his own ideas and his own school of psychological thought.

NOTES

C. G. Jung (recorded and edited by Aniela Jaffe), *Memories, Dreams, Reflections* (New York: Vintage Books, 1989).

Deirdre Bair, *Jung: A Biography* (Boston: Little Brown, 2003).

PART 2
THE SINNERS
*People Who Made Poor Use
of Their Saturn Transits*

13

BRITNEY SPEARS

American pop singer whose personal life has become a textbook for celebrity meltdown

THE CHOICE

In June 2004, Britney Spears was looking for a new direction in her life. It wasn't that the old direction had gone so badly. At twenty-one, she was one of the most successful pop singers of all time. She had sold millions of records and was known around the world. Spears had worked hard for her notoriety. In fact, she had been working virtually her entire life. She had started singing in public when she was just a small child, and since then her life had been consumed with gymnastics lessons, dance lessons, voice lessons, acting lessons, auditions, interviews, workouts, promotions, deals, contracts, and, of course, performing. This is not to say that Spears didn't love her work. When she had been forced to take a year off at the age of fourteen and actually go to high school, Britney had found it all very boring. The center of her life was performing, and she enjoyed the attention it garnered her. Even with the paparazzi, the general lack of privacy, the grinding schedule, and the cutthroat competition, Britney Spears still seemed to be having a good time. It was just that now **Saturn was squaring her natal Saturn** and she wanted more.

What Spears wanted was to become a grown-up. Throughout her life her parents, particularly her mother, had managed her career. By the time her parents were divorced in 2002, Spears was already a mega-star, the hub of a grand enterprise that included recording contracts, concerts, television appearances, product endorsements, and the hopes and dreams of millions of young fans. Her own development as a person had always seemed to matter less than the development of her image and her audience. Now she was going to change all that. She was going to make a decision that would change the course of her life and it would be entirely her decision. She had already played with this decision a few months earlier when she had married one of her buddies with Sagittarian impulsiveness, and then had the marriage annulled a few days later. That was a decision made in the fog of a transiting Neptune conjunction to her natal Moon, but now she was reacting to the clarity, to the unavoidable call to maturity, the natural need to establish an identity beyond the one mapped out for her by her parents and her managers that came from her **age twenty-one square of Saturn to its natal spot**. Britney Spears fell in love with dancer Kevin Federline, and within a few weeks she was announcing their engagement.

THE HOROSCOPE

At its most basic level—the Sun sign, Ascendant, and Moon sign—Britney Spears' horoscope seems remarkably pleasant and agreeable. With her Sun in mutable Sagittarius and sociable Libra rising, pleasing other people came easily for Spears. Even though her Moon in Aquarius reveals a stubborn inner core to her personality, it is still a very open and gregarious placement. There can be little doubt that the innocent, fresh-faced appeal with which Spears began her career was genuine, and that it is prominently seated in her horoscope. Sagittarius Suns are noted for the capacity for naiveté and for the playful, childlike delight that they can bring to even the most mundane matters. Spears' Libra Ascendant brings a likable grace and ease to these lively Sagittarian qualities while filtering out much of the brashness and abrasiveness for which Sagittarian Suns are also noted. Meanwhile, her Aquarian Moon provided Spears with a hidden idealism, hopefulness, and a confidence in the innate worth of

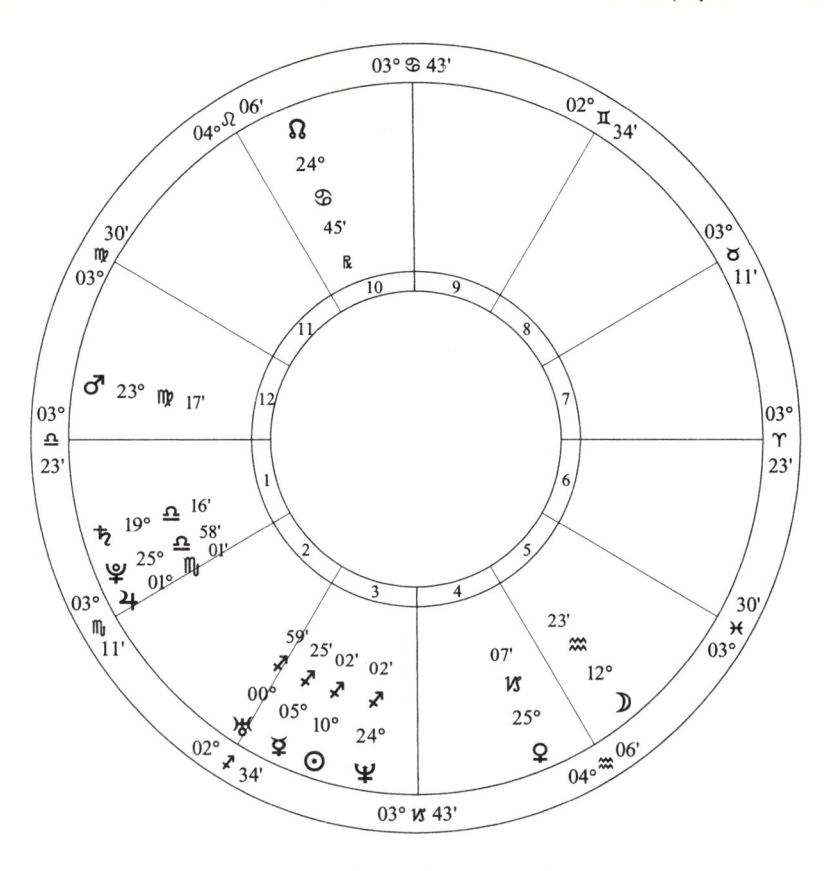

Britney Spears

December 2, 1981, 1:30 AM CST
Mahon, MS, 39N49 89W31

humanity that gives her gleeful Sagittarian spirit room to soar. Overall, the linkage of the three very positive signs provides us with the image of an energetic, optimistic, and well-meaning personality, a good girl that virtually everyone could like.

Unfortunately, the horoscope does not stop with these three signs. There are other factors in Spears' chart that are not nearly so positive, and describe anything but the likable goody-goody we have just met. First of all, Spears' Mars in the 12th House forms a nearly exact square with Neptune. This is a dangerous aspect that diverts expressions of anger and aggression into circuitous, non-productive and often self-destructive paths. There is a muddling of the physical energy of the person and a tendency to seek stimulation from unconventional sources. Substance abuse is always a possibility with this aspect, as is escapism of all sorts, ranging from chemical dependency to an irrational addiction to the trappings of glamour. Of course, there is also the possibility that the looping path of Neptune can lead all this pent-up Martian energy to a place of spiritual revelation and personal renewal, but the way to this higher level of Neptune is rarely smooth, and typically is punctuated by bizarre missteps and misery.

The second bad aspect in Spears' horoscope is the square of her Capricorn Venus by Saturn, Pluto, and Jupiter. It is the square to Pluto, the closest of these aspects, that is the most alarming. Early in her career, while still a virginal teenager, Britney displayed an adult awareness of sexuality and the power of a perfectly toned body that captivated her young fans and shocked their mothers. With Venus so violently assaulted by Pluto in her horoscope, this bombastic sex appeal came easily to the young singer. Though at the time, Spears tried to distance herself from sexual gyrations featured in her performances, explaining that she was only playing a part, the fact is that the lascivious vamp she portrayed on stage and in her videos had its source in the deepest levels of her personality.

The case could be made that the dynamic aspect between her angularly placed Venus and Pluto was the driving force behind Spears meteoric rise to pop music stardom. Spears was born with an innate understanding of the power of sex and a special gift for wielding it. The trine aspect between her Venus in Capricorn and her Mars in Virgo, two plain-speaking Earth signs, only adds to this capacity, providing a keen edge of desire to the well-honed athleticism of her dance moves. Unfortunately, though this kind of sex appeal can certainly sell music, it typically has a much less positive effect on the ability of the person to sustain sexual relationships. Power is always much more important than affection or physical pleasure when Pluto is involved with Venus. There is a need to keep the upper hand in a relationship and an unwillingness to compromise. Sex becomes the answer to everything or it becomes the prime arena for bargaining within the relationship. This is not to say that the difficulties provided for by this aspect could not be worked out and that an enduring, solid sexual relationship could not be achieved, but this would require a significant inner struggle and a willingness to surrender power for the sake of love.

THE LIFE

Britney Spears was born in a small town in Mississippi. Her father was a good-looking building contractor with a keen appreciation of alcohol and good times. Her mother was a school teacher who, in the opinion of some of her relatives, had "married down" and was often at odds with her husband's fun-loving ways (O'Leary, 2007). The Spears family was barely wealthy enough to provide young Britney with high-level gymnastic and dance lessons, and keep her busy with talent shows and contests, but Mrs. Spears had a vision. As she saw it, her daughter was a natural performer—singing and dancing along with the radio and television by the time she was two—and the mother was determined that Britney would make the most of these gifts. One account has Spears making her public debut in church at age four, another at her kindergarten graduation at age five.

Around age eight, **shortly after Saturn crossed her IC and about the time it made its first square to its natal place,** Spears was taken to an audition of child performers for a new incarnation of the old Disney Mickey Mouse Club. She was deemed too young for the show, but the judges were impressed enough to recommend that Spears' parents enroll her in the prestigious Off-Broadway Training Center in New

York. During the next three summers Britney trained at the center, and in 1991 she won a part in an off-Broadway play called *Ruthless*. In that same year, the Spears family, or at least Britney and her mother, relocated to New York City.

After her stint on stage, Spears once again auditioned for the new Mickey Mouse Club. This time she was hired and had the opportunity to perform with some of the best young talent in the nation, including her future beau, Justin Timberlake, and her future competitor, Christina Aguilera. Unfortunately, the show was cancelled in 1993, and, as Saturn squared her Sun, Spears' career seemed to have reached an impasse. Her parents returned to Louisiana and Britney was enrolled in a private school in nearby McComb, Mississippi.

Spears completed one full year of normal high school at McComb. She had a boyfriend. She went to the homecoming dance and to the prom but, after her experiences in New York City and on the Mickey Mouse Club, it all seemed rather tedious. Spears became so desperate to get back on stage that she auditioned for a part in an all-girl singing group, although she quickly figured out that she was not a team player.

Spears next big break came when **Saturn crossed her Descendant** in 1997. Again there are different accounts as to how it came about. In one version, Britney's mother sent a demo tape of her daughter's work to Jive Records in December 1996 (*People Weekly*, 1999). In another, her father hired an entertainment lawyer who brokered a deal in June 1997 (*People Weekly*, 2000). In either case, by the time the latter half of 1997 rolled around and **Saturn neared its first opposition to its natal place**, the process of making Britney Spears into a pop star was well underway. Spears was sent to Sweden to work with a top producer and songwriter in the production of her first CD. Through 1998, Jive Records invested a good deal of time and effort promoting their new singer, and by the summer of 1998 Britney was touring shopping malls and handing out tapes of her new single. She also opened for the all-male singing group, *N Sync (which included her comrade from the Mickey Mouse Club, Justin Timberlake). All this promotion paid off when the single, "Baby, One More Time," was released in October 1998, and the album by the same name came out in January 1999. Both reached number one in the Billboard charts, the first time this feat had been accomplished by a teenage singer. She followed this success in 2000 with another number one hit single and album, *Oops, I Did It Again*. Meanwhile, endorsement deals with companies like Pepsi and clothing designer Tommy Hilfiger were making the young star extremely wealthy (*People Weekly*, 1999).

Not all the attention the youthful singer received was positive. Many people were offended by the sexual content of Spears' work, especially in the videos she made to support her albums. The contrast between what Spears was doing on the television screen and her teenage innocence and Baptist upbringing was too great to be ignored. For her first video, "Baby, One More Time," Jive Records had recommended a fairly nonsexual theme, but Spears had held out for a routine featuring provocative schoolgirls dancing in short skirts and midriff-revealing blouses. After this, every video, every television performance, and every photo shoot seemed to be an excuse to up the ante, to reveal more flesh and further capitalize on her undeniable sex appeal.

By 2002, Spears' secondary progressed Mars was closing in on a conjunction with her Ascendant, an aspect that typically brings trouble and heartache. Britney was no exception to this rule. In 2002 she broke with boyfriend, Justin Timberlake, after he admitted in an interview with Barbara Walters that he and Spears had sex. A concert in Mexico City went sour after she made an uncharitable hand gesture to the paparazzi and the concert was cut short, supposedly because of an approaching thunderstorm. Her endorsement contract with Pepsi was not renewed, she took another company to court because she felt they had violated an endorsement contract, and her motion picture debut, a teen movie titled *Crossroads*, showed few signs of launching her into a career as an actress. But perhaps the most wrenching event of the year received little press coverage. That was the divorce of her parents. Apparently, without the task of making Britney a star to unite them, the differences between Mr. and Mrs. Spears had become too great to endure.

In 2003, with **Saturn crossing her Midheaven,** Spears seemed determined to put these defeats behind her. Her third album, released in 2001, had reached a number one ranking on Billboard's charts, but its sales had lagged somewhat behind her first two efforts. More importantly, other young female singers, such as Christina Aguilera, were now competing with Spears, both musically and in terms of sexual provocation. Preparations for Spears' fourth album, *In the Zone*, took on a quality of urgency. This would be Spears' chance to reestablish herself as the youthful queen of pop music. The best writers were hired. Hip hop superstars were brought in to help with the production. Most importantly, pop icon Madonna agreed to do a duet with Spears (Haskell, 2003). Madonna had long been an idol of Spears. Early in her career, the younger singer had compared herself to Madonna, explaining that she wanted to have a career as robust and long-lived as Madonna had enjoyed, but without the raunchy sex shows that Madonna had occasionally resorted to. Any hope of reaching this second ambition was put aside, however, when, at the MTV Music Awards Ceremony in September 2003, she and Madonna exchanged a long, open-mouthed kiss in front of a nationwide television audience (*Broadcasting and Cable*, 2003).

In the end, even though *In the Zone* earned some kudos for its more adult, hip hop sound, and it joined its predecessors at the number one spot on Billboard's chart, it did little to change the trajectory of Spears' career. From the point when **Saturn crossed her Midheaven in 2003**, the focus on the career of Britney Spears became continually less about her music and more about her; her partying, her clubbing, her boyfriends, and her not-so-private life. Her 2004 marriage to Kevin Federline and the birth of her two sons might have changed this but, in fact, these blessed events only gave Spears a brief respite. Now there were more areas of the life of Britney Spears for the public to scrutinize, including the care she was giving her children and, eventually, the deterioration of her marriage.

In November 2006, with Uranus squaring her natal Sun, Spears filed for divorce. Her behavior since has been everything any member of the paparazzi could want, with public displays of drunkenness, striptease, head shaving, and other monumental lapses in judgment. Nor have Spears' excesses escaped the notice of the court. The judge in charge of her divorce ordered Spears to submit to rehabilitation for her alcohol abuse and, after she refused to complete the program, temporarily gave custody of her two children to their father.

SATURN AT WORK

In some ways, Spears' relationship with her Saturn transits resembles that of the Dalai Lama. The circumstances of her career meant that she, like young Tenzin Gyatso, experienced the earliest of her Saturn passage—not in the personal realm of family and her relationship with her peers—but in the public arena of work and ambition. Thus when Saturn crossed her IC for the first time and made its first square to her natal Saturn, she began her apprenticeship as a performer in the Off-Broadway Training Center, and when Saturn reached her Descendant, she signed with Jive Records and began her ascent into rock-and-roll stardom. Though she was only twenty-two when Saturn made its first contact with her Midheaven, Spears was already at the peak of her career, both in terms of her power within her chosen industry and the expression of her talents.

The question is why Spears' next Saturn passage, the square to natal Saturn, didn't stop the freefall into self-indulgence and public disgrace that had come to characterize her life after the 2003 conjunction of Saturn to her Midheaven. The answer can be found in what happened to her in those early Saturn crossings. Typically, the Saturn passages we experience in our childhood bring us challenges of a personal and private nature, through which we establish a firm hold on our sense of self. We gradually learn to separate ourselves from the wants and needs of our parents, and we forge an identity for ourselves relative to our siblings and peers. In other words, we establish a sound basis for the mature person we will later become. Spears' concentration on her career during these early years diverted energy that might have otherwise been devoted to laying these important personal foundations, so that at age twenty-two, even though she was a veteran as a performer, as a person she was still a child.

For the Dalai Lama, this crucial gap in maturity was mollified by the traditions of his religion and the rigors of meditation and self-examination. Though he was not mature enough to deal with the crisis that beset his country when he was a teenager, he knew what he needed to do to gain this maturity. Spears seems to have convinced herself that marriage and motherhood would in themselves help her make up the gaps in her personal development. Of course, this has proved to be a highly flawed approach. Instead of making her more mature, the addition of a husband and two sons to her life only made her immaturity more apparent.

Britney Spears is young, and obviously has many changes and challenges ahead of her. The process of learning to be an adult will not be easy for her. Sagittarian Suns are typically slow to mature, even under the best of conditions. Given her background and the importance of Neptune in her horoscope, a return to religion and a renewal of faith is quite likely. Spears' next important Saturn passage does not take place until late 2009 and early 2010, when Saturn reaches her Descendant. Pluto will be crossing her IC at the same time. A significant and perhaps wrenching transformation is likely at this time.

SOURCES

Britney Spears, "A Major Minor: Singer Britney Spears, 17, Flexes Her Muscles in the Booming Teen Music Market," *People Weekly* 51:6 (February 15, 1999): 71.

Britney Spears, "Britney's Wild Ride: Your 12-Year Old Daughter's Favorite Popster is a Pouty Teen Temptress Who Sings 'Hit Me, Baby, One More Time.' Not to Worry Says Britney Spears, It's Only Show Biz," *People Weekly* 53.6 (February 14, 2000) 98.

Britney Spears and Lynn Spears, *Britney Spears' Heart To Heart* (New York: Three Rivers Press, 2000).

Robert Haskell, "Burning Spears: She's Got Competition These Days. But with a New Look, a New Album and No Justin Timberlake, Pop's Princess Aims to Reclaim her Throne," *W* 32.8 (August, 2003): 116.

Britney Spears, "Kissing Madonna Upstages MTV Awards," *Broadcasting and Cable*, 133.35 (September 1, 2003): 2.

Todd Gold, "A Summer Surprise: Britney Spears and Fiancé, Kevin Federline, Talk About the Ring, the Proposal and the Need to Nest," *People Weekly*, 62:2 (July 12, 2004): 52.

Kevin O'Leary, "How Did This Happen?" *Us Magazine* 668:52 (December 3, 2007).

14

O. J. SIMPSON

African-American football great who seemed to be living a charmed life until the day his wife and a man who was visiting her were brutally murdered

THE CHOICE

On the night of October 25, 1993, O. J. Simpson was standing inside his wife's condominium, screaming at her through a locked bedroom door. He was drunk and he was angry, and he knew that, legally, he had no right to be where he was. He and Nicole had been divorced for a year and he had forced his way into her home. But something had to be settled. Something had to be explained. Something had to be said. What it was, we will probably never know. It is unlikely that Simpson had a clear notion of what it was. All he knew was that he had the overriding need to put right, once and for all, his combative relationship with his ex-wife. And all we know is **that Saturn was less than a degree away from crossing his Descendant**. A decision, a very momentous decision, was being made at that moment. The fact that the police had just arrived, messing everything up, making it impossible for Simpson to say or do whatever it was that was on his mind, did not matter. There would be other nights.

THE HOROSCOPE

Simpson's horoscope, at least at first glance, gives no clue as to how he got himself into the situation we have just described. It is a very positive chart, full of optimism, charm, and good luck. Even when Simpson was a juvenile delinquent growing up in the slums of San Francisco, he was known for his smooth lines and effervescent personality. Everyone liked him, except possibly the members of rival gangs he occasionally had to thump. Three close trines dominate the chart: the Sun to Jupiter, Mercury to the Moon, and Mars to Neptune. Taken together they describe an upbeat, easygoing, quick-thinking person. The trine between the Sun and Jupiter is particularly important, because Jupiter is strongly placed within a degree of the IC, a very lucky placement. Luck comes to people with this placement largely because they always expect it to. Along with all this good news, we have Leo rising with a positively aspected Cancer Sun providing a healthy dose of self-confidence and an appealingly sensitive approach to other people.

Mars is strong in the chart, being in the 10th House and well-aspected. Along with the trine to Neptune, there is a sextile to both Saturn and Pluto. This sextile adds a physical toughness and self-discipline that is much needed in this easy horoscope, while the trine to Neptune alludes to almost magical physical abilities. These aspects to Mars are not altogether positive. The trine to Neptune provides an inclination toward deception and fuzziness with regard to the boundaries between fantasy and fact. With such an aspect, particularly with a Pisces Moon, there is the danger that the person will come to enjoy alcohol or other intoxicants far too much. Still, with the altruism and spirituality of Neptune coupled with the focus of Saturn and Pluto, the outlook is good.

Even the bad aspects seem to help Simpson. His Moon is square to Uranus and Venus. Given the happy-go-lucky quality of his trine aspects, Simpson might have been content to remain in the ghetto environment in which he seemed to be thriving. The hard contact between Uranus and his Moon gave him the restlessness, the need for new stimuli and broader vistas, and the ability to make radical changes in his thinking that he needed in order to break out of poverty and find a

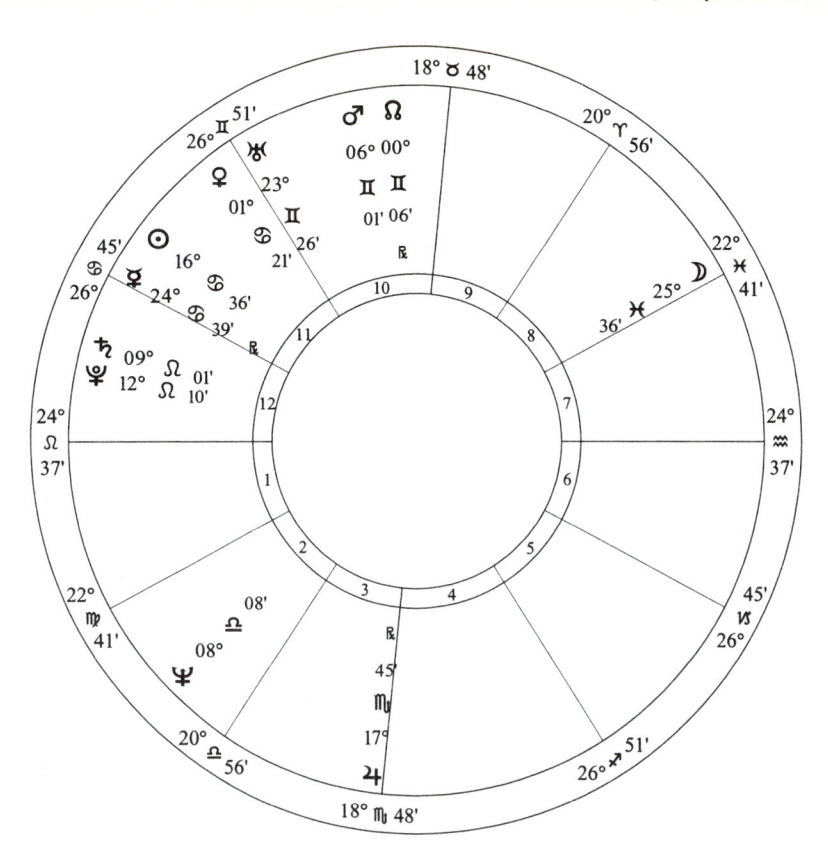

O. J. Simpson

July 9, 1947, 8:08 AM PST
San Francisco, CA, 37N46 122W25

better life. On the negative side, this square would cast a shadow over Simpson's relationships with women, indicating that he would choose women who are unusual or, in some way, a challenge to the social norm. At the same time, he would regard these women as unreliable, untrustworthy and out of control.

It is only when we look very closely at Simpson's horoscope that the real danger signals become apparent. Simpson's Moon forms a sesquiquadrate (135-degree aspect) with both Saturn and Pluto. The sesquiquadrate is generally regarded as an aspect of secondary importance and, in this case, the aspects are a little wide, each being at about a degree and a half of separation. But the fact that the Moon is at an almost equal distance between the two aspects, and it occupies the 8th House, the natural home of Pluto, makes it something we have to consider. This is an aspect with a large potential toward violence. It indicates a personality harboring deep resentments and a monstrous thirst for revenge. In some ways, this dark and downright mean aspect is good for the horoscope. It provides an edge to the personality, a killer instinct that Simpson certainly needed during his career as a professional football player. The problem was finding a way to vent all this negative energy once his playing days were over.

THE LIFE

The good fortune so strongly indicated in Simpson's chart came to the fore when **Saturn opposed its natal place**. Simpson had just entered high school and tried out for the high school football team. Since he was big for his age, the coach made him a lineman, but after a while Simpson got a chance to run with the football and his coach was amazed. At some point during this period, word got to the baseball great, Willie Mays, that there was a gifted young athlete in his old neighborhood who needed a push in the right direction. Mays decided to visit Simpson. Simpson later cited this visit as one of the most important events of his life. Mays showed the wild youngster what could be accomplished with his athletic skills if he was willing to discipline himself and cut his ties with gangs and crime. Simpson took the advice and, by the time **Saturn reached his Descendant in 1964**, he was the star of his school's football team.

The problem was that the high school Simpson attended was hardly a high-profile, football power. Even with O. J. Simpson running for them, they still had a losing season. Also, the discipline Simpson displayed on the football field did not extend to the classroom, and his grades showed it. As Simpson neared graduation, he found that no major colleges were interested in him. He entered a local community college instead, where once again he became the star player and, once again, he got some good advice. A recruiter from the University of Southern California told Simpson that if he brought up his grades there would be a place for him on the USC football team. The next semester Simpson concentrated on his studies, and in 1967 he was admitted to USC. That same year he married his high school sweetheart, Marguarite Whitley.

Uranus was opposing his natal Moon and squaring his natal Uranus when Simpson played his first game as a Trojan. Not only did Simpson distinguish himself on the field, he was also relaxed and charming with the reporters who flocked to the new star after the game. Thus began Simpson's long love affair with the media. It turned out that Simpson had two gifts to present the world. He had a phenomenal talent for running with a football and he was well-spoken, polite, and charismatic in the locker room afterward. The fact that he was a poor kid from broken home in a bad neighborhood made the latter quality even more remarkable, and even more valuable. At the same time that Simpson was establishing himself as a football player, he also began preparing himself for a second career in front of the cameras.

For a while it seemed that Simpson was on a fast track to success. In 1968, he won the Heisman Trophy, identifying him as the most outstanding football player in the country. In 1969, he was drafted by the Buffalo Bills as the number-one prospect. He immediately signed several lucrative endorsement deals and left behind his impoverished origins forever. Then, **in September 1969, Saturn squared his natal Saturn**, and, suddenly, there was a roadblock.

Simpson's coach at Buffalo was an advocate of the passing game. He didn't see too much potential in his new running back, except to occasionally catch the football. After seven solid years of being a star, Simpson was underused, underappreciated, and unhappy. The situation only got worse the next season when **Saturn reached his Midheaven.** At the time when Simpson's career should have been reaching new heights, he was injured and forced to sit on the bench. Even when he did get to play, it was in a secondary role. Even Simpson's golden relationship with the media was suffering. Sports gurus around the country were beginning to wonder aloud if Simpson wasn't just a flash in the collegiate pan who couldn't play at the professional level.

Once again, it was Uranus that came to save Simpson. As Uranus squared his Sun, the Buffalo team brought in a new coach, with a different attitude. This coach wanted to build a team around Simpson's phenomenal running ability. It took a couple of years for him to get all the supporting players he needed, but by the 1973 season the Bills were loaded and Simpson was primed to make football history. That year he broke the season record for yardage gained and established himself as a household name across America.

The next two years were good ones for Simpson. He continued to do his amazing work on the football field, and in 1974 he starred in his first movie, *The Towering Inferno*.

Simpson's celebrity status seemed both strongly established and secure. Then, in 1976, **as Saturn made its first return to its natal position**, his football career hit another snag. The managers of the Buffalo team began dismantling the supporting unit that was so important to Simpson's success. The coach resigned in protest and Simpson was distraught. He entered contract negotiations that year with the intent of leaving Buffalo and getting himself traded to another team. The fact was that Simpson never liked Buffalo and had never lived there. His wife and children still lived in Southern California and that was where he wanted to play, but the management of the Bills was adamant. They wanted to keep their star. In the end, Simpson accepted a multimillion-dollar deal and stayed in Buffalo.

This turned out to be a bad deal for both parties. For Simpson, the continual separation from his family was taking a toll on his personal life. A Cancer Sun with a Pisces Moon, Simpson needed a lot of love and emotional support. As his relationship with his wife became more strained, he went looking for this support elsewhere and, being both famous and good-looking, he had little trouble finding it. Simpson's wife was becoming increasingly jealous, particularly after the summer of 1977 when Simpson began keeping company with a pretty blond college student named Nicole Brown. For the management of the Buffalo Bills, the deal went sour **in late October of 1977, one month after Saturn conjoined Simpson's Ascendant**. Their million-dollar running back suffered a serious injury to his knee and had to sit out the rest of the season.

Although Simpson was traded to San Francisco the next season and played two more years, his football career was effectively over. However, Simpson seemed well prepared for this transition. Uranus was moving across his IC and conjuncting his natal Jupiter, an excellent aspect for positive change. Simpson was already making movies, and in 1979 he made the first of his soon-to-be-famous commercials for the Hertz car rental company. At the same time, he and Marguarite divorced and Simpson began living with Nicole. Then, in August 1979, his Uranus aspect took a tragic turn. His two-year-old daughter drowned in a swimming pool. It was reported that Simpson went into a rage in the hospital after his daughter died, and blamed Marguarite for the accident.

Despite this tragedy, Simpson's post-football career seemed to be rolling ahead. There were more movies and**, in 1983, when Saturn squared his natal Saturn,** he began appearing on *Monday Night Football* as a commentator. Also in 1983, he and Nicole became engaged. **In February 1985, a few months after Saturn crossed his IC**, Simpson and Nicole Brown were married. Also in 1985, he was elected to the Football Hall of Fame. Simpson remained a popular figure, even as his fame as a football player had begun to wane, and he was generally well-liked by the people who worked with him. No one seemed to doubt that O. J. Simpson was just a nice guy, except possibly his neighbors in the ritzy area where he and Nicole lived. Even before he and Nicole were married, there were complaints from these neighbors about loud arguments at the Simpson home.

In January 1989, the troubles in Simpson's home life finally made their way into the public eye. Police were called to the Simpson residence where they found that Nicole had been beaten and kicked out of the house. Even though Mrs. Simpson refused to press charges, O. J. was arrested and convicted of assault. Because of his celebrity, Simpson got off with community service and some half-hearted attempts at counseling. More importantly, the incident did not seem to tarnish his reputation. A short time after his conviction, Simpson co-starred in the first of a series of comedies titled *The Naked Gun*.

Simpson's career seemed to have survived the scandal. The same could not be said for his marriage, however. After the 1989 incident, Nicole sought counseling. In January 1992, she asked Simpson for a separation, and in **March 1992, one month after Saturn opposed Simpson's natal Saturn,** she filed for divorce. With his Sun in emotionally needy Cancer and his Moon in equally emotional Pisces, it is not surprising that Simpson had problems letting go of the relationship. However, Simpson carried this need to cling to frightening extremes. After the divorce, he stalked Nicole and terrorized her, leading up to the incident on October 25, 1993. This time Simpson was not charged. Nicole once again refused to pursue the issue. Simpson went home to consider his options. The one he apparently did not consider was leaving his ex-wife alone.

Eight months later, on June 12, 1994, Nicole Simpson was killed outside her home. Ron Goldman, a young man who apparently had just dropped by to return a pair of sunglasses Nicole had left behind in a restaurant, was also murdered. Suspicion immediately centered on O. J. Simpson and he was charged with the crimes. Simpson was under some very explosive aspects at that time. Both transiting Uranus and transiting Neptune were opposed to his natal Mercury, indicating bad decisions, while his secondary progressed Mars was squaring his natal Neptune, an aspect that would be consistent with an ill-conceived act of violence. More importantly, perhaps, Jupiter by secondary progression was separating from the slow retrograde conjunction it had been making to Simpson's IC for most of his life. A long streak of good fortune was ending. After a sensational, nationally televised trial, Simpson was acquitted by a jury, but few of the millions of people who had closely followed the trial on television agreed with the verdict. In the court of pubic opinion, Simpson was a murderer. A jury in civil court concurred and the families of both Nicole Brown Simpson and Ron Goldman were granted a huge judgment after it was found that Simpson had caused the wrongful deaths of these two people.

Saturn crossed Simpson's Midheaven in May 2000. In August 2000, he was granted custody of his children by Nicole Brown Simpson. Sometime in early 2006, Simpson approached an agent with an idea for a book. He said he was willing to provide information about the murders of Nicole and Goldman *as if* he had committed the crimes. The project, to be titled *If I Did It*, got underway in April. **Saturn arrived at its natal place in Simpson's chart in October 2005, January 2006, and June 2006.** When news of the book deal, which was to be accompanied by a television special, was released there was a groundswell of outrage, and in **November, just as Saturn first connected with Simpson's Ascendant**, the project was aborted. **In August 2007, one month after Saturn made its last contact with Simpson's Ascendant,** the rights to the unpublished manuscript were given to the Goldman family as part of Simpson's still unpaid civil judgment. They published *If I Did It* as Simpson's confession to the crime.

SATURN AT WORK

What is perhaps most interesting about O. J. Simpson's Saturn transits is that they have most often coincided, not with his moments of athletic triumph and glory, but with periods of defeat and depression. When Saturn squared his natal Saturn and crossed his Midheaven in 1969 and 1970, he was trapped on a team that seemed to have little use for his special skill. Then, in 1976, with Saturn returning to its natal place, he had to watch while management dismantled the team that had supported him during his most productive years. Meanwhile his efforts to negotiate a trade for himself were stymied. The next year, as Saturn crossed his Ascendant, Simpson suffered a serious injury that more or less put an end to his glory days.

Simpson's next Saturn passages, in 1983 and 1984, when Saturn squared his natal Saturn and crossed his IC, seem to have been more positive. He began his career as a TV commentator, married, and a short time later was inducted into the Hall of Fame. Still, this period also corresponded with the beginning of the domestic squabbles that would later destroy his relationship with Nicole. Finally, we have the passage of the opposition to natal Saturn in 1992, which coincided with his and Nicole's divorce, and the conjunction of Saturn to his Descendant, which coincided with his invasion of Nicole's home.

It would appear, then, that the good fortune in Simpson's horoscope was none of Saturn's business. The fact that he possessed this remarkable gift for running, as well as the discipline to harness that gift, and the savvy to profit from it, were not the issues that came up during his Saturn transits. Saturn was more concerned with what Simpson was going to do when his long streak of good luck stopped and his natural gifts were not enough the get him the fame and emotional security he needed. Repeatedly, during his Saturn passages, Simpson was asked to call up resources beyond his physical advantages and charisma; skills and discipline did not come as easily to him. In 1969 and 1970, he performed rather well. Despite his dissatisfaction with how his coach was using him, Simpson remained upbeat and never fell into the trap of self-pity. In 1976 and 1977, he was less successful. He later admitted that the dismantling of the team threw him into a depression and it was generally noted that his prolonged contract negotiations cast a dark shadow over the 1976 season (Davis, 1994). Likewise, the 1983 and 1984 transits brought the beginning of acrimony between him and his future wife, even though, overall, Simpson seemed to prosper. It was not until his Saturn opposition in 1992, when Nicole filed for divorce, that Simpson's inability to pass these tests became terribly apparent.

The key to Simpson's downfall seems to be hidden in the sesquiquadrate aspects between his Moon and Saturn and Pluto. The potential for violence provided for by these contacts, a potential that was quite evident during Simpson's early days, had been vented in a positive way on the football field, as long as Simpson was playing the game. Since these are relatively minor aspects, this was all that was necessary to keep that negative energy from showing itself elsewhere in his life. After he left football, however, Simpson lost this means of venting his aggression. At this point the resentful, vengeful, and destructive qualities of these aspects began to display themselves in Simpson's personal life.

Biographers of O. J. Simpson find it remarkable how Simpson began preparing himself financially and professionally for life after football even before he began his pro career. Unlike many sports heroes of the time, he deliberately courted the media and worked hard to create an appealing image. During a period when other African-Americans were aggressively challenging the white establishment, Simpson presented himself as a friendly and nonthreatening black man (Davis, 1994). As a result, Simpson moved smoothly from his career as a football player to the role of bankable movie star and popular TV personality. And yet, Saturn was directing Simpson's attention elsewhere. Saturn was calling on him to prepare himself emotionally and psychologically for this transition. Because Simpson failed to meet this challenge, all his other preparations did not matter. After Nicole's and Goldman's murders, he was suddenly regarded as one of the most dangerous and threatening black men around, and he lost his career in movies and television.

SOURCES

Don Davis, *Fallen Hero* (New York: St. Martin's Press, 1994).

Sheila Weller, *Raging Heart: The Intimate Story of the Tragic Marriage of O. J. Simpson and Nicole Brown Simpson* (New York: Pocket Books, 1995).

Pablo Fenjves, with O. J. Simpson, *If I Did It: Confession of the Killer* (New York: Beauford Books, 2006).

15

MATA HARI
(Margaretha Zelle MacLeod)

Dutch-born courtesan who faked her way to international fame as a dancer, only to be falsely accused and executed as a spy during World War I

THE CHOICE

In 1890, a pretty and somewhat spoiled little Dutch girl named Margaretha Zelle got the shock of what was to be a lifetime full of shocks and surprises. Her father, a prosperous hatter who had developed something of a reputation as an ostentatious spendthrift in the small community in which they lived, declared bankruptcy. This sudden decline into poverty was devastating for young Margaretha. To make matters worse, the personality of her father changed radically. Before the bankruptcy, Mr. Zelle had been generous and extravagantly indulgent with his daughter. Now he became contentious and abusive. This happened as **Saturn crossed Margaretha's Midheaven**. The next year, when **Saturn made its adolescent opposition to her natal Saturn**, Margaretha's parents were divorced. The year after that, her mother died and Margaretha had to be placed with relatives.

During this same period, Margaretha Zelle grew to her full height of five feet, ten inches, making her almost a giant among the Dutch girls and boys of her time. While the rest of her body was developing at this extraordinary rate, her breasts remained small. Pretty little Margaretha,

153

who had once charmed everyone with her dark good looks, became an awkward teenager, too tall, too flat-chested, and too poor to ever attract a husband. Her relatives decided to send the unfortunate girl away to a college for kindergarten teachers.

THE HOROSCOPE

Looking at her horoscope, it is easy to see where the future Mata Hari got her famous sex appeal. Scorpio is her rising sign, giving her the capacity to make every gesture and word ooze with sexual provocation. She has Mars, the planet of masculine, aggressive sexuality in bold, fun-loving Leo; and Venus, the planet of feminine, receptive sexuality, in the emotionally volatile Water sign of Cancer—a very sexy combination. Also, her Venus forms a trine aspect to her Moon in Pisces. Women with this aspect are often able to project a kind of beauty and sex appeal that transcends physical limitation. On top of this, we have the confidence of her Sun in Leo and the audacity of Jupiter in the First House. Despite the opinion of her relatives, Margaretha possessed a pronounced sex appeal.

There are two problem areas in this horoscope. The first is the conjunction of the Moon and Saturn in her 4th House. To some degree, we can see this aspect playing itself out in the early death of her mother, but its most damaging influence goes deeper. It is an aspect that restricts the ability to surrender oneself emotionally. It brings about an armoring of the self against emotional pain and a need to establish control over emotional exchanges. At its most extreme, it is an aspect that inhibits the ability to express love. On the positive side, the conjunction to practical, tough-minded Saturn deters some of the romanticism and flights of fantasy to which the Moon in Pisces is so prone. Unfortunately, by doing this, the aspect also limits the ability of this Pisces Moon to find the emotional connections it so desperately needs.

The second trouble spot is the square between Margaretha's stellium of planets in Leo (Mars, Mercury, and Uranus, along with the Sun) to her 1st House Jupiter. Jupiter opposes Pluto, forming a T-square that centers on Uranus. There is much that is positive about this set of aspects. It

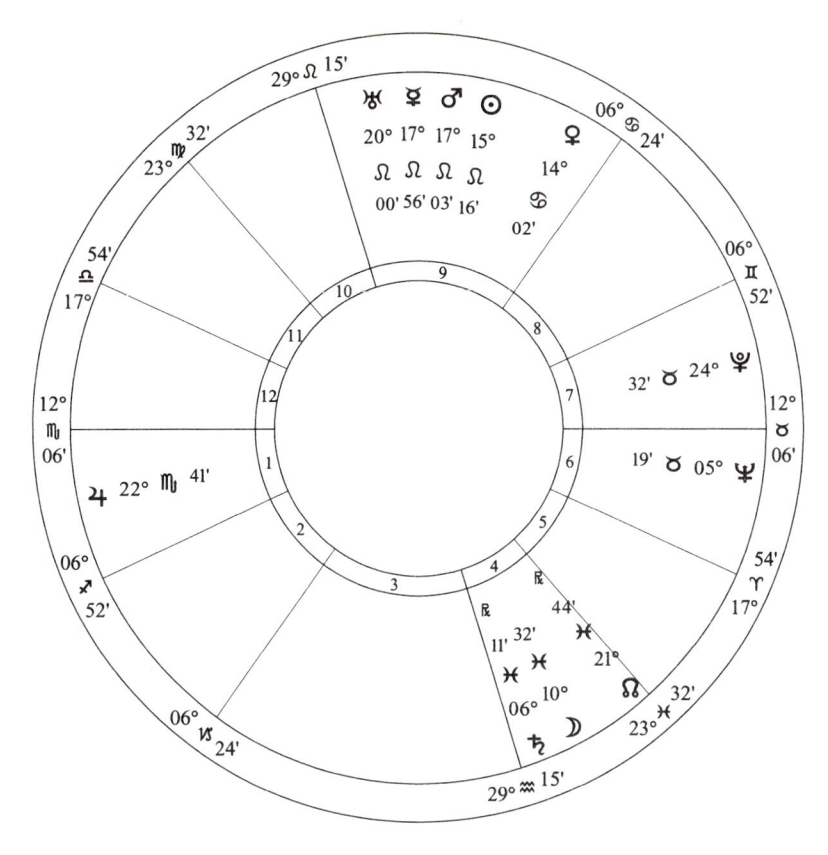

Mata Hari (Margaretha Zelle MacLeod)
August 7, 1876, 01:00 PM local time
Leeuwarden, Netherlands, 53N12 05E46

provides for an expansive, extremely vital personality that loves drama and demands attention. It is the aspect of someone who defies limitations, takes uncommon risks, and always expects the best result. It is an aspect of optimism, daring, phenomenal energy, and overwhelming self-confidence. It also might be considered a lucky aspect. The combination of Jupiter and Uranus is often connected to incidents of amazing good fortune, but a lot of this good fortune comes from a willingness to take the kinds of big risks that can bring enormous rewards.

The negative side of this set of aspects comes largely as an extension of its positive side. When risk-taking becomes habitual, when the big payday becomes the only payday worthwhile, and when optimism begins to overcome good sense, the charm of these Jupiter aspects is quickly lost. The most troubling element of this combination is the very close conjunction of Mars and Mercury. Although this aspect provides for a dynamic and highly original mind (when combined with the conjunction to Uranus) and bombastic communication skills, it is also an aspect of impulsive, reactive decision-making. Combine this with the expansiveness of Jupiter and we have a pronounced capacity for overstatement, overcommitment, and underappreciation of all obstacles. Decisions made too quickly for the purpose of immediate gratification, and statements made without proper thought or preparation would be a huge problem for Margaretha.

THE LIFE

By 1895, Margaretha had made two momentous discoveries. The first was that she had no intention of becoming a kindergarten teacher. The second was that, despite the fact that she failed to meet the standards of beauty of her time, she still had the ability to attract the attention of men. These discoveries came to Margaretha just as transiting Pluto was squaring her natal Moon and the pressure for her to find a husband was building. At this point, Margaretha's lucky Jupiter aspect seemed to intervene. She came across a paragraph in what passed for the personals section of her local newspaper, in which a captain in the Dutch army announced he was seeking a wife. Captain Rudolf MacLeod was a bachelor in his forties, who had spent most of his life living in various colonial posts for Holland. The advertisement had been placed for him by a friend who had decided the aging officer could use the extended sick leave he had been granted by the military to look for a wife. Margaretha, who had a weakness for both older men and uniforms, leapt at this chance for matrimony. MacLeod apparently leapt at Margaretha. The two were married only two months later.

Interestingly, Saturn was not involved in this rush into wedded bliss. **Saturn arrived at its next transit, a conjunction with Margaretha's Ascendant,** about six months after the wedding. It was at about this early point in her marriage that Margaretha was learning, much to her distress, that her new husband had no intention of giving up his bachelor ways. He continued to spend much of his time boozing with his friends and visiting prostitutes, just as he had done when he was single. Moreover, MacLeod attempted to dominate his new wife and keep her on a strict budget.

Of course, no one dominates a Leo Sun, and MacLeod's budgets hardly agreed with Margaretha's strong Jupiter aspects. The marriage quickly became a battleground. Still, the ill-matched couple managed to conceive a son, who was born in 1897. A short time later, Captain MacLeod took his family to the Dutch colony on Java. Margaretha spent the next three years of her life at various posts in Southeast Asia. **During this period, Saturn made its age twenty-one square to its natal place.** Unlike most of the other military wives, Margaretha took careful notice of the customs and activities of the native population of her new home. She even wore the native costume on occasion. Though her interest in these matters was spotty and often superficial, she still absorbed something of the ambiance of the region.

Also during this Saturn passage, Margaretha had her second child, a daughter. The problems in her marriage had not abated. Even though MacLeod was very fond of his children, he still found himself frequently at odds with his strong-willed wife. This situation only worsened when their son died in 1899. The boy had been poisoned by a servant conspiring with a solder who had a grudge against the captain, but MacLeod blamed Margaretha. The couple stayed together (mostly because Margaretha had nowhere else to go) until MacLeod retired and the family returned to Amsterdam in 1902. Then they quickly separated.

For a time MacLeod and Margaretha fought over custody of their daughter, but by 1903 Margaretha was beginning to concede. Perhaps she recognized that the child would be better off financially with MacLeod. Or perhaps she had decided that a child in tow would greatly inhibit her ability to realize the dreams she had been secretly harboring since childhood. She was bound for Paris.

Margaretha arrived in the cultural capital of Europe, the city of light, art, and fashion, with little money and no contacts. She lasted only a few months. Her ambition seems to have been to become an artist's model, but her tiny—now somewhat saggy—breasts precluded nude modeling and left her with few options. Then lucky Jupiter struck again. Back in Amsterdam, Margaretha met a pleasure-loving French diplomat and she was soon able to return to Paris as his paramour.

Baron Henry de Marguérie was as uninterested in an emotionally binding relationship as was Margaretha, but he was a good friend and a very canny advisor. He proposed that Margaretha try to make some money dancing. Margaretha had no training in dance, but she did possess long legs and a natural grace. She also had a Leo Sun's exultant self-confidence and an impeccable sense of presentation. With the baron as her impresario, Margaretha made her debut as a dancer in the salon of a noted Parisian socialite.

Calling herself "Madam MacLeod," Margaretha put together a dance that used elements of rituals that she had seen or heard about in Asia, along with a bit of striptease and a costume of her own design (cleverly engineered to cover her breasts while exposing everything else). The audience was fascinated. She was invited by Emile Guimet to repeat her performance in his new museum of Oriental art and culture. He also insisted that she assume a new stage name, something with an air of Oriental mystery. The name that was chosen was Mata Hari. Dancing as Mata Hari for the first time on March 13, 1905, Margaretha's exotic and sexually charged gyrations were not only accepted as a legitimate interpretation of Hindu temple dancing, they made her immediately famous.

Saturn was crossing Margaretha's IC at the time of her debut, and again later in the year when, now using the name Mata Hari, she was triumphantly touring Europe with her unique act. Still, Margaretha was not prepared to completely give up her old life. In the midst of her stunning success, she made one last visit to Amsterdam to see her daughter. She sought to work out an agreement with MacLeod to spend time with the girl. MacLeod responded to this overture by officially filing for divorce in April 1906, just as **Saturn was conjuncting Margaretha's natal Saturn.** The ex-captain cited his wife's morally suspect career as grounds for the divorce.

Despite the incredible success Margaretha was enjoying as Mata Hari, her position in the performing world was never secure. Those knowledgeable in the art of dance quickly surmised that Margaretha was an amateur with no training, while other performers just as quickly capitalized on the success of Mata Hari by performing their own versions of "ethnic" dances. Then there was the matter of Mata Hari's biography, which seemed to change with each interview she gave. The ethnological source of her dance was also questioned. Experts pointed out that there were no dancers in Hindu temples and the so-called rites Mata Hari was performing had no basis in fact. Fortunately for Margaretha, her fans were still more interested in her body than in the veracity of her story.

Now that she was an international sensation, Margaretha was able to attract the attention of men of great wealth and power. Though she made quite a bit of money dancing before large audiences and in private salons, the bulk of the funds needed to support Margaretha's increasingly luxurious lifestyle came from her male benefactors. By 1910, she was being supported by a French banker named Xavier Rousseau. He bought her a home in Paris and four thoroughbred horses. (Margaretha was an accomplished horsewoman.) Margaretha apparently felt so comfortable in the relationship that she sent her maid to Holland on a mission to kidnap her daughter, which was foiled by MacLeod. Then, **as Saturn crossed her Descendant**, disaster struck. Rousseau's bank failed and he was forced to give up his mistress. At thirty-five, Margaretha Zelle MacLeod found herself once again in search of a job.

At first, the situation seemed under control. Her agent was able to book her for performances at one of Paris' elite venues, but this good news was fleeting. When she tried to join the company of the famous Sergei Diaghilev, she was humiliated. By the time **Saturn made its next square to its natal position in 1913,** Margaretha was performing in Sicily on the same bill as a troop of trained dogs. Interestingly, it was at the same time that she gave a private performance for an Italian aristocrat in which she danced the notorious "dance of the seven veils" from *Salome,* the scandalous play written by Oscar Wilde and made into an opera by Richard Strauss. The noble was so impressed that he had her pose for a painting of this mythical destroyer of virtuous men and embodiment of depraved feminine sexuality.

In 1914, tired of scrambling for jobs, Margaretha called on one of her former boyfriends, a rich German who was now an officer in the German army. With some reluctance, her ex-lover invited the aging dancer to Berlin, where she performed her act and searched for new benefactors. Ominously, considering what would happen later, she was living in Berlin when World War I began.

By the end of 1914, Margaretha was back in Holland, living a relatively quiet life supported by a new Dutch lover. This really didn't matter, unfortunately, because the British intelligence service had already pegged her as a potential German spy. They needed no more than her connection to various German men (she was reputed to have counted the son of the Kaiser as one of her lovers) and her presence in Berlin in August 1914 to make the assumption. A year later, when Margaretha grew bored with Holland and decided to return to Paris, the British gladly passed their suspicions onto the French.

Unfortunately for Margaretha, this information fell into the lap of Georges Ladoux, an underachieving French intelligence officer who desperately needed to catch a spy, any spy. Equally unfortunate for Margaretha was the fact that she further weakened her position by falling in love. In Paris she met and became smitten with a young Russian officer named Vadim de Masloff. Overwhelmed by her fame and exotic beauty, Masloff was equally smitten with Margaretha. When Masloff returned to the front and was wounded, Margaretha was determined to go see him. To do so, she needed a pass from the French intelligence service. This placed her directly in the hands of the already suspicious Georges Ladoux.

Ladoux offered Margaretha money to spy for the French. Margaretha, foreseeing a big payoff that would allow her to support herself and her new lover in style, agreed to the plan. She didn't realize that Ladoux's offer was a trap designed to prove the Frenchman's suspicions that she was working for the Germans. In February 1917, after making an abortive attempt to enter Germany and conducting some freelance spying for the French in Spain, Margaretha was arrested. The evidence against her was flimsy and the most damaging documents were outright fabrications, but these were minor problems for the prosecution. After all, they were trying Mata Hari, a woman who had made a living out of seduction and deception, the embodiment of Salome and unbridled feminine sexuality, the *femme fatale* who led men to their doom. The verdict was a forgone conclusion.

Margaretha was arrested and sentenced to death as Uranus made its middle-age opposition to its natal place. This is an aspect under which many people enjoy major breakthroughs and arrive at important achievements in their careers. For Margaretha, the achievement was calmly rising at 4 AM on the morning of October 15, 1917, carefully dressing herself, walking unassisted to the site of her execution, and standing straight and proud before the firing squad that would end her life.

SATURN AT WORK

The history of Margaretha Zelle's Saturn transits is a study in missed opportunities. At fifteen, when Saturn made its first conjunction with her Midheaven, she could have learned the value of thrift from the bankruptcy of her flamboyant father, but she did not. Then a few months after her impulsive marriage to MacLeod, when Saturn crossed her Ascendant and she discovered what a bad choice she had made, she could have filed for a separation. Instead she chose to remain in her husband's cruel hands. Once she traveled to the Dutch East Indies, Margaretha's options were much more limited, but she could have chosen to use this period of isolation and idleness to truly educate herself about the culture of the native peoples (or on any other subject, for that matter), but instead, Margaretha wasted her time flirting with young officers and fighting with her husband. And finally, when Saturn crossed her IC and made its return, she could have used her great good fortune and newfound fame to establish her own financial independence, but instead, she covered her tracks with lies, spent lavishly, and made herself dependent on wealthy male protectors.

This is not to say that making good choices at these junctures would have been easy for Margaretha. It would have required her to overcome the impulsiveness and unfounded optimism to which her Jupiter-dominated horoscope was so prone. It would have also required her to make use of the realism implicit in her Moon to Saturn conjunction without falling victim to the depressive, self-destructive qualities of this aspect. There is evidence that, at some level, she understood this. Her attempts to reunite with her daughter, both occurring during a Saturn transit, indicate that she knew she needed to reestablish a connection with a normal life and reassume her responsibilities as a mother, but these attempts failed. In the end, Margaretha's bad choices had left her with few options. The firing squad very probably saved Mata Hari from a sad fade into obscurity as a forgotten celebrity and an aging prostitute.

SOURCES

Russell Warren Howe, *Mata Hari: The True Story* (New York: Dodd, Mead & Co., 1986).

Julia Wheelwright, *The Fatal Lover: Mata Hari and the Myth of Women in Espionage* (London: Collins & Brown, 1992).

Toni Bentley, *Sister of Salome* (New Haven: Yale University Press, 2002).

16

HERMANN GÖRING

Nazi leader who became the head of the German Air Force and the Gestapo under the regime of Adolf Hitler

THE CHOICE

In late October 1922, just as **Saturn made a quick conjunction with his natal Saturn,** Hermann Göring met the man who would change his life. The man he met was not particularly impressive. He was just another common German soldier left idle, hungry, and disheartened at the end of World War I, just another angry young man anxious to find someone to blame. Göring, on the other hand, was a war hero and had been (after the demise of the legendary Baron von Richthofen) the commander of Germany's most elite air force unit during the war. Still, it was Göring who found himself overwhelmed when he heard his new idol address the small, but rapt, audience. It was he who surrendered his own ambitions of forming a political party and gladly subjugated himself to the party headed by this sallow little corporal who spoke so forcefully about the injustice of the Versailles Treaty and the inevitable triumph of the German people. The party that Göring joined that night was called the National Socialist Party, and his new master was Adolf Hitler.

THE HOROSCOPE

Göring's horoscope is an odd one in that there are no close aspects to the Sun, Mercury, or Venus. The only aspect to the Sun is a wide (five and a half degrees) square to Jupiter and a sesquiquadrate to Pluto. The latter aspect is considered a minor one, but it takes on increased importance with Pluto's sign, Scorpio on the Ascendant. Both Scorpio and Pluto have a combative, martial character that further throws the emphasis in this horoscope toward Mars, the one inner planet that is really shaking things up in the chart. Mars is opposed to Saturn, sextile Pluto and Neptune, widely conjunct with Jupiter, and in a quincunx with Uranus. Göring was a natural soldier. The opposition to Saturn and the sextile to Pluto gave him self-discipline and a need for order and a fixed hierarchy. These aspects also provided a knack for violence and mayhem.

The opposition between Saturn and Mars can be very negative in its influence. It is an aspect that narrows the focus of Mars' energy to the point that it becomes harsh, judgmental, and even cruel. It is an aspect of people who prefer to see problems in black and white terms, and who favor solutions that are direct and uncompromising. The sextile between Mars and Pluto strengthens this tendency and adds a yen for power, but Pluto is so close to Neptune in this chart that the influence of one cannot be considered without examining the other.

The close conjunction of Pluto's will to power and Neptune's tendency to erode boundaries and fog judgment is so incongruous with the influence of Saturn and Pluto that it implies a second tier to this personality. Here Jupiter, with its wide conjunction to Mars and wide square to the Sun, becomes an ally. So, while Göring was able to maintain his tough-minded, decisive Scorpio Ascendant persona as a soldier and statesman and earn the title of "Germany's Iron Man," there was always another side of his personality that refused to accept the hard edges of his Saturn universe and laughed at the discipline and uncompromising judgments that it called for (Overy, 1984). This was the side of his personality that loved art, luxury, and display. It was the side of his personality that allowed him to appear jovial, cultured, and reasonable to foreign journalists and dignitaries, even while the Saturn-Pluto side was plotting, organizing, and brutally crushing his opposition. It was also this Neptune-Jupiter side of Göring's personality, with its blurring of boundaries and its inclination toward dependency, that made him so susceptible to the influence of drugs.

Some attention must also be paid to the conjunction between Göring's Scorpio Moon and his Uranus in the 12th House. Though the aspect is wide, it is still filled with ominous undertones. It tells us that women—particularly independent, unusual women—will play a large role in Göring's life, and not always in a good way. The placement of Neptune and Pluto in the 7th House shows that Göring's relationships with these women will have a fateful (Pluto) impact on his life and often work against his better judgment (Neptune).

THE LIFE

Hermann Göring was a man for whom there was no higher calling than to be a soldier. This had been his dream since he had assumed the rank of subaltern in the German army when **Saturn crossed his Descendant in 1912.** Unfortunately, during this same transit a tawdry drama was playing itself out within his family. Göring's mother had been having an affair with a wealthy Jewish friend of the family for years. The man was Göring's godfather and, in many respects, more influential in his life than was his elderly and frequently absent father. Shortly after Hermann's graduation, the godfather broke off the affair, and Göring's father belatedly became aware of his wife's betrayal and moved the family from the glamorous castle that the godfather owned to more prosaic digs. Many years later, Field Marshall Göring, the second most powerful man in Germany, would force his godfather to surrender ownership of that castle to him.

For a young man with such a warrior's mentality, the onset of World War I must have seemed like a godsend. However, it was not until 1915 that he began to see action. It was early in this year that Göring left the infantry and took flight training to become an observer. As the battle for the skies evolved and airmen began to shoot at each other, he was soon involved in dogfights with Allied planes. In these one-on-one battles, Göring proved himself to be both daring and skilled. He quickly amassed an impressive record of "kills" and earned himself a couple of medals. **Saturn was squaring in natal Saturn (the age twenty-one square)** and Göring was finding his place in the adult world. To be sure, it was a bloody and risky place—Göring was seriously wounded at least once—but it was a place well-suited for his natural courage and taste for glory.

Of course, this all came to an end in November 1918, when the war ended. Göring took over the Richthofen unit just in time for the surrender, although he refused to give up his planes and had his pilots fly them into Germany. Still, peacetime was not a complete waste for Göring. He took a job with the Fokker Company to demonstrate their planes in Sweden. There he became something of a celebrity, giving air shows and flying wealthy Swedes from place to place. It was during this heady period of his life that Göring met Carin von Fock, the wife of a Swedish count, and fell in love. **By the time Saturn crossed his Midheaven in September 1920,** he and Carin were lovers, a fact only barely concealed from her remarkably stoic husband. For a short time, the illicit couple tried to live together in Stockholm, but soon the public scorn became too intense and Carin agreed to leave both her husband and her child and flee with Göring to Munich, where they were married in February 1923.

In November 1923, after his historic meeting with Adolf Hitler, Göring the soldier once again heard the call to battle. By now he was the head of Hitler's SA or storm troopers, and Hitler was organizing a *putsch*, a violent takeover of the government of Bavaria. This was to be the first step of a revolution that would sweep the weak Weimar government of Germany from the political stage. Saturn had just squared Göring's natal Sun and Uranus was hovering near his IC. He was ready. He marched shoulder to shoulder with Hitler and several hundred SA men through the center of Munich. For a short while, he must have felt some of the glory he had known during the war. Then he was shot.

The bullet passed through Göring's groin, narrowly missing an artery. Bleeding profusely and in intense pain, he was taken from the scene of the battle by some of his men. Then he and Carin escaped

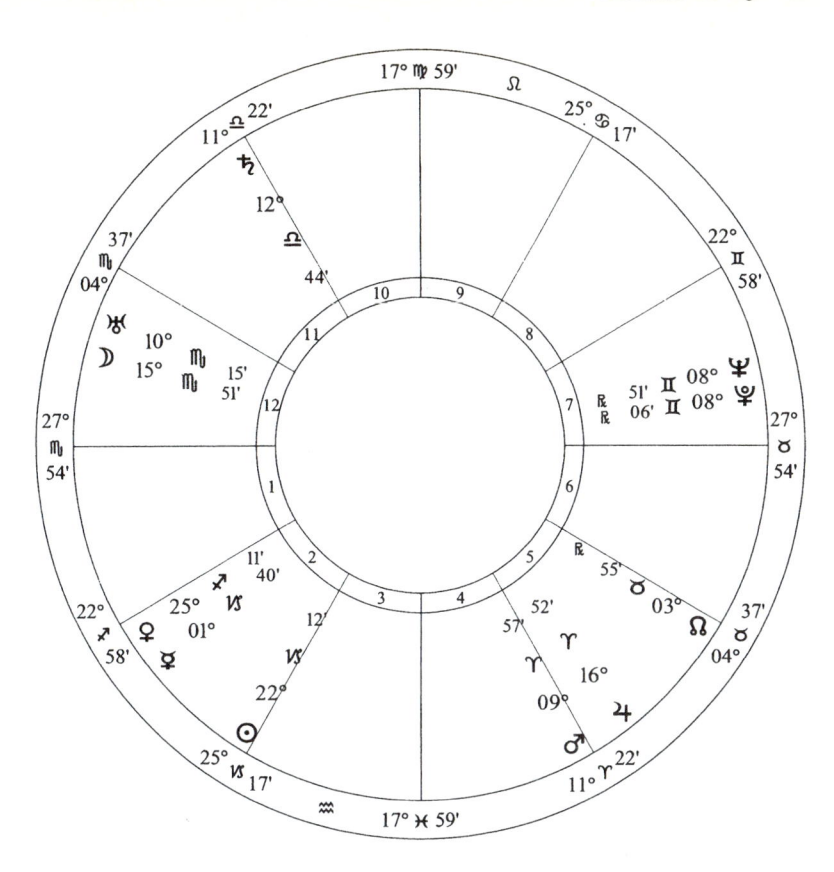

Hermann Göring
January 12, 1893, 4:00 AM MET
Rosenheim, Germany, 47N51 12E07

to Italy. Hitler's first grab for power had been ignobly defeated and Göring was a wanted man in Munich. He began a desperate period of exile. The recovery from his wounds was slow and excruciating, and he was forced to watch from a distance while Hitler and the other perpetrators of the Beer Hall Putsch stood trial and received their punishment. To make matters worse, Göring was unable to complete the one mission given to him by his imprisoned leader. Hitler ordered Göring to make contact with Benito Mussolini, whose Fascist party had taken over Italy only a couple of years earlier, and secure aid for the struggling National Socialist Party, but despite Göring's repeated entreaties, the new Italian dictator refused to see him.

As much as all these troubles weighed on his mind, Göring's real problem had nothing to do with politics. In the course of treatment of his gunshot wound, Göring had been introduced to morphine. Soon he was addicted. As his political and money troubles mounted in Italy, Göring's addiction grew stronger. When he and Carin went to stay with her parents in Sweden, his condition was so alarming and his behavior so violent that his wife had him committed to a mental institution. There he was forcibly weaned off the drug, but his dependence on morphine never ended. Even though he was apparently able to kick his habit for periods of time, Göring would remain an addict for the rest of his life.

A year after he had been pronounced sane and released from the mental hospital, and two months **after Saturn crossed his Ascendant**, Göring returned to Germany. His homecoming was hardly auspicious. He was still broke, working as a salesman for an aircraft company, and Hitler wanted nothing to do with him. The National Socialist Party was no longer a gang of thugs intent on revolution. It had become a viable political party. Hitler no longer needed warriors; he needed politicians. So Göring decided to change as well. By threatening to sue for back pay, he persuaded Hitler to allow him to campaign for a seat in the Reichstag. He won.

Göring took to his new role with all the enthusiasm and flamboyance he had shown as a soldier. Hitler decided that with Göring's status war hero and his charming aristocratic wife, the new Reichstag representative could be used to woo support from German business interests and from the upper crust of society. In this milieu, the former flying ace proved to be an extraordinary asset for the party. **In 1930, as Saturn squared his natal Saturn,** there were new elections and the Nazi Party was catapulted from an obnoxious fringe group within the Reichstag to the second most powerful political party in the country. Hitler acknowledged Göring's contribution by making him the leader of the Nazi contingent of representatives.

Hermann Göring was once again at the top of the Nazi heap. Not only had he regained his prestige within the party, he had also profited lavishly, and not altogether legally, from his position in the Reichstag and his growing list of contacts throughout the business world. After years of financial uncertainty and outright poverty, Göring was becoming a wealthy man. And yet, even as he was beginning to enjoy his new power and prosperity, tragedy found him once more. In 1931, as Saturn crossed his natal Sun, his beloved wife, Carin became ill and in October she died.

At the time of Carin's death, Göring had yet to commit any crimes against humanity. In fact, aside from graft and fomenting revolution, both endemic in Germany at that time, he was relatively blameless. By the time Saturn reached his Descendant ten years later, however, he would be counted among the worst criminals of the century. In 1934, along with Heinrich Himmler, he oversaw the bloody purge of Ernst Röhm and his supporters. His constant plotting and thirst for power led to the ouster or worse of many other competitors within the Nazi state, while his minions set up the first concentration camps to deal with enemies outside the party. The power he gained through these machinations made him one of the chief architects of the German war machine that would soon devour Europe. As head of the Luftwaffe, he rained down death and destruction on Spain, Poland, France, and Britain. As the master of the German economy, he organized extensive slave labor operations throughout Europe. As president of the Reichstag, he helped develop anti-Semitic laws that were designed to marginalize and brutalize Germany's Jewish population, and as the head of the Gestapo he saw to it that they were ruthlessly enforced. He advocated forced emigration of German Jews and then internment in his slave factories. And, finally, Hermann Göring stands as the grand overseer of the mass murder of six million Jews across Europe.

During the period of Carin's illness and death and Hitler's rise to supreme power in Germany, 1931 through 1933, Pluto opposed Göring's natal Sun, indicating a major transformation. Pluto aspects to the Sun generally coincide with a major restructuring of the identity, often caused by the person being carried away or overwhelmed by forces beyond human control. For Göring, this unstoppable force was the Nazi Party. He identified himself with the party in a way that even Hitler could never do. When he said, "I have no conscience. Adolf Hitler is my conscience," he was, in fact, announcing the utter surrender of his own personality to the nefarious goals and twisted morality of the Nazi Party (Irving, 1989).

Not surprisingly, considering this transformation, the two major Saturn transits that followed Hitler's takeover of Germany in 1933 seem to coincide with events that were more significant to the Nazi regime than to Göring. **When Saturn crossed Göring's IC in 1936**, Hitler occupied the Rhineland, his first open defiance of the Versailles Treaty and his first test of the willingness of the European powers to oppose his will. **When Saturn opposed Göring's natal Saturn in late 1938 and early 1939,** Germany swept into Czechoslovakia, again extending its power and territory without bringing about a war.

And yet, it seems likely that these transits coincided with other events of a more personal nature, probably involving Göring's on-and-off addiction to morphine. We know that in 1937 a dentist prescribed a low dose of morphine for Göring, a dose that would have been sufficient to renew his addiction if he had, as he claimed in 1933, kicked the habit. We also know that by the end of the war he was taking codeine, a much less addictive drug. Unfortunately, the true story on these transitions is denied us, since Göring's personal papers disappeared at the end of the war.

It wasn't until **Saturn reached Göring's Descendant in 1942** that we can definitely see the influence of the transit. It was during this period that Göring's relationship with his idol began to fall apart.

Prior to the war, Göring had been one of Hitler's advisors who called for caution. He understood that war was inevitable, but he wanted to postpone it until Germany was economically and militarily ready to take on all of Europe. After the entry of the United States into the war and German stagnation in Russia shattered Hitler's hope for a quick victory, Hitler began to spend less time with his second in command and more time with men like Martin Bormann and Joseph Goebbels, who told him only what he wanted to hear. In 1942, Göring lost his preeminence in the area of munitions production to Albert Speer, the first outward sign that the Führer was beginning to reassess his opinion of "the iron man."

During the period between 1933 and 1942, Göring displayed periods of remarkable energy and leadership, during which he seemed involved in every aspect of the Nazi regime. He also succumbed to long periods of idleness when he either seemed to be recuperating from illnesses or enjoying his vast estate and impeccable art collection (all of which were gained for him at the point of a bayonet). After 1942, the latter condition seemed to dominate. **In May 1945, just as Saturn made its next square to his natal Saturn**, Göring surrendered to the Allied forces. As Hitler's successor, he hoped to be recognized as the legitimate leader of the defeated German nation. Instead, he was regarded as a common criminal. Over the next several months, the many sins of his Nazi past were brought to light in the Nuremberg trials, and Göring, still defiantly playing the role of the iron man, was sentenced to be hanged. He committed suicide shortly before this ignoble sentence could be carried out.

SATURN AND WORK

In trying to determine where Hermann Göring went wrong in his life, it is easy to focus on his first Saturn return when he made the disastrous choice to follow Adolf Hitler, but, in many ways, his downfall began when Saturn crossed his Midheaven and he fell in love with Carin von Fock. Previous to this affair, he was a war hero with a good job. He was respected by everyone and adored by many. The choice Saturn brought Göring when it reached his Midheaven during this period was a choice between holding on to his honor, to his pride as an officer and a warrior, or surrendering to the psychosexual need to somehow relive the unsavory drama of his childhood, in which his mother was unfaithful to his father. Göring chose the latter and, because of that choice, he quickly became an outsider, just another unemployed soldier without honor or prospects, waiting desperately for the man who could restore his strength and give him hope of a glorious future.

It might be said that Göring was making a choice for love, and that his devotion to Carin, at least to a degree, justifies his actions. Certainly Göring's affection for his wife is one of the most humanizing of his qualities. And yet, Carin was even more thoroughly seduced by Hitler and the Nazi movement than was Göring, and her anti-Semitism was more virulent that his. Her influence in Göring's life only made it more difficult for the ex-pilot to see how truly negative his choice to follow Hitler had become.

In this regard, Göring's life serves us an example of how a bad choice, even a bad choice made with the best and most romantic of intentions, can have disastrous results when it is made during a Saturn passage. Saturn brings us standards of virtue and good behavior that are simply not amenable to our piteous cries for love, and we violate them at our peril. Sometimes, of course, true love is worth the risk, in which case we have to accept our fate. Göring chose not to accept his fate. He chose to rebel against Saturn's judgment, and when Hitler came along offering him a means of throwing off his poverty and renewing his tarnished honor, the warrior jumped at the opportunity. And it was this choice, a bad choice compounding a previous bad choice, that turned the decorated war hero into a murderer.

SOURCES

R. J. Overy, *Göering: The Iron Man* (Boston: Routledge and Kegan Paul, 1984).

David Irving, *Göring: A Biography* (New York: Wm. Morrow & Co., 1989).

17

JANIS JOPLIN

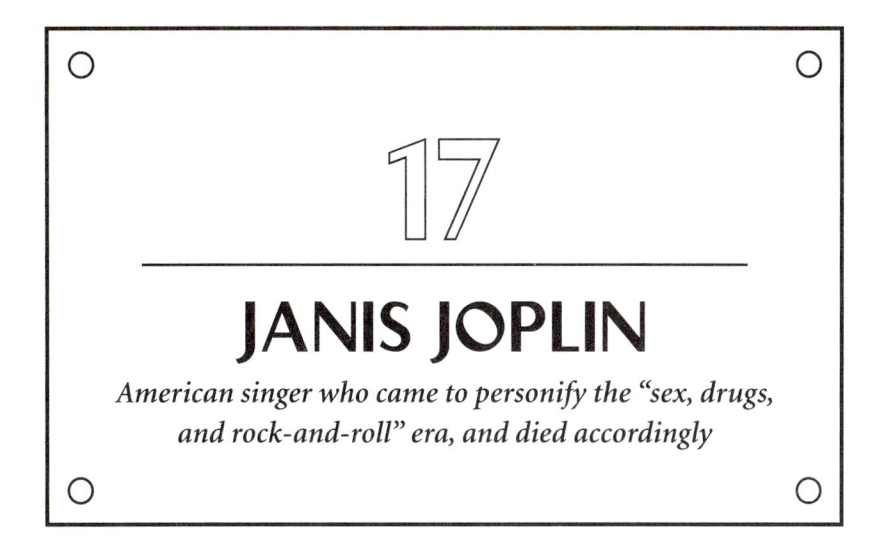

American singer who came to personify the "sex, drugs, and rock-and-roll" era, and died accordingly

THE CHOICE

At age fourteen, Janis Joplin found herself in hell. It was called high school. Prior to her fourteenth year, Janis had been a cute, freckled-face pixie—lively, well-behaved, and popular at school. Then, in **November 1956, Saturn opposed its natal place**, her adolescent Saturn passage. Her body was changing. The freckles were replaced by rampant acne and her weight ballooned. Her bra size didn't. This trying Saturn passage was immediately followed by another, **the conjunction of Saturn with her Midheaven**. Now it was not just her body that was changing. Her place in the world had also changed. She became an object of ridicule and rejection. Older kids laughed at her new body and the pixie-like charm that had made her well-liked in grade school now had become grotesque and ineffective. Suddenly, through no fault of her own, Janis Joplin was transformed into something no Capricorn Sun wants to be—a failure.

Looking at her horoscope, there can be no doubt about how this young woman was going to react to her new status. That Capricorn Sun, practical and conservative as it may be, forms trines to both Neptune and revolutionary Uranus while her Mercury, Venus, and Ascendant are in Uranus' sign, Aquarius. Janis Joplin reacted to the ridicule she experienced in her high school by rebelling. If she could not be accepted by her peers in conservative Port Arthur, Texas, then she would fly in the face of their conventions. She began dressing like a beatnik and affecting mannerisms and speech that announced to one and all her rebellion, her defiance, and her independence from the accepted norms.

Thus began a cycle that would come to define Janis Joplin. The more Joplin rebelled against the conventions of Port Arthur, the more Port Arthur rejected and defamed her. By her senior year in high school, Janis had gone from being that strange kid who dressed in black and affected a loud, cackling laugh to a tough-talking outcast who cussed like a farmhand, got drunk with boys, and stayed out all night. Worse yet, it was generally assumed that she was also promiscuous, a slut, and this meant there was no limit to what her tormentors could say or do to her. Years later, after she had achieved worldwide fame and recognition, it is no wonder that Janis Joplin still recalled her high school years with extreme pain and regret.

THE HOROSCOPE

Going back to Joplin's horoscope, we must consider both her Mercury and her Moon. Her Mercury in Aquarius makes a strong opposition aspect to Pluto. It is also in close semisquare (45-degree) aspect with her Mars. Tough talk came easy for Joplin. People with Mercury to Pluto aspects are completely ruthless when they are placed on the defensive. They hold nothing back and their criticism and insults can be both devastating and decidedly indelicate. There is also a gut-wrenching, over-the-top quality with Mercury to Pluto aspects that is aptly expressed in Joplin's singular style of singing.

The problem with Joplin's Mercury aspects is that the toughness and combativeness they provide are exactly contrary to the needs of her Moon in Cancer. Joplin's Moon is rather isolated in her chart. In a horoscope dominated by Air and Fire signs, it and Jupiter are the only bodies in a Water sign and it makes no strong aspects. In fact, the only aspect to the Moon is a quincunx to Mercury. And yet, the needs of

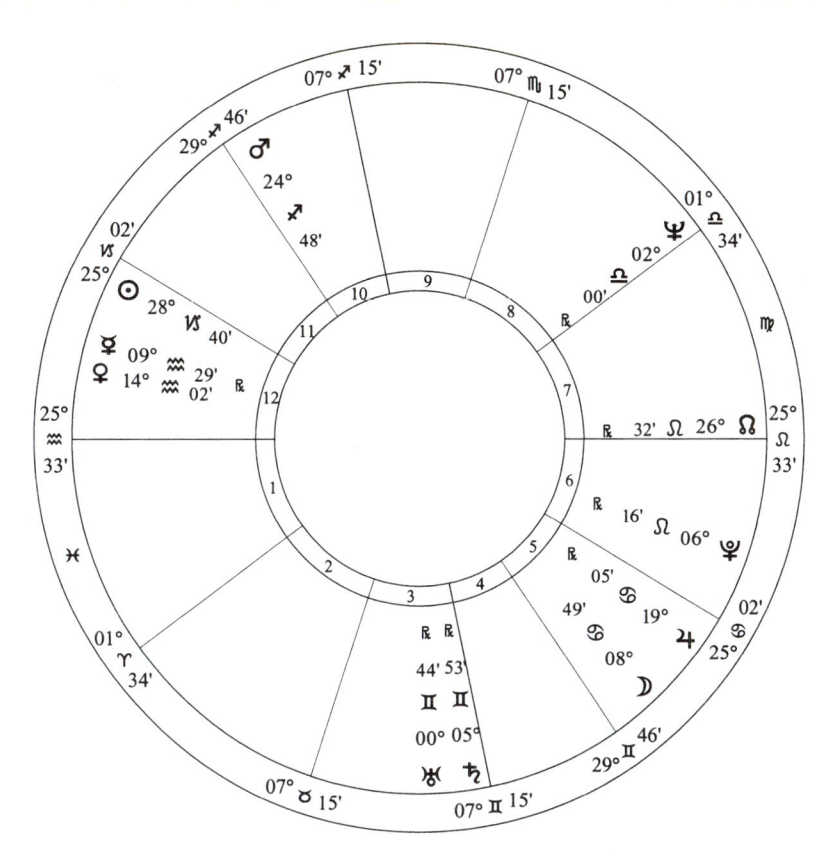

Janis Joplin
January 19, 1943, 9:45 AM CWT
Port Arthur, TX, 29N54 93W56

the Moon can never be ignored. For Joplin, this meant an overwhelming need for emotional security and warmth, a need to hold people close and develop strong, enduring connections. All of these qualities were disrupted, both by the rebellious tendencies of her Sun to Uranus aspect and the defensive contentiousness of her Mercury. Certainly Joplin's Mercury talked a good game and she exulted in being unlike anyone else in her high school, but her Moon needed love and acceptance, and it took every insult leveled at her to heart.

THE LIFE

In 1961, a year after her graduation from high school, Uranus crossed Joplin's Ascendant and Saturn conjoined her Sun. After a semester at a local college learning secretarial skills, she took a typically Uranian leap into the unknown and moved to California. It was not the breakout move she might have anticipated. Joplin lived with her aunt during most of her stay and worked as a keypunch operator. Still, it gave her a taste of the freedom that would become her goal.

Back in her hometown of Port Arthur in 1962, Joplin once again enrolled in the local college. She drank, hung out, partied, and even tried her hand at singing. In high school she had excelled in visual art, but now music, in particular folk music and blues, was becoming her overriding interest. Soon she was gravitating toward Austin, Texas, where there was a lively college atmosphere, a growing counterculture, and opportunities for her to get on stage and sing. By the beginning of 1963, Joplin had enjoyed enough success as a singer in the Austin area to convince herself that she should make another assault on California, only this time she was going there as a singer.

In San Francisco, Joplin quickly settled into a free and easy bohemian lifestyle. She found work as a singer but did not make much money, and devoted a great deal of her time and energy to just hanging out and having a good time. Drugs were an immediate lure. In Austin, Joplin had become as well-known for her hard drinking as for her singing. She had also taken Benzedrine and other amphetamines. In San Francisco, Joplin quickly moved on to injecting speed and later to experimenting with heroin.

Between June 1963 and February 1965, **Saturn crossed Joplin's Ascendant and squared her natal Saturn**. It was a period full of opportunity for the young singer. Though folk music was still thriving, rock-and-roll was continuing to excite young audiences and a new appreciation for African-American music such as blues was developing. Joplin's remarkable voice came to the attention of many people during her stay in San Francisco, people who could have started her on her way toward a thriving career. But bad choices consistently derailed her opportunities to succeed. Sometimes it was the booze and the drugs that caused her to miss auditions or sabotaged an important performance. Other times it was her loud and often abrasive personality. Joplin had lost none of the defensive vulgarity and capacity for blistering verbal assaults that she had developed in high school. Some of her fellow musicians simply didn't care to have her around and she was banned from singing in at least one bar after she insulted the manager.

The one conscious choice Joplin made during this prolonged Saturn passage turned out to be disastrous. In the fall of 1964, Joplin acquired a new boyfriend. Even her most liberated friends warned her against this new relationship. They considered this new man in her life unstable and hopelessly self-destructive. Joplin had had many affairs prior to this with both men and women. None of them had been serious. With this lover, however, the nurturing capacity of her Cancer Moon was activated. He was, after all, even more helplessly addicted to speed than she was. **By the time Saturn completed its last square to her natal Saturn**, both Joplin and her boyfriend had resolved to quit drugs and to get married, but the boyfriend's resolve proved too weak. After following her lover to Seattle, where he was locked up in a mental hospital with amphetamine-induced paranoia, Joplin, now a ninety-five-pound wreck, meekly returned to Port Arthur.

Back in Texas with her family, Joplin seemed determined to abandon all her freewheeling ways. She quit drinking and swore off amphetamines. She bought a new wardrobe of conservative clothes and pinned her wild hair back in a bun. She went back to college, majoring in sociology and, for a while at least, appeared to have become a model of propriety. For a while she still maintained hopes of marrying her errant boyfriend, but it soon became evident that he was living with another woman. Despite this disappointment, Joplin soldiered on in her new lifestyle and abstained from all her bad habits for almost a year. During this time she avoided performing.

This period of Joplin's life points to another tendency described in her horoscope. This was her innate conservatism. Not only did she have the Sun in Capricorn, but she was born with Saturn less than a degree and a half away from her IC. Saturn is also trine to her Sun, though the orb is fairly wide. Despite the exultant rebellion described by the Grand Trine between Joplin's Sun, Uranus, and Neptune, there remained a core within her personality that was thoroughly practical, businesslike, and ambitious. People who knew her even during the wildest periods of her life commented on this quality. They noted how hard she worked on developing her singing style and how closely she studied the work of other vocalists, both on recordings and in person. Janis Joplin needed to be a success, and she understood that her drinking and drugging were holding her back. In this context, her efforts to control her substance abuse, though clumsy and ultimately unworkable, were praiseworthy. What is unfortunate is the fact that she was unable to separate the means to her success, performing as a singer, with the abuse of alcohol and drugs.

It was finally Joplin's need to sing that brought her back to her old haunts and her old habits. She returned to the venues in Austin that had been the scene of her earliest successes and was greeted with open arms. The old Janis was back. She began drinking and smoking marijuana again. The only difference was that now she seemed to be in control of her consumption of alcohol and she was still determined to stay away from the speed and heroin that had previously brought her so low.

In June 1966, only a few months after she had put aside her straight disguise and resumed her singing career, an old friend from San Francisco came to visit her. He told her about a band called Big Brother and the Holding Company that was looking for a "chick" singer. He had recommended Joplin. This time drugs and alcohol did not cloud her judgment and Janis hurried back to San Francisco to audition. The band members were impressed, even a little overwhelmed. Joplin was now an ambitious Capricorn on a career track, and nothing was going to stop her.

The next year, as Joplin's progressed Sun came within two degrees of her natal Ascendant, she got her big break. Singing with Big Brother and the Holding Company at the Monterey Pop Festival, she stole the show from established groups like the Who and the Mamas and the Papas. She electrified the audience and launched her career. But it was not all good news. Even though she had come back to San Francisco with a vow to stay away from speed, by the time of this breakthrough performance Joplin was once again injecting amphetamines. In the heady atmosphere of her newfound success, it was easy for her move on to other drugs, including heroin.

Janis Joplin's rise to fame and fortune was remarkably fast and short-lived. It extended only through the period during which her progressed Sun moved across her Ascendant. A year after her performance at the Monterey Pop Festival, she broke with Big Brother and the Holding Company to further her solo career. A year after that, she was touring with a new band she had organized and she was already fretting about signs that her career was flagging. In this short period of time, Joplin managed to establish herself as an icon of popular music and as one of the greatest blues singers of all time. In her singing, at least, she managed to overcome both her own troubled youth and the troubles of her bedeviled generation, and give voice to the pain and troubles of all humanity. Unfortunately, she never totally escaped the shadow of those dark years in her Port Arthur high school and the emotional damage they had caused her. Just three years after her triumph at Monterey, Joplin died from an overdose of heroin.

SATURN AT WORK

Since Joplin was born with Saturn in a close conjunction with her IC, her Saturn passages were naturally concentrated. The adolescent opposition of Saturn to its own place is difficult enough. She had to endure this at almost the same time that Saturn transited her Midheaven. This would be a daunting one-two punch for anyone to endure. The problem for Joplin is that this combination of challenges came when she was very young and inclined to react to them in the most extreme and fearful way. She elected to protect the sensitive Cancer Moon side of her nature by creating an aggressive, tough-talking, rebel-against-anything persona that would become her favorite shield against the world.

The problem was that this protective front, which was so effective in keeping away the people she did not like, also kept at a distance all the people she did like. Created out of the fearful reaction of a fourteen-year-old high school girl with a personality already prone to extremes (Sun trine Uranus, Mercury opposed Pluto) the persona Joplin created in high school became her own worst enemy. No lover (of either gender) or multiple lovers augmented by powerful narcotics was able to pierce it. It also prevented her from taking full advantage of her remarkable talents for many years.

When Joplin went through her second Saturn passage in the early sixties in San Francisco, she had the opportunity to put aside her fears and drop this hardened persona. At this point in her life, she was surrounded by people who could have loved her, and opportunities to find a satisfying release from her fears in her singing and yet, despite all these offers of help and all the opportunities she had to begin her career as a singer, Joplin could not find the courage to accept her vulnerability and her weaknesses. Instead she persisted in covering up her insecurity with tough talk, booze, and drugs.

This crucial failure of courage did not make itself evident in any single event or decision. Rather it played out through a long series of minor failures and seemingly insignificant choices. It was a failure defined in increments, the most substantial of which was her decision late in the passage to attach her hopes of matrimony to an addict even more abject than she. And, as often happens, this failure to answer Saturn's call brought Joplin to the lowest point in her life.

It was this failure that defined the remainder of Joplin's life. Her brief escape into ultra-conventionality and her equally brief period of living her old life without hard drugs were simply rest stops on the road to self-destruction. The fact that Joplin became famous along the way, even though it is clearly indicated by her secondary progressions, seems to be almost a footnote in the story being told by her Saturn transits. She had chosen, almost by default, to hold on to her fears and to maintain the loud, vulgar, impenetrable shield that protected her emotions. Now she was entering truly dangerous territory.

It is tempting to speculate about what might have happened to Joplin if she had survived just a few months longer, until Saturn returned to its natal place and brought her next Saturn passage. Would an older, more mature and successful Janis Joplin have been able to make the adjustments she so desperately needed to make in order to escape her drug addictions and inability to accept love? That, unfortunately, is a question that will never be answered.

SOURCES

Ellis Amburn, *Pearl: The Obsessions and Passions of Janis Joplin* (New York: Warner Books, 1992).

Alice Echols, *Scars of Sweet Paradise: The Life and Times of Janis Joplin* (New York: Henry Holt & Co., 1999).

18

PAUL GAUGUIN

*French painter famous for his paintings of Tahiti
and his love for Tahitian women*

THE CHOICE

In April 1876, the judges of the great French Salon, the name given to the officially sanctioned exhibition of artwork held annually in Paris, faced a daunting task. Forty-five hundred works had been submitted; from these they had to choose only a few hundred to be hung in this prestigious exhibition (Sweetman, 1985). The lucky artists who made the cut had a chance of winning a gold medal and fame that could secure their place in the history of art. More importantly, they received the approval of the highest authorities in the art world. Just to have a piece hung in the Salon was an important validation of an artist's accomplishment, something to boast about to folks back home, and very often the first step toward a thriving career. In 1876, the jury selected for exhibition a small, unremarkable landscape, the first submission ever of an untrained amateur painter who had just experienced the passage of **transiting Saturn across his Descendant**. This delighted neophyte was Paul Gauguin.

Paul Gauguin had not pursued the normal career track of a great nineteenth-century painter. He had not attended the state art school

183

or worked in the studio of an established Salon painter. Gauguin had spent his youth as a sailor, and at the time of his submission was still a lowly paper pusher, working for the French stock exchange. He had started sketching as a pastime while he was in the navy, and only became interested in painting after he settled in Paris, so his acceptance into the Salon was a heady event. It was immediately followed by another important invitation. When he went to his sometimes-mentor in painting, Camille Pissarro, to report this accomplishment, the grand patriarch of the Impressionist movement asked him to exhibit with the Impressionists in the future. The paintings of these artists, including Claude Monet, Pierre-Auguste Renoir, and Edgar Degas, were deemed too radical to be displayed in the 1876 Salon and they had been forced to organize a separate exhibition. Gauguin was not entirely committed to the Impressionist movement, but he was happy to hobnob with these rebellious and exciting young painters, particularly now that he could be viewed as their equal.

THE HOROSCOPE

Looking at the horoscope of Paul Gauguin, it is hard to understand why he waited so long to start his career as a painter. With Venus in his 10th House forming a T-square with the Moon on the Ascendant and Neptune on the Descendant, it seems that it would have been a natural choice. Of course, this is not the most energetic or direct of T-squares. Its most prominent feature, the Moon in Virgo, is naturally indecisive and desultory. This lack of focus is increased by the close opposition to Neptune, creating a dreamy, evasive, and extremely sensitive personality. The square from Venus in Gemini adds an easy charm and keen aesthetic judgment, but it also doubles the natural sensitivity of the Moon and provides for an avoidance of conflict and a tendency to place peace, comfort, and aesthetic pleasure above all other concerns.

The sensitive, charming, and somewhat feminine personality described by this T-square sounds very unlike Paul Gauguin as he was described by his contemporaries. To these people, Gauguin was a rough-edged, self-involved egotist, charming to be sure, but also something of

Paul Gauguin 185

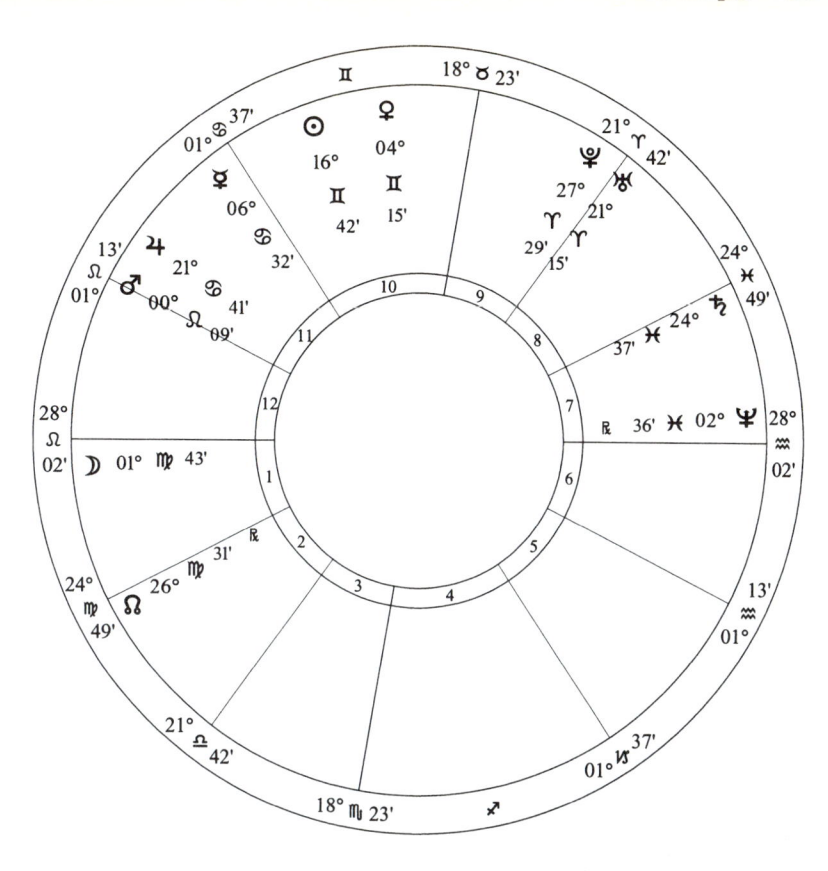

Paul Gauguin
June 7, 1848, 10:00 AM local time
Paris, France, 48N52 02E20

a scoundrel. The reason for this discrepancy is Pluto. Pluto forms a trine to the Moon and a strong square aspect to Gauguin's Mars. The square to Mars, in particular, adds a tough, ruthless quality to the personality. Gauguin's Leo Ascendant is also a factor, covering the pronounced sensitivity of his Moon with a deceptive layer of bluster and flamboyance. This is where Gauguin got his intensity and focus. It is also the source of his bold and often callous egotism. The influence of the Moon in his horoscope and its T-square were expressed, to a large extent, only in his paintings.

Perhaps the most dangerous aspect in Gauguin's chart is also one of the best. His Jupiter in the 11th House makes an almost exact square with Uranus. This is an aspect indicating sudden changes in fortune and lucky breaks. It is also an aspect indicating an often destructive addiction to the grandiose, a tendency to overdo, overspend, and overextend. Here optimism always rules, whether it is warranted by circumstances or not.

THE LIFE

Paul Gauguin was born into a distinguished family. On his mother's side he was connected to Spanish royalty. At the time of his birth, his great-uncle was viceroy of Peru. For this reason, and because of political instability in France, Gauguin's father decided to move the family to South America shortly after Paul was born. Unfortunately, the elder Gauguin died of a heart attack before the family arrived in Lima, and Gauguin's mother was forced to place herself and her two children in the care of their Peruvian relatives. Gauguin tended to exaggerate his contact with primitive culture during his years in Peru, but all we really know is that his mother collected some Peruvian ceramics that he treasured.

By the time Paul was seven, a revolution in Peru had uprooted the family once again and they were back in France. His mother's situation was somewhat desperate until Gustave Arosa, a wealthy Spanish businessman living in Paris, stepped in to provide guidance and financial help to her and her children. What Gauguin thought about this unusual arrangement, **which began as Saturn opposed his natal**

Saturn, is unknown. He was apparently a quarrelsome and unruly child, with no great ambitions. When he turned seventeen and it was time to choose a career, despite Arosa's contacts, there seemed only one option open for the boy: the merchant marine.

Again, we know little about Gauguin's experiences as a sailor, both in the merchant marine and in the French Navy, except for his boasts of endless sexual conquests. We have no record of his reaction to the death of his mother, which occurred while he was away on a long voyage and **when Saturn crossed his IC.**

In 1870, France went to war with Prussia and suffered a quick and ignoble defeat. This had little effect on Gauguin's life as a sailor except when he returned to Paris immediately after the conflict. He found that his mother's home had been destroyed by the Germans and that many of the precious objects they had brought from Peru, including the ceramics, were lost. This is the first record we have of a genuine emotional reaction from the young Gauguin. He was devastated—**Saturn was square to its natal place**.

At this point Gauguin decided it was time to put himself in the hands of his mother's protector. Arosa did a lot of business with the French stock exchange and he arranged for Gauguin take a low-level job there. The work was tedious, but the pay was excellent, and—now back in Paris—Gauguin had an opportunity to cultivate his nascent interest in painting. Now that he had a steady job, Gauguin began to move quickly, perhaps too quickly, toward becoming a conventional citizen. Pluto was crossing his Midheaven in 1871, 1872, and 1873—it was a time for transformations. He met a strong-willed young Danish woman named Mette Gad at a party, and began to court her. They were married within a year; the next year he became a father. **By the time Saturn reached Gauguin's Descendant and he had his triumph at the 1876 Salon,** he was living two lives—one as an upstanding businessman, and the other as a bohemian artist allied with the most radical painters in Europe.

There was one other change in Gauguin's life in 1876, one which would have a much more immediate effect on his life than his admission to the Salon. His boss at the stock exchange, Arosa's friend, retired and a new boss arrived who owed no loyalty to Gauguin's protector. A short time later, the name of Paul Gauguin disappeared from the company's list of employees.

Not that Gauguin was particularly worried. France was in the midst of a speculative frenzy and there was plenty of money to be made. Paul's next job is a mystery, though it was apparently the source of a rift that developed between Arosa and himself, indicating that what Gauguin was doing might not have been entirely legal. A year or so later, he moved to yet another job and the money was still coming in. He had forced his wife, who loved to spend as much as he did, to move to cheaper, more bohemian lodgings where he could maintain a studio and have easier access to his artist friends. Everything seemed to be going Gauguin's way. Then, **as Saturn passed over Gauguin's Midheaven,** the boom suddenly went bust.

Soon Gauguin was out of a job and scrambling for a way to support himself, his wife, and their five children. He tried to make money selling his artwork in Rouen. He tried to get started as a salesman in Copenhagen. Nothing seemed to work. Mette knew what she was going to do. She moved back in with her family. What was Paul going to do? Finally, in 1885, **as Saturn squared its natal place,** he retreated back to Paris to make one last attempt at succeeding as a painter. He hadn't entirely given up on his family. He took one of his younger sons, Clovis, with him.

At first it seemed that Gauguin's good luck had deserted him. During their first winter in Paris, Gauguin and his son starved and, when Clovis became ill, Gauguin was forced to beg for money to buy medicine. Finally, he was able to persuade his sister to pay for a boarding school for the boy. His own financial situation, however, remained a day-to-day struggle. And yet, as a painter, Gauguin was making progress. He wanted to create paintings that were even more radical than those the Impressionists were doing and he decided the key to finding this new style was the primitive artifacts he had seen in Peru as a boy. Gauguin became obsessed with finding strains of primitive culture that survived despite the overwhelming influence of the modern Western world. He first looked for this primitive source in Brittany and then in the French colony of Martinique, with only middling results. He even made an attempt to start an artist's colony in southern France with the troubled Vincent Van Gogh. After that now-famous disaster, Gauguin returned to Paris, shaken, but still looking for the big break that would end his hand-to-mouth existence.

It seemed like good timing. **Saturn was crossing Gauguin's Ascendant** just as Paris was opening its huge 1889 Universal Exhibition, featuring a giant tower built by a Mr. Eiffel. Gauguin and the small band of followers he was developing decided to stage an exhibition of their paintings to coincide with the colossal event. Unfortunately, the art show produced no profits, but what was going on inside the Universal Exhibition changed Gauguin's life forever. For the first time, he saw a variety of primitive cultures, along with their art, showcased in one place. For a man seeking a return to the primitive in European painting, it must have seemed like a smorgasbord of visual delights. Oddly enough, it was only the Polynesian exhibits that did not impress Gauguin.

It took a while for the information Gauguin gleaned from the 1889 Universal Exhibition to be processed by his exceedingly lunar personality, but by the next year he had determined that he was going to leave France and that his destination, despite his initial impression, would be the French outpost in Tahiti. After this, it just became a matter of raising money and arranging passage. Gauguin didn't arrive at the Tahitian capital of Papeete until June 1891; it was September of that year before he finally moved away from the town, with its pervasive European influence, and established himself in a hut where he could live alongside the natives. **Transiting Saturn opposed his natal Saturn in October.**

What followed was the most productive and perhaps the happiest period of Gauguin's life. He found himself a teenage native girl whom he called his "wife" (despite the fact that he was still maintaining an often acrimonious correspondence with Mette back in Copenhagen), and he painted. During the next two years he created some of his most sumptuous and important Tahitian paintings. Then he packed up the fruits of his joyous labors and traveled back to France to show the world the wonders he had created.

The world certainly took notice. His exhibition in Paris was the hit of the season. Unfortunately, the resulting sales were minimal. The only good news was a surprise inheritance from a long-lost uncle, which was enough to finance a return trip to Tahiti. But first Gauguin had to visit some of his old haunts and show off his new prosperity, along with his new girlfriend, a beautiful and very young Javanese. While parading along a waterfront in Brittany, Gauguin got into a fight with some sailor who insulted his girl. Secondary progressed Mars was on his Ascendant and his secondary progressed Sun was conjunct with his Mars. His display of aggression could have only one result. The aging ex-sailor was so badly beaten in the fight that he ended up in the hospital with injuries that he would suffer with for the rest of his life.

Gauguin's second arrival in Tahiti **in 1896, the year Saturn crossed his IC**, was an exercise in misery. He immediately began to fight with all the Europeans in Papeete, from the simple shopkeepers to the island's Catholic bishop. His health was poor—both because of his injuries and for other reasons. His former "wife" quickly deserted him when she saw that his genitals were covered with syphilitic sores, and his uncle's money quickly ran out. By 1897, Gauguin was starving. He could barely afford food, let alone paint. He was so beset by difficulties that he attempted suicide, but failed. The next year he was reduced to taking a menial job with the Tahitian Department of Public Works.

Meanwhile, back in Paris, things were looking up for Gauguin. **As Saturn squared its natal place**, his Tahitian paintings began to find buyers. The result was not the kind of windfall the artist was always expecting, but it was enough to allow Gauguin to quit his job and resume painting full-time, or at least as much as his health would allow. And yet, despite his growing success, Gauguin's misery only increased. By now the missionaries in Tahiti were warning the natives to stay clear of the crazy white painter, and he had trouble finding models. He had few friends in the European community, particularly after he started publishing a satirical newsletter criticizing the government and society there.

In November 1901, Gauguin sold his house in Tahiti and moved to a new Polynesian paradise in the Marquesas Islands. At first, the new start seemed to be exactly what the painter needed. He acquired a new teenage "wife," and labeled his new abode the "House of Pleasure," but now Gauguin was undergoing a prolonged conjunction of transiting Pluto to his Sun and this period of happy activity did not last long. Soon Gauguin's new wife, now pregnant, had deserted him, and many of the paintings he had begun after he first arrived in the Marquesas remained unfinished. His physical complaints returned, and so did his obsession with fighting with any available representative of European authority. As he had in Tahiti, Gauguin became a man apart, isolated from his own people, and only provisionally accepted by the natives. He died alone on May 3, 1903.

SATURN AT WORK

On one level, we can see the life of Paul Gauguin as an example of triumph over adversity. As an artist he was a visionary outsider who succeeded against all odds and brought the world objects of incredible beauty that will enrich our culture forever. Saturn was very much involved in this accomplishment. From Saturn's conjunct to his Descendant, when he was accepted by the Salon, to its crossing of his Midheaven, when he denied the comforting support of his day job, to Saturn's square to his natal place, when he left his family and went to paint in Paris, to Saturn's conjunction with his Ascendant, when he saw the Universal Exhibition in Paris, to Saturn's opposition to its natal place, when he finally began living and painting the way he had always envisioned, to the next square of Saturn to its own place, when his work began to attract buyers, progress on his professional front followed Saturn's lead.

And yet, despite the success he had as an artist, Gauguin remained a failure as a human being. His character flaws and reprehensible behavior, in the end, prevented him from enjoying the success that he had won. Young Gauguin, the newly married office slave who had a yen for painting, or even the harried, starving artist who refused to give up his son, had a remarkable ability to make friends and inspire loyalty from other people. Old Gauguin, the syphilitic misanthrope who died a painful death on a distant South Seas island, had succeeded in alienating himself from nearly everyone who had contact with him. This was his failure.

The key indicator of this failure was Gauguin's inability to record any reaction to the death of his mother when Saturn crossed his IC in 1867. Since Gauguin wrote virtually nothing about his relationship with his mother, we can only guess at his attachment to her. And yet, given that he was a boy growing up without a father, it must have been significant. His reaction three years later to the destruction of her house and the belongings that had been left there was, as he confessed, very strong. This indicates that there was an attachment to his mother that he was unable to express.

What this points to is an inability on the part of Gauguin to deal with the emotionality and sensitivity provided for by his Moon to Venus to Neptune T-square. His Pluto aspect to the Moon and to Mars, along with his Leo Ascendant, gave him the means of covering the feminine qualities this powerful T-square implies, but these aspects did not give him a means of reclaiming the emotional sustenance that we all require from our Moon, our Venus, and even, to a lesser extent, from our Neptune. It was for this reason that Gauguin was unable to face his feelings about the loss of his mother. This, in turn, caused him to rush into a marriage with a woman who could never share his love of art or support his ambition to become a painter. For a while, Gauguin's overwhelming optimism and a coincidental boom in the stock market allowed the artist to cover up these errors in judgment and compound them by bringing five children into the world. But when Saturn reached his Midheaven, the truth had to be told. The stock market crashed and Gauguin was forced to make an agonizing choice between his career as an artist and his family.

The result of this choice was two-fold. On the one hand, it gave Gauguin the freedom he needed to succeed as a painter. On the other, it deprived him of the wife and family that had become the surrogate for his disowned emotional self. The more alienated Gauguin became from his family over the next several years, the more distant this soft, feminine, feeling side of his personality became and the more unsavory his behavior became. The split between Gauguin the artist, and Gauguin the scoundrel, was made. There are some who might say that this split between genius and human concerns was necessary in order for Gauguin to produce all the great works of art he did, but Saturn makes no such allowances.

SOURCES

Wayne Anderson, with Barbara Klein, *Gauguin's Paradise Lost* (New York: Doubleday, 1976).

David Sweetman, *Paul Gauguin: A Life* (New York: Simon & Schuster, 1995).

19

LEE HARVEY OSWALD

Alleged assassin of President John F. Kennedy, although he did not live long enough to stand trial

THE CHOICE

In November 1953, a judge in New York City ordered a teenager placed in an institution for troubled youth. Lee Harvey Oswald had come to the attention of authorities in New York because of habitual truancy, but once psychologists began to evaluate the youngster, they immediately came to the conclusion that he had a propensity for violence and was therefore dangerous. This was hardly news to his brothers or to other people who knew the family. At least one witness reports watching him chase his older stepbrother with a knife, and only months earlier he had drawn a knife on his sister-in-law after she asked him to turn down the TV. To these people, along with his teachers and nearly everyone who had prolonged contact with Lee, the judge's ruling was overdue. It came, not surprisingly, when Lee Harvey Oswald was **fourteen years old and one month after his adolescent Saturn opposition.**

The only interested person who strongly disagreed with the judge's ruling was, unfortunately, Lee's mother. Marguerite Pic Oswald Elkdahl was likely just as unstable and psychologically troubled as her son. She doted on Lee, her youngest, probably because of the shabby way she had treated him early in his life. When Lee's father died, only two months after the boy was born, Marguerite had put his older brother and stepbrother in an orphanage, and placed Lee with various relatives and foster parents until he was old enough to be taken to the orphanage himself. **When Oswald was five years old, and Saturn moved across his Ascendant**, his mother finally came to claim her three boys from the institution. By this time she had remarried, and Lee happily entered into what promised to be a warm and loving family. Instead he found constant contention and bickering. Marguerite could not get along with her new husband and when he left her three years later, Lee was once again deprived of a beloved father figure.

By the time Oswald and his mother arrived in New York City to live with his stepbrother in 1952, the salient features of his personality seemed firm. He was demanding and physically abusive with his mother, who seemed to live only to please him. He rarely attended school and, when he did, showed little interest in his classwork and even less in his classmates. He was withdrawn, arrogant, and showed no inclination for group activities. He was also belligerent at school and often got into fights with other students. Lee showed little emotional connection with his own family, with the possible exception of his older brother. He ate his meals alone in his room with his books and his classical records.

Lee's mother reacted to the judge's order to institutionalize her son by packing her bags and fleeing the city. This was not difficult for Marguerite. Since leaving the orphanage, Lee had already lived in more than a dozen different places with his mother. Lee and Marguerite returned to her hometown of New Orleans, out of reach of the New York court system. Lee's behavior did not change. If anything, he was more abusive toward his mother. But there was light at the end of the tunnel. Soon he would be able to follow the example of his brother and join the Marine Corps.

THE HOROSCOPE

With a Libra Sun, Capricorn Moon, and Cancer rising, Oswald's horoscope is loaded with cardinal energy and initiative. And yet, there are

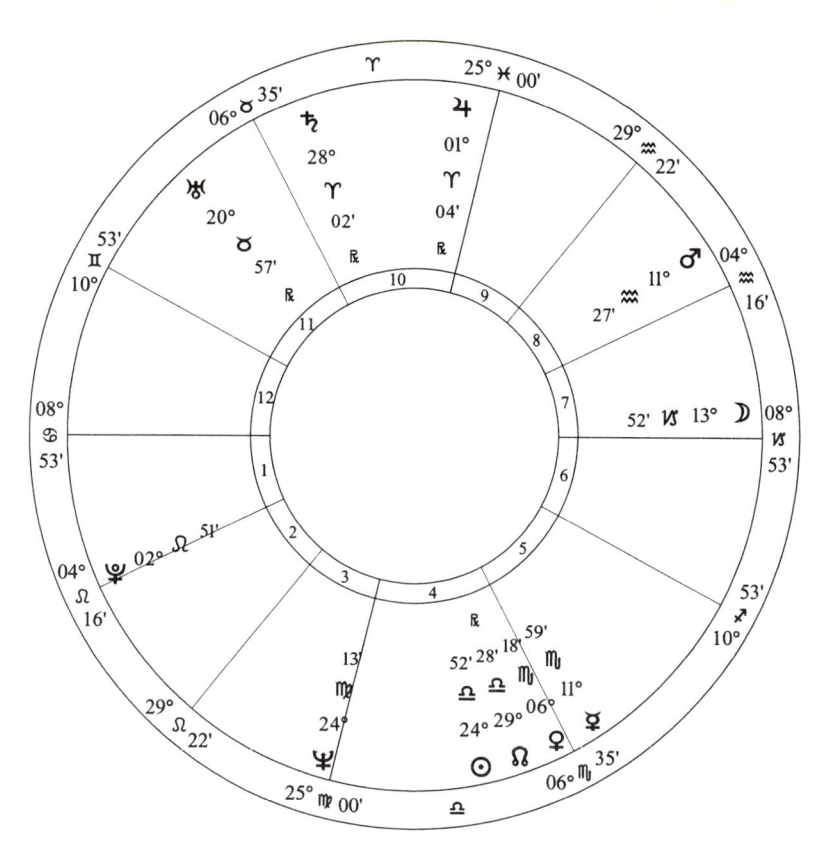

Lee Harvey Oswald

October 18, 1939, 9:55 PM CST

New Orleans, LA, 29N57 90W04

several prominent monkey wrenches in these extraordinarily active works. First of all, Saturn is opposed to the Sun. This is a classic representation of a stressed relationship with father figures. Typically the father is distant, sometimes deceased, sometimes abusive, and often absent. For Lee, who had only a brief contact with a father figure in the form of his stepfather, this was a central theme in his life. It could be said that the reason he displayed so much animosity toward his mother was because he saw her as depriving him of that father figure. Saturn opposed to the Sun also indicates a lack of self-confidence, restrictions in the ability to express ego drives, and difficulty in relating to figures of authority. At its worst, it provides for periods of intense depression and self-destructive urges. On the positive side, it is an indicator of tough-mindedness, self-discipline, and determination, bringing focus and seriousness to the personality.

Jupiter is also opposed to the Sun, though widely, and it is conjunct with Oswald's Midheaven. This latter position might be considered a lucky aspect. It provides for expansive ambitions and unfettered optimism. And yet, these qualities are so much in contrast with the restrictive indication of his Saturn to Sun aspect that the two almost become an endless inner debate of "Yes, you can," "No, you can't." In some situations, the placement of Jupiter helps to mollify the negativity of Oswald's Saturn, adding confidence and generosity. In others, it will only exacerbate the problems this Saturn to Sun aspect represents. The fact that Jupiter is opposed to Neptune, which is on Oswald's IC, provides yet another dimension to the problem, adding a delusional, quixotic quality to Jupiter's irrepressible optimism.

Next, we have the square of Pluto to Venus. This indicates a powerful sexuality that is somehow blocked or denied proper expression. This is furthered by the wide square between Venus and Mars in cool and abstract Aquarius. Because of their financial situation, Oswald and his wife were frequently separated during their marriage and, even when they were together, it was often in the home of a relative or friend, so their sexual relationship was often restricted. Also, Oswald was often abusive with his wife, both psychologically and physically. More importantly, however, this aspect restricted Oswald's ability to express affection on a personal level to anyone. We have to view this aspect in relation to his strongly placed Capricorn Moon. Together they provide for great difficulties in dealing with and showing love for women.

The most worrisome of the bad aspects in Oswald's horoscope is the extremely close (less than half a degree of separation) square between Mercury and Mars. On the positive side, this aspect provides for an extremely active and quick mind. On the negative, it is an indicator of a violent temper and a tendency to verbally and intellectually bully other people. There is a general lack of tolerance in the person's thinking and a strong tendency to lash out when presented with ideas that differ from one's own. In Oswald's case, the aspect is so close that its combative, intolerant tendencies were often disruptive to his ability to think and behave rationally. Certainly, the close sextile between Mercury and the Moon does something to lessen the negativity of his Mars to Mercury aspect. It caused him to seek an answer to his loneliness and sense of rejection in books. Unfortunately, the ideas he took from his reading only served to make him more of an embattled outcast.

THE LIFE

This influence of his Mars to Mercury square, the tendency to follow impulse over rationality, is clearly evident in the thinking of the sixteen-year-old Lee Harvey Oswald. On one hand, he longed to join the Marines. His older brother had given Lee a copy of the Marine Corps manual when he was twelve, and the youngster had read it through so many times he practically knew it by heart. Oswald was so anxious to become a Marine that he attempted to join when he was sixteen, only to be rejected. On the other hand, by the time Oswald was sixteen years old, he was an avowed Communist. He had begun studying Communism while in New York, and he arrived in New Orleans with firm, even passionate political beliefs. Why this young Communist would choose to join an organization that served the designs of a capitalist government that he saw as imperialistic and oppressive seems to make no sense, unless you are a conspiracy theorist, but it represented the kind of incoherence in thinking that Oswald would display repeatedly during his life.

Oswald was finally able to gain entry into the Marine Corps when he was seventeen, but he quickly fell into the same pattern in the military that had characterized his performance in public school. He failed to fit in with his fellow soldiers. His vociferous Communism put off most, and his loner ways alienated the rest. He was disrespectful with his superiors, lackadaisical in the performance of his duties, and he resisted discipline. Within the next two years, Oswald would be court-marshaled twice, and he would suffer a nervous breakdown. When he was finally released from the Corps in 1959, it was with no regret on either side.

By this time Oswald had a new plan, a new light at the end of the tunnel. He was going to defect to the Soviet Union. A month after his discharge, Lee went to Moscow and presented himself to the authorities there as a defector. To his surprise, the Russians were not impressed. In fact, they wanted no part of this oddball ex-Marine. Oswald became so distraught over this unexpected turn of affairs that he attempted suicide in his Moscow hotel room. Now the Russian bureaucrats were faced with a situation that could possibly become embarrassing. Dead Americans, even crazy ones, tended to draw unwanted attention. They began to reassess his application. Finally, in January 1960, **one month after Saturn crossed Oswald's Descendant,** they agreed to accept him.

Oswald was sent to Minsk by the Soviet government. He was given a job in a sheet-metal factory there and his own apartment. At first, Oswald enjoyed his new life as a Communist. His status as an American defector made him something of a celebrity, and, for the first time in his life, he was popular. But as the novelty of his position began to wear away, Lee became more and more dissatisfied. He deeply disliked the menial work he was assigned, and his requests to be sent to college fell on deaf ears. He became bored with Minsk and with his fellow workers, and he was learning that the Soviet brand of Marxism was oppressive and inflexible. The final blow came when a young woman he was particularly enamored of refused his proposal of marriage. By early 1961, Oswald was already making enquiries about leaving the Soviet Union.

Displaying the same lack of coherence in his thinking that he had shown when he joined the Marines, Oswald proposed marriage to another young Russian woman at the same time he was approaching American officials about returning to the United States. Marina Prusakova later admitted that she was more impressed with the fact that Oswald had his own apartment than by anything else. Still, she agreed to marry him. The hurried ceremony took place while **Saturn squared Lee's natal Saturn in April 1961. When Saturn returned to this square in retrograde in July, Oswald made a formal application to leave the Soviet Union (much to Marina's surprise)**. Since he now wanted to leave Russia with his new wife, **it took until just after Saturn made its last square to natal Saturn in January 1962 for permission to be granted.**

Lee Harvey Oswald and his now-pregnant wife arrived in Fort Worth, Texas, in June 1962. He had hoped, as a defector reversing his defection, to return to the celebrity status he had enjoyed during his first months in Russia. This was not to be. Oswald quickly found that he was just another anonymous American who was going to have to find some way of making a living in a capitalist society. This was a real problem since—outside of his training as a sharpshooter in the Marines—Lee had virtually no job skills. It was October before Oswald secured a full-time position. The first thing he did with his steady income was to order a rifle and a pistol through the mail.

In April 1963, Oswald made his first attempt at an assassination. His target was a local right-wing political activist and ex-general named Edwin Walker. Oswald had already taken time to survey the area around Walker's home and plan the operation, although he had to ride on a bus with his rifle hidden beneath his Marine overcoat in order to carry out his mission. But luck was with General Walker that night. Oswald's shot glanced off a window frame and grazed Walker's hair. When Oswald read in the newspaper the next morning that Walker had survived his attack, he was extremely disappointed.

Almost immediately, Oswald's restless mind was off on a new track. Only a couple of weeks after he took a shot at Edwin Walker, Oswald arrived in New Orleans. He stayed with relatives and spent his days handing out pro-Castro leaflets under the auspices of an organization called Fair Play for Cuba. Oswald was the only member in the New Orleans branch of this organization. Castro and defection to Cuba had apparently become Oswald's new hope, his new light at the end of the tunnel.

After getting into a brawl with anti-Castro activists and debating Cuban emigrants on the radio, Oswald traveled to Mexico City where he hoped to gain entry into Cuba. He was certain that the Cubans would be happy to admit him after his activism on their behalf. Oswald was shocked when they flatly refused him, and he returned to Dallas a deeply disappointed man, with no future and no light at the end of the tunnel. Seeing the state her husband was in, Marina begged one of her friends for help. One woman made a call to the Texas School Book Depository in downtown Dallas and got Lee a job there.

At this time, transiting Neptune was conjuncting Oswald's Mercury and squaring his Mars, a long-term aspect that made Oswald's already disjointed ideation even more prone to delusion and fantasy. Also, Oswald's secondary progressed Sun was nearing an opposition to his natal Uranus. The combination showed that he was entering a period of his life which, given his history of violent, irrational behavior, could be particularly explosive and dangerous. Oswald accepted the job at the book depository, but decided not to live with Marina and his child, who were staying in the home of a friend. Instead he took a room in Dallas under an assumed name. A couple weeks after Lee started his new job, the route of President John F. Kennedy's November 22 motorcade through Dallas was published in the newspaper. The dejected, hopeless Lee Harvey Oswald could not have helped but notice that the car carrying the president would be passing by the building in which he worked.

SATURN AT WORK

For Lee Harvey Oswald, his first adolescent Saturn opposition was a time when crucial decisions were being made about him, rather than by him—and given his disordered mental state, this was probably not a bad idea. By choosing to evade the order of a New York judge and flee the state with her son, Oswald's mother was sending her troubled son a message, a message that he clearly understood and would never forget. She was telling him that his violent, abnormal behavior was okay, that the intervention and treatment proposed by the state were not necessary. With this message in mind, it was only a matter of time before young Oswald's propensity for violence caused someone harm.

Oswald's next Saturn passage, the conjunction with his Descendant, also provided another opportunity for outside authorities to steer him onto a less self-destructive path. The Russian bureaucrats who reviewed Oswald's application for entry into their country understood that Lee Harvey Oswald had no more need to be a Russian than the Soviet Union had need of Lee Harvey Oswald. If Oswald had accepted their judgment and returned home to the United States, he would have been forced to make compromises in his quixotic search for fame, and might have found a way to live a productive life. Instead, he came off his Jupiter high and into a self-destructive Saturn low, so dismal that he tried to kill himself, and the Russians acquiesced. This decision allowed Oswald a brief taste of the recognition and validation he so needed and would continue to seek once his status as a celebrity in Minsk wore away.

The square of Saturn its own place, which quickly followed Saturn crossing Oswald's Descendant, gave him two chances to make a new start. First of all, he found a wife and the opportunity to build a relationship with a woman that could have helped him grow out of the tremendously unhealthy and hurtful relationship he had developed with his mother. Secondly, he was given the opportunity to return to the United States and make a new beginning.

Oswald failed miserably on both counts. His relationship with Marina soon developed all the negative qualities that had long characterized his situation with his mother. Oswald was as demanding, abusive, and emotionally distant as a husband as he had always been as a son. As a returning American citizen, Oswald also failed. Hungry for the brief period of fame and popularity he had enjoyed in Minsk, he arrived home with hopes far out of step with the stark realities of his new life. If Oswald had used the best part of his Saturn to Sun natal opposition, if he had formed a long-term plan, worked hard and diligently, and been patient, he might have overcome the problems that faced him but, instead, he remained lost in his Jupiter/Neptune dreams of finding a new society, a new world where he would be once again celebrated and loved. He identified this new world as Cuba, only to be devastated when the Cuban government refused him entry.

One might ask, "Where was Saturn in Oswald's chart on November 22, 1963? Wasn't this day the most important turning point in his life?" Saturn was not making a significant aspect in Oswald's horoscope on the day John Kennedy was assassinated. It didn't need to be. Oswald fired his rifle at President Kennedy for the same reason he had attempted to assassinate General Walker a few months earlier—because he had no other options. When Saturn squared his natal Saturn for the last time in 1961, Oswald had made a decision not to accept the situation in which the earlier bad choices, both his and his mother's, had placed him. The only way out of his position as a low-paid, insignificant, menial laborer, a man without any light at the end of the tunnel, was to take the life of someone who was far more significant to the world than himself. This final act of violence and ultimate self-destruction became Oswald's way of realizing his Jupiterian dream of glory or, at least, what his deluded mind saw as glory. So, what Lee Harvey Oswald did on November 22, 1963 cannot be seen as his destiny. Instead, it should be viewed as the product of a life defeated by delusional thinking, unrealistic goals, and too many bad choices.

SOURCES

Gerald Posner, *Case Closed: Lee Harvey Oswald and the Assassination of JFK* (New York: Random House, 1995).

20

BILL CLINTON

President of the United States whose many accomplishments were largely overshadowed by his sexual improprieties while in the White House

THE CHOICE

In May 1969, **just as transiting Saturn squared his natal Saturn**, a young American named William Jefferson Clinton, who was studying at Oxford on a Rhodes Scholarship, faced what seemed an impossible dilemma. He had just received from the draft board in his home state of Arkansas an order to report for induction into the United States Army. He had been drafted. This painful moment of truth was a common experience for many young men of Bill Clinton's generation, the generation that came of age during the Vietnam war—but for him it was particularly jarring. While attending Georgetown University, Clinton had worked in the office of J. William Fulbright, the powerful senator from Arkansas. Fulbright was a noted opponent of the war and under his tutelage Clinton gained an awareness of the futility and immorality of that struggle that few could match. At the same time, however, Bill Clinton's supreme ambition was to be a politician and he understood that to openly oppose the draft or even to evade it could become a severe impediment for him later on.

During the months prior to receiving his notice, Clinton had counted on the influence of family and friends to at least delay this moment of decision. His induction had already been postponed twice and, as luck would have it, it would be postponed again because the notice had reached him in the middle of his last term at Oxford. July was the new date set for his induction, unless he could find some way out. Clinton returned to the United States in June and immediately began looking for people who could help him. One alternative was to enter the ROTC program at a university. Clinton was able to gain admittance to the law school at the University of Arkansas at the last moment and he was accepted into their ROTC program, but this solution was hardly satisfactory. First of all, Bill Clinton did not want to go to the University of Arkansas. He knew that with his intellect and credentials, he could get into a much more prestigious law school if he just had the time. The other problem was the fact that, as part of the ROTC program, he would be obligated to serve three years in the military after law school, delaying his plans to enter politics.

In September, Clinton somehow persuaded the head of the ROTC program to allow him go back to Oxford to complete another term there. Meanwhile, the United States government changed its policy on draft eligibility, instituting a lottery system. **In December 1969, just as retrograde Saturn was exactly square with his natal Saturn once again**, Bill Clinton's birth date came up number 311 (out of a possible 365) in the lottery. Immediately, he went from an unwilling soldier-in-waiting to a young man who would never have to worry about the draft again. Clinton quickly withdrew from the University of Arkansas and from the ROTC program, and spent the rest of the school year in Europe. He later claimed that his being skipped by the draft was just a matter of luck, ignoring the desperate finagling that went into keeping the draft board at bay until that fateful day in December. The fact remains that if Bill Clinton had simply accepted the notice he received in May and reported for induction in July, he very likely would have already been on his way to Vietnam by the time his lucky number came up in the lottery.

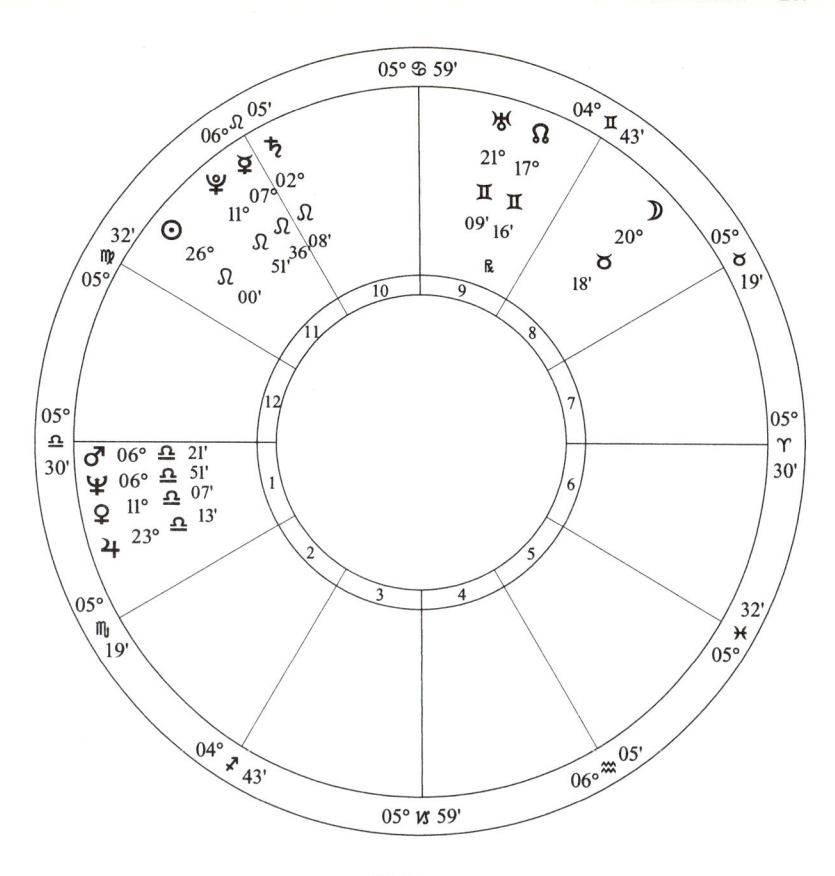

Bill Clinton

August 19, 1946, 8:51 AM CST

Hope AR, 33N40 93W35

THE HOROSCOPE

The outstanding feature of the horoscope of Bill Clinton is the conjunction of three planets—Mars, Neptune, and Venus—directly below his Libra Ascendant. This is a powerful and extremely complex arrangement. The three planets form sextile aspects with another stellium—Saturn, Mercury, and Pluto in Leo—creating a gestalt of energy that is on the one hand pleasantly easy and charmingly clever and on the other fraught with stunning contradictions and dangerous complacency. Jupiter is also in the 1st House, adding its irresistible optimism and steamroller confidence to the mix. This emphasis on the 1st House emphasizes to an inordinate degree the persona or outer personality. In other words, there is very little of Bill Clinton's personality that is concealed from the public eye. It is a personality in which the penchant for theatrics and the broadcasting of personal dramas, all very typical for a Leo Sun sign, are taken to the maximum degree. For better and for worse, virtually everything that happens within the heart and soul of Bill Clinton happens in a public arena.

The centerpiece of this complex system of aspects is the very close conjunction of Mars, Neptune, and the Ascendant. At first glance, this seems to be a very dynamic placement, and it does provide the capacity for great bursts of energy and enthusiasm. But Mars, which is typically weak in Libra, has its physical energy and aggression further diffused by Neptune, creating a situation in which self-indulgence and self-deception are all too common. There will always be a battle between the competitive zeal of Mars and compulsive congeniality of Libra, just as the directness of Mars will frequently be at cross-purposes with Neptune's tendency to sidestep problems and avoid confrontation through vagueness and incomplete truths.

The positive aspects that both Mars and Neptune receive from Saturn and Pluto help to guard against the inclination toward escapism and substance abuse so frequently seen with Mars and Neptune aspects, and the overall strength of Venus in the chart provides for an openness and charm that make the abruptness and confusion of the Mars and Neptune conjunction much easier to take. Still, there is a nebulous and indefinite quality about this Mars to Neptune aspect (a quality that will be apparent to everyone because of its placement on the Ascendant) that is hard to trust. The perception of dishonesty inherent with Neptune and the natural tendency of Mars to offend will always be in the public eye, regardless how much it is corrected by Saturn or sweetened by Venus. Thus we have the image of "Slick Willie" that Clinton has never been able to shed.

There is one part of Clinton's horoscope that is private. That is his Moon in Taurus in the 8th House. The Moon squares his Sun, aptly describing the difficulty with father figures that plagued Clinton's youth. His birth father died before he was born and he spent his early years defending his mother against abuse from his alcoholic and philandering stepfather. On another level, this Moon placement represents a need for security—in particular, security represented by a strong feminine presence in his life. There is a deep, psychosexual element to this need. There is also a practical element, a need for security in the form of material wealth. In his youth Clinton was notably uninterested in financial affairs. He was generous with money when he had it, and unabashed about letting other people pay when he didn't. When Hillary Rodham entered his life, however, he found someone who not only filled his deep-seated need for a strong female companion; he also found someone who recognized the necessity of money, both as a political tool and a means to personal security. Clinton's ability to project this need for security, in all its forms, onto his wife transformed the pair into the ultimate power couple. It also freed Clinton to explore all the reckless vagaries arising from his Mars to Neptune conjunction.

THE LIFE

Bill Clinton grew up a star. Adored by his mother, well-liked by his peers, he set out to shine in every field available to him. By the time he was in high school, he had already been identified as a leader. He was chosen as a delegate to Boys Nation and with that elite group he visited Washington D.C. in 1963, and shook hands with President John F. Kennedy. And yet, there was another side of young Clinton's life that was not so glorious. Living with an alcoholic stepfather forced

Bill into the role of peacemaker and protector for his mother and his younger half-brother. In May 1962, **five months after Saturn made its adolescent opposition to his natal Saturn**, his mother divorced his stepfather only to marry him again. Even though he was frustrated by his mother's decision, Bill wanted to show his solidarity with both her and his half-brother, so he officially had his name changed from Blythe, his birth father's name, to William Jefferson Clinton.

From his high school in Hot Springs, Arkansas, Bill Clinton went to Georgetown, University in Washington D.C. During the summer after his sophomore year, Clinton worked in the campaign of Frank Holt, who was running for governor of Arkansas. Holt lost the election but Clinton gained valuable contacts in Arkansas politics, contacts that landed him a part-time job on the staff of J. William Fulbright. Working on Capital Hill gave Clinton the thirst to pursue a political office of his own. **In the spring of 1967, as Saturn crossed his Descendant,** he ran for student council president at Georgetown and lost, suffering the first major defeat of his budding political life. Around this same time, Clinton broke up with his steady girlfriend and began playing the field, both on the Georgetown campus and in Washington. As Saturn moved retrograde in opposition with his natal Mars and Neptune, Clinton's stepfather died. Despite their painful history together, Clinton grieved. The next month **Saturn made a second conjunction with his Descendant** and he received better news. Clinton was chosen as a Rhodes Scholar and given a scholarship to study at Oxford University in England.

After his struggles with the draft were ended, Clinton gained admittance into Yale University to study law. It was at Yale that he met another brilliant student and future political leader, Hillary Rodham. The ambitious duo quickly formed a bond. Also while attending Yale, Clinton worked on the presidential campaign of George McGovern, gaining important experience in practical politics and establishing contacts. By the time he left Yale and took a teaching job at the University of Arkansas, Clinton was primed for his first attempt at gaining an elected office. In March 1974, **just a couple of months before Saturn crossed his Midheaven,** Bill Clinton officially announced his candidacy for the United States House of Representatives. It was an uphill battle for Clinton. He was challenging an incumbent who was popular and well-established but, with the help of the Watergate scandal in Washington and a core of devoted supporters, including Hillary Rodham, Clinton almost pulled off the upset, coming close enough to a win to establish himself as the rising star of Arkansas politics.

In October 1975, **just as Saturn reached his natal Saturn**, Bill Clinton and Hillary Rodham were married. A few months later, **with Saturn still moving near its natal place,** he announced that he was running for attorney general in Arkansas. Clinton won this post easily and in 1978 he was ready to run for governor. For the energetic and charismatic young politico, winning this seat proved much easier than holding it. Clinton entered the governor's office with a coterie of youthful reformers and the intention of showing his Rhodes Scholar and Yale University buddies that Arkansas could be lifted out of the doldrums, but his efforts proved clumsy and unworkable. By the end of his term, he faced opposition from established interests like the timber industry and from a large portion of the general population who resented the fact that he had increased the fee for car registration. It didn't help that shortly before the election, several hundred Cuban refugees lodged in Fort Chaffee in Arkansas rioted. In November 1980, **just as Saturn crossed his Ascendant and began a conjunction with his natal Mars and Neptune**, Bill Clinton lost his bid for reelection.

The chastened ex-governor of Arkansas was certainly still young enough to start a new career, but for Bill Clinton there was no career except politics. Following the advice of Dick Morris, a political guru who had advised Clinton during his first run for governor, Clinton made some changes. For one thing, he needed to adopt a more conservative, middle-of-the-road approach. For another, his wife, who was still calling herself Hillary Rodham, would have to take his name, in keeping with the social conventions that still meant a great deal to an Arkansas voter. And finally, Bill Clinton would have to apologize for his registration tax and all the other errors he had made during his first term. Clinton's apology was televised in February 1982. It worked. **By the time Saturn squared its natal place in December 1982**, he had again been elected as governor. The next year, **with Saturn still squaring his natal Saturn,** Clinton pushed through a major education reform bill which became the show piece of his tenure as governor.

Clinton went on to win three more terms as governor of Arkansas, but by now he was eying a bigger prize. By 1987, he was considered a possible contender for the Democratic presidential nomination. At that time, Neptune was crossing his Midheaven and people considering his candidacy began asking questions about the governor's personal life.

It is not known when Clinton's womanizing began, but by the time he had established himself in the governor's office, it had apparently become habitual. His affair with Gennifer Flowers had been ongoing for some time and he was rumored to have had sexual rendezvous with several other women. In 1987, it was thought that these rumors could be fatal to a Clinton presidential campaign and, to the surprise of many, Clinton announced he would not pursue that office. By 1991, however, the pressure to move up had become too great. After all, he couldn't remain governor of Arkansas forever. **In November 1991, just as Saturn opposed his natal Saturn,** Bill Clinton announced that he would be a candidate for president of the United States.

As had been predicted, Clinton's extramarital affairs, in particular his affair with Gennifer Flowers, quickly became an issue in the campaign. Another nasty stumbling block for the candidate was his narrow escape from the draft in 1969. But Bill Clinton managed to overcome these questions about his past and his character and win the election. Much as he had done during his first term as governor, Clinton entered the White House with a bold agenda. A key piece of that agenda was creating some sort of government-controlled health insurance system to cover the millions of uninsured and underinsured Americans. Hillary Clinton was put in charge of exploring this issue and she was immediately met with vociferous opposition from conservatives and the insurance companies. Meanwhile, during the congressional elections of 1994, Republicans made a concerted effort to take a majority in both houses of Congress. Running on a promise to fight for lower taxes, smaller government, and family values, they succeeded.

In 1995, President Bill Clinton seemed to be in trouble. Conservative Republicans ruled Congress and appeared intent on forcing their radical agenda into law. Meanwhile, Clinton and his wife were being hounded by investigations into their financial affairs—in particular their dealing in a land development scheme called "Whitewater." The embattled president responded to this challenge by forcing the Republicans into a budgetary showdown, a virtual shutdown of the government. The government shutdown demonstrated not only the firmness of Clinton's leadership, but also the doctrinaire roots of the so-called "Contract with America." Meanwhile, Clinton carefully shifted his own positions in a more moderate direction. Health care reform was abandoned, as were other Clinton initiatives that had proved unpopular. Raising money for the 1996 campaign also became a priority, and even though many complained that his methods (such as allowing wealthy donors to sleep in the White House) were improper and even crass, the president remained unabashed. By the time **Saturn crossed his Descendant in September 1996,** Clinton had established a substantial lead over his Republican opponent, and in November he easily won reelection.

One other event occurred during this period that had much more to do with relationships. In February 1997, as **Saturn made its last crossing over Clinton's Descendant,** the president resumed his sexual affair with Monica Lewinsky, a young intern who had formerly worked in the White House. Clinton had been having sex with Lewinsky since 1995, but he had arranged for her to be transferred to the Pentagon in April 1996, promising to bring her back to the White House after the election. He reneged on that promise, and in May 1997 broke off the relationship. What Clinton didn't know was that Lewinsky was sharing details about their relationship problems with another worker at the Pentagon, Linda Tripp. Tripp recorded Lewinsky's account and the recording eventually found its way to the office of Ken Starr, who was heading the Whitewater investigation.

The Monica Lewinsky scandal became public in January 1998. **On August 17, with Saturn a degree beyond a square with his natal Saturn and turning retrograde,** Clinton was questioned by attorneys from Ken Starr's office about his affair with Lewinsky and other matters, including the allegations of Paula Jones. The questions were persistent, detailed, and, some would say, malicious—and the president's answers were painfully obtuse. Once this grueling session was ended, President Clinton went on national television to apologize to the American people for his immoral behavior, though he continued to maintain it was a private matter. Meanwhile, Congress considered impeachment proceedings against the president on charges that he lied to a federal official about the affair and interfered with a federal investigation. In December 1998, the proceeding began, and in February 1999, **two months before Saturn made its last square**, the matter was put to a vote in the Senate and failed. Clinton had been saved from the worst public humiliation a president of the United States could face, but his presidency and its legacy had been irreparably damaged.

SATURN AT WORK

In later years, Bill Clinton tended to treat the fact that he had avoided the draft as if it was the result of blind luck. In fact, his letters and actions during 1969 indicate it was a period of intense moral turmoil. When he received his draft notice in May 1969, Bill Clinton was being called upon to stand up for his moral convictions. He chose not to. Certainly, he had good reason. As a draft resister, he could have gone to prison and he would certainly have never been elected governor of a conservative state like Arkansas. Clinton placed the survival of his political career and his dream of one day being president ahead of his moral opposition to the war in Vietnam. When he received his lottery number in December of that year it was almost as if he were being rewarded for his ethical waffling, as if Saturn was giving him a pass; but, in reality, he was being asked another question. To what extent would this divide between his personal morality and his public career go?

We cannot point to a date and say this is when Bill Clinton's compulsive womanizing began. More than likely it was a gradual process.

Neptunian addictions so often are. In any case, this moral vagary, this refusal to take responsibility for decisions made in a relationship, even relationships that seemed unimportant and short-lived, became Bill Clinton's answer to the question posed in December 1969. In his political life, he would continue to fight for good things, for effective public education, for universal health care, for sound economic policies, and for social programs to help the sick and the poor. In his private life, he would become a lying, predatory philanderer. And as his political life advanced, more or less in lockstep with his Saturn transits, this divide only became wider and more dangerous.

During those dark days of the Monica Lewinsky scandal, many supporters considered Bill Clinton's enemies to be villains—willing to waste millions of tax dollars and drag the country through a slimy mess of sexual skullduggery that had nothing to do with public policy, just for the pleasure of shaming a political foe. And yet, when we continually ignore our responsibilities, we repeatedly fail to do the things we know we should do. We shouldn't be surprised, then, when Saturn comes at us hard. The viciousness with which President Clinton was attacked during this period only reflects the degree to which he had divorced himself from the corrective, disciplined function of Saturn in his horoscope. He had chosen the self-indulgence of Neptune over the rigors of Saturn, and when Saturn squared its natal place in August 1998, Bill Clinton had to pay, and pay dearly, for that choice.

SOURCES

David Maraniss, *First in His Class: A Biography of Bill Clinton* (New York: Simon & Schuster, 1995).

Haynes Johnson, *The Best of Times: America in the Clinton Years* (New York: Harcourt Inc., 2001).

Nigel Hamilton, *Bill Clinton: Mastering the Presidency* (New York: BBS Public Affairs, 2007).

21

ANDREW CUNANAN

A charming California-born hustler who went on a five-week killing spree that ended after he murdered fashion mogul Gianni Versace, and then committed suicide

THE CHOICE

In October 1990, Andrew Cunanan was living his dream. He didn't really have a job. He was living with a friend and her husband in San Francisco, taking care of their child and working part-time. His financial situation was tenuous, as it had been all his life, and his future was undecided. And yet, none of this mattered to Cunanan. He had just met a man named Gianni Versace, an Italian clothing designer who had made himself rich and become an international celebrity because of his daring and sexually provocative designs. Cunanan and Versace met at a party given in the great designer's honor, and Versace had immediately taken a shine to Cunanan. Cunanan was charming and good-looking, and he had a gift for telling a good story, whether it was true or not. The next night, or maybe two, Cunanan was a member of Versace's "posse," experiencing the chauffeured lifestyle of the privileged few for whom money was no object and the only goal was having a good time and being in style. During this string of glittering nights, **Saturn was transiting Cunanan's Midheaven.**

THE HOROSCOPE

At first glance, Andrew Cunanan's horoscope does not seem particularly dangerous. In fact, there is much in it that is positive. His Virgo Sun is placed in the creative 5th House where it is trined by Saturn and the Moon, and forms an almost exact semisextile to Jupiter. These are all easy aspects, indicating an outgoing and balanced personality, someone with a gently conformist attitude who would be regarded favorably by people in authority. Since he has both the Sun and the Moon in Earth signs, we can expect a practical, materialistic attitude tempered with a good dose of optimism because of the Sun to Jupiter semisextile.

The good news continues when we consider Cunanan's Mercury. It is placed in Libra, in a conjunction with both Jupiter and Uranus, and in a sextile with his Venus. This combination greatly reinforces the openness and the optimism provided by Jupiter's contact with his Sun and indicates an extremely active, inventive mind. As a child, Cunanan displayed remarkable memory and perceptiveness. He started reading at an early age and loved showing off to visitors by spewing forth facts about art, history, or anything else, and reciting memorized verses from the bible. He was quickly pegged as the smart one among his siblings, and became the darling of his mother.

The only problem evident in this portion of Cunanan's horoscope is a tendency toward laziness. The aspects are all so easy and Jupiter is so emphasized that hard work could become an anathema. It is so easy for a person with this sort of horoscope to get what they want by being clever, charming, or just plain lucky that they never develop the ability or the need to strive. This tendency toward lazy self-indulgence is furthered by the placement of both Cunanan's Moon and Ascendant in luxurious Taurus.

When we look at the situation in Cunanan's 1st House and the conjunction of his Taurus Moon with Saturn, we begin to see trouble looming. In one sense, this aspect provides the self-discipline and ability to focus on working hard, which this horoscope very desperately needs. But, on the other hand, it is an indicator of persistent depression

Andrew Cunanan 219

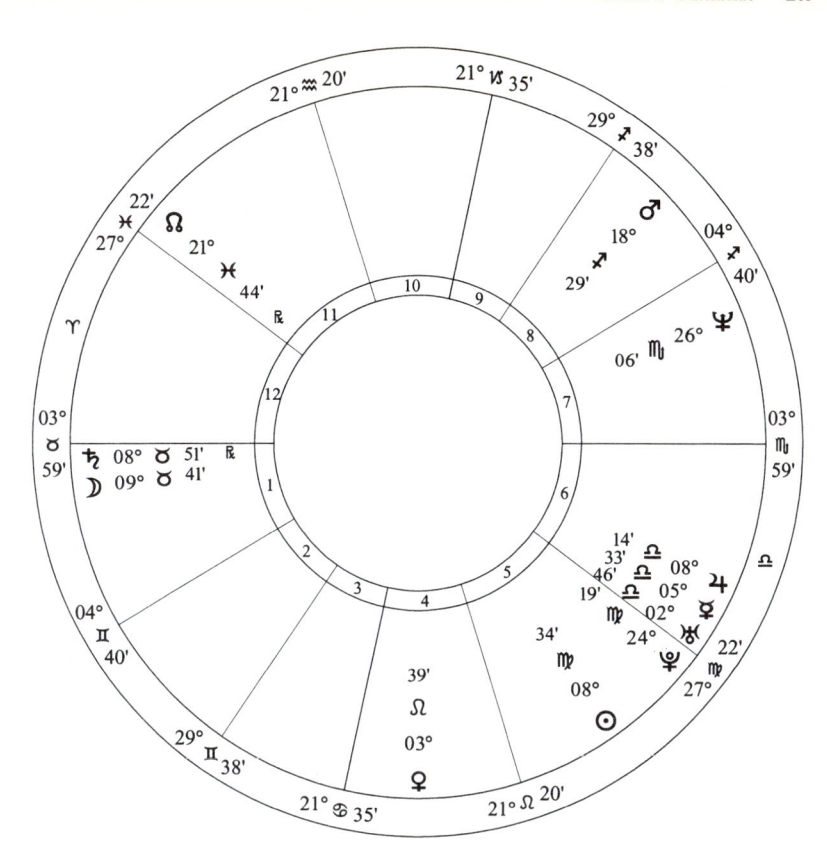

Andrew Cunanan

August 31, 1969, 9:41 PM PDT

National City, CA, 32N40 117W05

and self-criticism. Since the conjunction is powerfully placed in the 1st House, this self-criticism would tend to greatly undermine the extraordinary self-confidence evidenced by the aspect to Cunanan's Sun. There is also a tendency with this aspect to be hard and judgmental with other people, and to withhold affection. This quality is reinforced by the wide square from Saturn to Cunanan's Venus in Leo.

This all brings us to Cunanan's Mars and the wide square it makes to Pluto. The orb in this aspect is relatively wide, but since it is an applying aspect and Mars is in the 8th House, which is naturally associated with Pluto, we must give it due consideration. Also, it is the only aspect Mars makes in the horoscope with the exception of a sesquiquadrate (135-degree aspect) to his Venus. The Mars to Pluto square carries with it a reputation for deep resentment and violence. It is the classic indicator of a person who will be either a victim or a perpetrator of violent crime (although this is hardly true in every case). Since this aspect is weak and since there are so many other things, mostly positive, going on in Cunanan's horoscope, we would not expect it to be a dominant factor. Still, its presence in the background of this easy, somewhat self-indulgent, yet constantly self-questioning personality has to be a matter of concern.

THE LIFE

It is likely Cunanan never told Versace his real name. In fact, Cunanan probably revealed very little about his background or his life that was true. Even though he was only twenty-one at the time, Cunanan had already become a master at fabricating exaggerated and exotic personal histories for himself, and he had even developed an alter ego named DeSilva, which he used whenever he could. These false histories were all designed to hide one shameful fact. This was not his homosexuality. Cunanan was very open about this, at least with his many friends in San Francisco's Castro district. Nor was it his biracial parentage. Cunanan's father was Filipino, but Cunanan reveled in his exotic look, though he often led people to believe he was Jewish. The scandalous fact that Cunanan was determined to hide from everyone who knew him, the one painful truth that he tried his best to deny, was that Andrew Cunanan was poor.

Cunanan's father had struggled to support his wife and four children, of whom Andrew was the youngest, on his meager U.S. Navy pension. The elder Cunanan showed plenty of initiative, but his various business ventures tended to be unsubstantial and short-lived. Cunanan's mother was a homemaker, totally devoted to her children, particularly Andrew. Sometime during Andrew's childhood, his father found stable employment as a stockbroker. Still, the money he brought home was barely enough to sustain the middle class lifestyle to which the family aspired.

Andrew seems to have suffered very little during his childhood because of these financial difficulties. As his mother's favorite, as the favorite of the entire family, really, he was seldom denied anything. He was allowed to indulge his taste for the best designer clothing and other fine things. Cunanan showed a remarkable concern for fashion and style even as a child, and he always sought to look his best. A handsome boy and very bright, he understood very quickly that the appearance of affluence was almost as good as affluence itself.

In the fall of 1983, **as Saturn reached his Descendant and just before it made its adolescent opposition to its natal place,** Andrew Cunanan got a big break. Thanks to his intellect and, possibly, his almost fawning attitude toward the institution, the young scholar was admitted to Bishop's High School. Bishop's was a private school with an excellent academic reputation, but it was not the challenging class work that lured Cunanan to the school. Rather, it was the social opportunities it afforded. Bishop's was where the cream of San Diego society sent their children. Here Cunanan had the opportunity to hobnob with the scions of genuine wealth. Old money, new money; Bishop's had it all. Here Cunanan could observe the lifestyle of wealth, learn its language and its social graces. For Cunanan, Bishop's was much more than a high school; it was a training ground for the kind of life he wanted to live.

Despite his economic disadvantage, Cunanan fit in well at Bishop's. He was popular with his fellow students and did well with his studies. In fact, his high school years at Bishop's may well have been the best years of Cunanan's short life. Of course, none of his peers at Bishop's were allowed to meet his parents or visit his home. He didn't so much lie about his origins as create a smoke screen of tall tales, innuendo, and the strategic dropping of a name that kept the issue in a state of flux. His friends at Bishop's understood that Cunanan was not being honest with them, but they didn't seem to mind. He was so much fun to be around. At times he seemed wild and crazy, a totally uninhibited lunatic. On other occasions he was affable and devastatingly charming. Always he was stylishly dressed and socially alert. In a word, Andrew Cunanan was "cool."

The only problem Cunanan had with high school was that it had to end. Andrew graduated as Pluto opposed his natal Moon, an oppressive aspect that coincided with an oppressive time for Cunanan. He started college with vague ambitions of becoming an art historian, but his real career began when he moved out of his family home and started rooming with a female friend from Bishop's. The young woman, of course, came from a wealthy family and she introduced Cunanan to many of her moneyed friends. In this way, the education Andrew had begun at Bishop's on how to live rich was continuing.

By the time Cunanan left Bishop's, his homosexuality was apparent enough to become an embarrassment for his parents. One advantage of living with his high-school friend was that in her milieu Andrew's sexual orientation was accepted, even welcomed. On a broader scale, however, there could not have been a worse time for a young homosexual to acknowledge his sexuality. It was 1987 and the terror of AIDS was shaking the homosexual world. Not surprisingly, the fear of AIDS became an overriding factor in Cunanan's sex life.

Meanwhile, the chances of Cunanan or his family ever achieving anything near the wealth of Andrew's friends at Bishop's only got slimmer. In 1988, Cunanan's father abruptly fled San Diego and returned to the Philippines in order to avoid being charged with stealing money at the brokerage where he worked. Now Andrew's mother had to support herself and Andrew on just her husband's Navy pension. Given the lifestyle to which Cunanan was currently becoming accustomed, this was an impossible task.

Fortunately for Cunanan, his arrangement with his female friend made it possible for him to postpone dealing with this family disaster. Even after his friend married, had a child, and moved to San Francisco, Cunanan remained a fixture in her household. Despite his mother's financial hardships, Andrew was still able to enjoy all the benefits of his friend's wealth and dabble freely in the homosexual night life of the notorious Castro district of San Francisco. He even got to hang out with Gianni Versace. What did he have to worry about?

And then Versace left San Francisco. The significance of this departure would only become apparent to Cunanan much later, but it was the beginning of what would become a very mean ending. A few months later, his rich friend left California with her husband and child, and Cunanan was forced to move back in with his mother and face the bitter reality of being poor.

By the time Saturn squared his natal Saturn in January of the next year, Cunanan was working as a lowly clerk in a store and taking classes at a local community college. He desperately tried to keep up appearances by abusing his credit cards and selling drugs on the side, but the anger and self-disgust he felt because of his reduced circumstances was apparent. He became abusive toward his mother, rejecting her smothering affection, threatening her, and, on at least one occasion, physically attacking her. Cunanan also developed a taste for sadomasochistic pornography during this depressing period. He even performed in some of these films, and he claimed to some of his friends that he was becoming a homosexual prostitute. More importantly, Cunanan was becoming addicted to methamphetamines, drugs that seemed to increase his erratic behavior.

About three years after his fall into poverty, with Neptune on his Midheaven and his progressed Sun conjoined with his natal Uranus, Cunanan did make a change in his life. He found a benefactor, a wealthy, older man who was willing to buy him the nice things he craved and grant him entry into the privileged circles in which he felt so at home. This relationship soured after a few months, but Cunanan was quickly able to find another rich protector among San Diego's elite. Sex apparently did not play a decisive role in these arrangements. Rather it was Cunanan's wit and his urbane sense of style that made him a desirable companion.

Meanwhile, Cunanan had relationships with other homosexual men in San Diego. For the most part, these were passing encounters. One of his lovers was a young man named David Madson. After he and Madson broke up and Madson moved to Minneapolis, Cunanan confessed to a friend that he greatly regretted losing Madson, and that Madson was probably the only man he had ever loved. To what extent he made these feeling known to Madson is unclear.

In July 1996, Cunanan's situation took another nosedive. He argued with his second benefactor over a car and the relationship was terminated. Meanwhile, his mother had moved in with Cunanan's sister and was living on food stamps. Cunanan was effectively homeless. For a while he was able to stay with friends and get by with drug deals and the credit cards his benefactors had left him, but by April of the next year, the cards had been canceled and the largess of his San Diego friends was drying up. Depressed, broke, and overweight, Cunanan had to do something drastic. He told his friends that he was using the last of his credit to go to San Francisco to make a new start. Instead he bought a one-way ticket to Minneapolis.

Cunanan took a pistol with him to Minneapolis. What he originally had intended to do with the weapon is unknown. The first murder he committed there, the bludgeoning of Jeffrey Trail, a friend of Madson's, was apparently committed in a sudden and horrific rage. At that point there was no turning back. He kidnapped Madson, took him to a wooded area, and shot him. His next two murders were committed in the process of stealing cars and money. Cunanan used these vehicles to travel to Miami, where Gianni Versace lived in a magnificent mansion. When Cunanan confronted the designer on the front steps of his home, it is likely that Versace did not even know the real name of his attacker, if he remembered him at all. Cunanan shot him nonetheless. Then, hiding out in a nicely appointed houseboat, Cunanan waited as the police closed in. He committed suicide before they could reach him.

SATURN AT WORK

When Saturn crossed his Descendant in 1983 and he was admitted to Bishop's, Cunanan faced a very simple choice. Would he use his good fortune as an opportunity to create wealth for himself, or would he be seduced by the mere trappings of wealth? The fact that Cunanan made the wrong decision and went chasing after the appearance of wealth can be excused in many ways. We could blame his youth, his overindulgent mother, his felonious father, a horoscope with too many soft aspects and too much Jupiter, or the self-esteem issues inherent to the conjunction of Saturn and the Moon in his 1st House. All these excuses apply, but none of them diminishes the destructive repercussions of his error. The fact that Cunanan had a second chance to make the right choice when Saturn opposed its natal place the next year only compounded his problems.

Cunanan lived under the shadow of this bad decision for the rest of his life. Despite all the fun he had at Bishop's, despite his academic achievements there and the many contacts he made or could have made with wealthy, accomplished people, Cunanan never profited from his schooling except to the extent that what he learned there about the ways of the very rich allowed him to, at least for a while, find people who were willing to pay his way. We can only guess at what Cunanan was thinking after his last night of clubbing with Gianni Versace, when he experienced the full weight of Saturn on his Midheaven. It was, no doubt, the peak of his life as a poor man posing as a rich one, but, at the same time, it was a moment that made the hollowness of Cunanan's position, his self-delusion, and all the missed opportunities of his life become painfully apparently.

Cunanan had the opportunity to change his course, both during the conjunction of Saturn to his Midheaven and, later, when Saturn squared his natal Saturn. And yet, among all the statements recorded by Cunanan's friends, including the well-to-do people he got to know at Bishop's, there is no indication that Andrew came to any of them pleading for help finding a job. Given his intelligence and breadth of his knowledge, Cunanan could have done many things to support himself. Instead he chose to sell drugs or his body.

Pride might have been a factor in Cunanan's unwillingness to seek gainful employment but, from what we know of his horoscope, the self-criticizing, self-punishing depression indicated in the conjunct of his Moon with his natal Saturn seems a more likely culprit. In fact, Cunanan began committing suicide about the time Saturn squared its natal place and he was coming to grips with his mother's poverty. Over the next five years, he sank deeper and deeper into this depression. At the same time, the wide Mars to Pluto square in his natal chart went about its natural function of accumulating anger and resentment against friend and foe alike. Then, at some point, either when he purchased a one-way ticket to Minneapolis or immediately before he struck the first blow at Jeffrey Trail's head, Cunanan decided to let this anger pour forth and compound his own self-destruction with the destruction of five innocent lives.

SOURCES

Maureen Orth, *Vulgar Favors: Andrew Cunanan, Gianni Versace, and the Largest Failed Manhunt in U.S. History* (New York: Delacorte Press, 1999).

22
JERRY SIEGEL

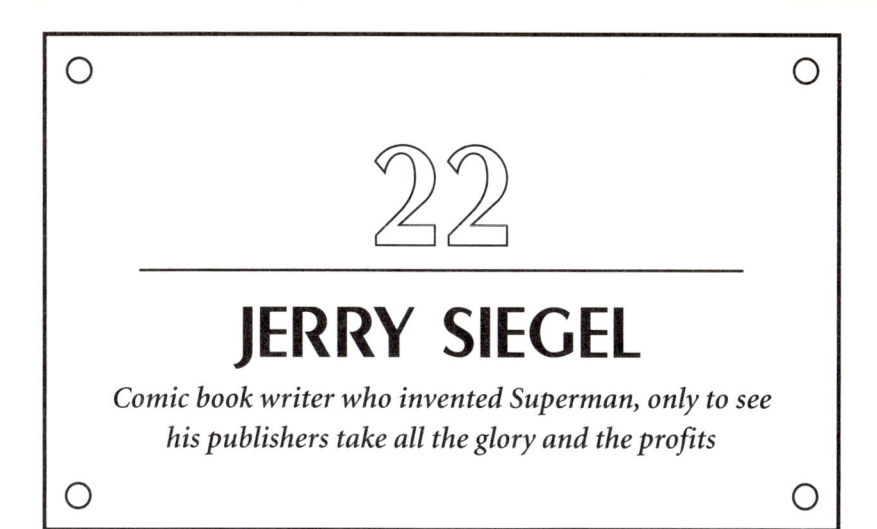

Comic book writer who invented Superman, only to see his publishers take all the glory and the profits

THE CHOICE

For Jerry Siegel, turning fifteen was the best of times and the worst of times. In the fall of 1929, around the time of his fifteenth birthday, he started his own "fanzine." It was a magazine filled with short stories he had written, stories that had been rejected by his favorite science fiction magazines, laboriously typed on a manual typewriter and mimeographed at school. He made ten copies and no one knows how many he sold, though he paid for an ad in a science fiction magazine. The ad certainly cost him much more money than the project made, but it established his name in the small world of science fiction fans.

A few months later he achieved another dose of fame when a parody he had written was published in the school newspaper. It was fame strictly limited to his suburban high school and, though he relished the exposure, Siegel was far too shy and socially inept to capitalize on it. At the same time, he met another dreamy loner with a fascination for pulp magazines and comics, Joe Shuster.

In later years, Jerry Siegel spoke of these events often. He seemed to have total recall. Of the third event that occurred during this period he rarely, if ever, spoke. It was as if it never happened. Siegel's father, a hard-working Jewish immigrant who had put aside his own artistic ambitions to make money in the haberdashery business, who had always encouraged his youngest child to read, draw, and dream, was shot to death in his shop by a robber. **Saturn was opposing its natal position at this time**, the adolescent opposition, while transiting Pluto was squaring his natal Moon. Siegel was making his passage from pampered child to troubled teenager in the midst of a flurry of good fortune and one great tragedy.

THE HOROSCOPE

Siegel's horoscope is a document filled with indications of both extraordinary good fortune and hard times. First of all, Uranus and Jupiter, the eternal augurs of sudden good luck, are in a conjunction just a few degrees above his Ascendant. Uranus forms a marvelous trine to Siegel's Moon in Libra, giving us an exuberant and optimistic personality, and in some ways personalizing this lucky streak. On the other hand, there is a very close square between Uranus and Jupiter to Siegel's 9th House Mars. This is not so positive, for it describes an impulsiveness and feelings of absolute certainty that will occasionally work against him. There will be a strong tendency to rely too heavily on sudden good fortune, and not enough on hard work and preparation.

Siegel's Venus is almost directly on his Midheaven. This is another harbinger of good luck, particularly in one's career. It is an indicator of an artistic personality, or at least a person with a deep appreciation for beauty, harmony, and the good things in life. The fact that Venus is trine to Siegel's Neptune and sextile his Moon strengthens this tendency toward a career in the arts. This is a placement that allows for a great love of comfort and a tendency to avoid conflict, qualities that can be very pleasant but also troublesome, particularly when combined with the laziness inherent to his Jupiter-Uranus combination.

Offsetting the overall good qualities of these aspects, Siegel has one very bad aspect in his horoscope. Or perhaps we should say two. His natal Saturn and natal Pluto are in a tight conjunction and both form a very close square to his Moon in the 8th House. This is a one-

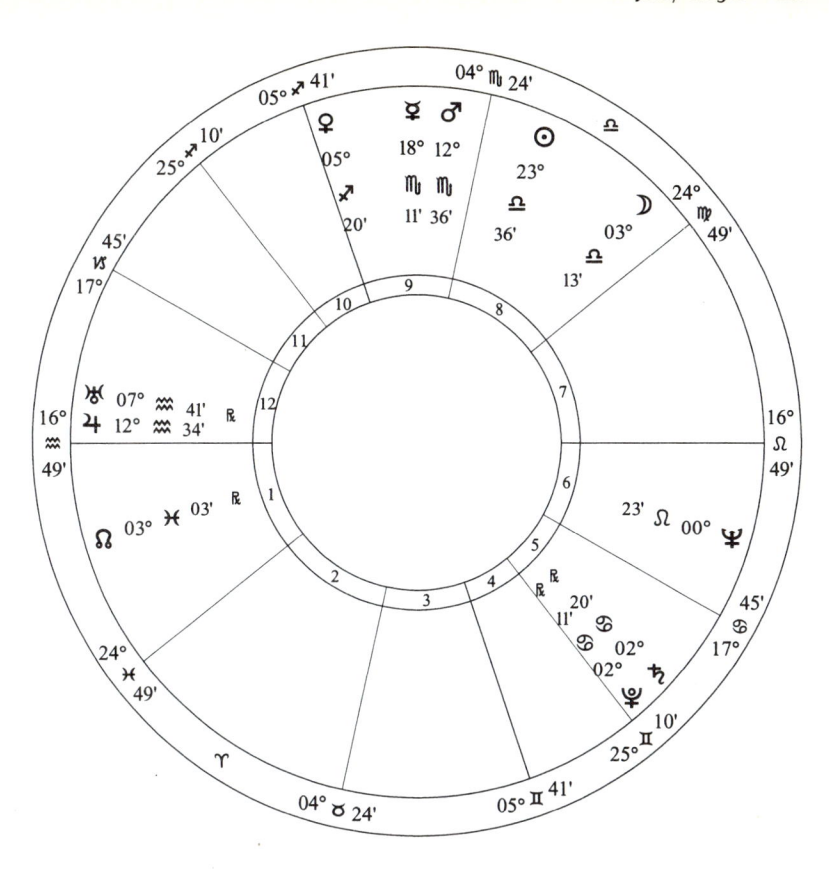

Jerry Siegel
October 17, 1914, 3:00 PM EST
Cleveland, OH, 41N30 81W42

two punch to Siegel's emotional solar plexus. Saturn provides for a tendency to hold people at a distance and to withhold affection. Pluto adds jealousy and an emotional wariness that can easily develop into paranoia. Power and control are big issues with this combination. There is a keen awareness of the economy of submission and dominance. More important, both these aspects block and confine the effusive emotionalism of the Moon, Saturn for the sake of control and decorum, and Pluto in order to better concentrate ill will and empower an old grudge.

THE LIFE

For Siegel's five older siblings, his lucky streak must have seemed to have begun while he was still a child. While they were forced to work in their father's store and seek jobs at an early age, Siegel was pampered and protected by their mother. He never had to work in the store and never felt the pressure to add to the family's income. While they had grown up knowing poverty and hard times, by the time Jerry was born, their father, Mitchell Siegel, had become successful enough to move the family to a comfortable suburb outside Cleveland. Even after Mitchell was killed, Siegel's mother continued to insist that her youngest child should be able to stay at home and keep her company.

Of course, there was a price to be paid for this good fortune. Siegel grew into a boy obsessed with pulp fiction and comic strips. In school he never seemed to mix with his classmates. He was a loner, aloof and distracted. Through high school and even beyond, he had no girlfriends and seems to never have dated. His overbearing mother may have had something to do with this. Members of Siegel's family, interviewed much later, attested to her formidable personality. These same relatives characterized Jerry as a "nerd" who never played baseball with other kids and talked constantly about the stories he was writing or the pulp fiction he was reading.

Not surprisingly, considering the importance of Uranus and Jupiter in this chart, Jerry Siegel's nerdish, introverted life was changed by a sudden burst of inspiration. It happened one hot summer night while he was still in high school. He woke up with the idea for a new comic strip character, a man with fantastic strength who wore a cape and could leap tall buildings. He jotted down his ideas for the character he would call "the Superman" in a rush of sweaty enthusiasm, and, the next morning, hurried to the home of his buddy Joe Shuster. Shuster was a natural draftsman who had taught himself how to draw by copying pictures from the Sunday "funnies." The two teenagers worked all day and finished six weekly installments of the adventures of "The Superman." Siegel wasted no time is sending their samples to publishing syndicates.

There was nothing particularly original about Siegel's and Shuster's creation. There were already other superpowered characters in the pulp magazines. There were men with super strength and heroes with secret identities—some who even flew and wore capes. What Siegel did was simply put all these elements together in one character, but he tapped into the heroic archetype as no one had done before.

Siegel was often a bit vague about the exact date of his night of inspiration, but the documents and rejection letters he hoarded show that it must have been in 1933. This was **also the summer that Saturn crossed his Ascendant**. Superman became more than just another character to the young writer. He became an intrinsic part of his persona. Throughout his life, Siegel would identify, or seek to identify himself as the "creator of Superman" (Jones, 2004)

At first the reaction to Siegel and Shuster's new comic was hardly overwhelming. The first newspaper syndicate they submitted the strip to turned it down immediately. Other publishers seemed to consider the project, only to put it aside or reject it after a long delay. In the meantime, Siegel and Shuster graduated high school and produced some detective comics that were published. The pay was dismal. Both continued to live with their parents and work part-time at other jobs, but Siegel refused to give up hope. Quietly, persistently, he sat in his attic room, pecking away at his typewriter and dreaming big dreams for his Superman.

Siegel had to wait for **February 1938, when Saturn squared its natal place** for his dreams to be answered. That month he and Shuster received word from a company called Detective Comics that they wanted to publish Superman, not as a weekly newspaper strip as the boys from Cleveland had imagined, but as a comic book. Siegel and Shuster didn't hesitate to sell their rights to the character for $130. Then they scrambled to rework their first Superman serial to fit in a comic book form. A couple of months later they saw it published in a magazine called *Action Comics*.

By the summer of 1938, Superman was proving to be a publishing phenomenon, selling out everywhere, with young fans demanding more. Soon the character was given his own comic and a deal was made to start a newspaper strip. Siegel and Shuster were signed to a ten-year contract and were being paid enough to hire other artists and writers to help them sustain the growing work load. This sudden wave of prosperity gave Siegel enough confidence to ask out the girl who lived across the street from his mother's home. He had been watching her come and go for years—now that he was actually getting a paycheck, he could approach her with his head held high.

The girl's name was Bella and she was still in high school. She was also very probably the first woman Siegel had ever dated. Siegel's mother strongly objected to the relationship and when Jerry suddenly announced that he intended to marry his teenage sweetheart, her objections became shrill and strident. Still, Jerry would not be deterred. He had been waiting a long time to free himself of his mother's control, and he intended to do it at a physical, financial, and emotional level. He and Bella were married little more than a year after the triumph of his Superman comic. A short time later they moved to New York.

Even while he was enjoying the first blush of marital bliss and basking in the glory accorded him by his fellow pulp fiction writers and artists, Jerry Siegel was having doubts about the deal he had struck with Detective Comics. Superman was everywhere, from comics to radio, from lunchboxes to pajamas, and the money being made by his publishers was skyrocketing. Little Detective Comics soon became National Periodical Publications, a public company with enormous financial resources. Meanwhile, Jerry and Joe Shuster were still being paid by the page. Jerry wrote angry letters to his publishers. He bickered, complained and, at one point, he and Bella marched in front of National's offices carrying placards. Occasionally, Siegel's constant protests resulted in more money for him and Shuster, but Siegel was not satisfied. His creation was making a lot of people rich and he wasn't one of them.

As Siegel's bitterness grew, his personal life was also suffering. In 1941, his mother died. Since many in his family considered her death to be a direct result of his marriage to Bella, Siegel cut himself off from his family. Around **1942, when Saturn crossed his IC,** he bought a house in an upscale suburb of Cleveland, far from his childhood home. The new house was mostly for Bella. Siegel was spending more and more time away from his wife in New York City.

In 1943, when Uranus passed over his IC, Siegel was drafted. He was stationed in the United States far from any battle, but he did meet someone who would figure very prominently in the only battle that ever interested Jerry Siegel. This was Albert Zugsmith, a young lawyer with a fancy for popular entertainment. Zugsmith began filling Siegel's head with notions of the riches he could reap and the revenge he could wreak if only he, the creator of the most popular comic book character in the world, had the right lawyer.

The turning point didn't really come until **1944, when Saturn made its return to Siegel's natal Saturn.** At this time, he learned that his publishers were bringing out a new version of Superman called Superboy. The character, based on Superman as a youngster growing up, was very close to an idea Siegel had developed for National years earlier, only to have it rejected. For Siegel this was the last straw. Very soon the ten-year contract which he and Shuster had signed would run out and Siegel had already decided that he was going into court to fight for the rights to his Superman. Zugsmith would be his champion.

The battle began in 1947. From the very first, despite the persistent reassurance he and Shuster were getting from Zugsmith, it was a terribly unequal fight. Siegel had, after all, signed a contract. **In May 1948, with Saturn on Siegel's Descendant** and Pluto on his Ascendant, the inevitable verdict was handed down. Siegel and Shuster could *not* have back the rights they had signed away in 1938. A cash settlement was worked out giving the two men around $100,000 each, much of which went for legal fees, and their names would no longer be associated with Superman in any of his many profitable incarnations.

After the verdict, Albert Zugsmith went on to become a successful movie producer. Joe Shuster, who had been slowly going blind for years, withdrew from the comic book business and lived the rest of his life as an invalid, dependent on the care of his brother. Jerry Siegel fumed. He found other work. There were many people in the comic book industry who were willing to help him. And yet, none of his new ideas found anywhere near the audience that Superman enjoyed. For one thing, the comic book industry, which had expanded exponentially after the introduction of Superman in 1938, was now on a downward slide. For another, Siegel seemed to have lost his creative edge. Often his benefactors were embarrassed when they read the scripts he brought them. The loss of his Superman seemed to have destroyed something within the writer.

By 1959, Siegel's financial situation was desperate. Bella, long abandoned in Cleveland, had filed for divorce as soon as the results of Jerry's lawsuit were known. Predictably, Siegel had rushed into another marriage, this time with Joann Kovac, a young woman he had first met during the triumphant days after the sale of Superman. She had posed for Shuster for his first drawings of Lois Lane. Siegel's new wife went to the bosses at National Periodical Publications and demanded justice for her impoverished husband. She was insistent enough that the old grudges were laid aside for a while and Siegel was contracted to write new stories of Superman.

This happened **just as Saturn made its second opposition to its natal place** and as secondary progressed Jupiter moved slowly to conjunct his Ascendant. Siegel took full advantage of his homecoming and did some of the best writing and storytelling of his career. Yet Siegel was still angry and still plotting. National's copyright on Superman was up for renewal in 1965. Jerry began laying plans for a new lawsuit.

Siegel's second attempt to secure return of his rights to Superman was even less successful than his first. The only thing it accomplished was to make him unemployed. In 1968, Siegel moved to California along with his second wife and their daughter. There he worked for Disney for a time and then was forced to take a job as a file clerk in a government office.

In 1975, shortly before the release of the first Superman movie, Siegel made one last plea for justice, but this time he bypassed the courts and went directly to the public. He prepared a press release detailing his account of his battle with National and sent it out to over a hundred newspapers. By this time, National Periodical Publications had become a part of Warner Communications, a huge company with a public image to protect. To avoid a scandal, the corporation agreed to give Siegel and Shuster a pension and medical insurance. More importantly, at least for Siegel, they returned the byline of the boys from Cleveland to every presentation of Superman.

SATURN AT WORK

It is hard not to sympathize with Jerry Siegel in his long battle with National Periodical Publications, but the cold, hard fact of the matter is that he was wrong. The agreement he signed with what was then the humble Detective Comics Company was fairly standard and their treatment of Shuster and himself, measured by the standards of the time, was generous. Seigel's publisher was playing the game according to the rules. It's no wonder that they reacted with amazement and then outrage when Siegel refused to play by those rules.

Siegel represents perhaps the most extreme example we have of the passage of Saturn over the Ascendant coinciding with the development of a persona. Siegel framed his persona around the idea that he was the creator of Superman to such an extent that it warped his judgment. The fact that someone owned the rights to this persona was not simply a financial or legal issue with Siegel. It was an insult to his very being.

The deal with Detective Comics was struck just as Saturn made its first waning square to its natal place, the first step toward adulthood. Siegel embraced this transformation with enthusiasm, starting a career, rushing into a marriage, and breaking with his mother in rapid succession. Such was Siegel's enthusiasm that mistakes were made.

This became obvious when Saturn crossed his IC in 1942, and he found himself falling out of love with his young bride, permanently estranged from his family, and nursing an insistent grudge against his employer.

This leads to Saturn's first return and National's decision to publish Superboy. For the executives at National Periodical Publications, Superboy was simply a business decision. Some of their competitors had had success with young characters with whom their teenage audience could identify. National decided to follow this trend and introduce stories about Superman when he was a teenager. The fact that Siegel had proposed this idea a few years earlier meant little to them. The character was a younger version of the same character to which they owned the rights, and the stories they were using bore no resemblance to ones that Siegel had written.

Again, Saturn gave Siegel choices and he chose to see the Superboy comics as a call to arms. He had Zugsmith at his elbow, promising a big payoff. (Some people, most notably Joe Shuster, later suspected that Zugsmith had been paid by National to incite Siegel to sue.) He had the years of outrage, watching millions flow into the coffers of his publishers while he remained a working stiff, albeit a well-paid working stiff. And mostly he had the sense of having his most precious possession, a creation that was in so many ways an extension of himself, stolen and controlled by a group of soulless capitalists.

When Saturn reached Siegel's Descendant, the folly of his bad choices became all too evident. He not only lost the suit and his job, but he also had his and Shuster's names stricken from any future publication of Superman. As far as the public would know, Superman was now divorced from Jerry Siegel and Joe Shuster. This was not the only relationship in Siegel's life that suffered a sudden change. It was just two months after Saturn contacted his Descendant that Jerry's first wife filed for divorce.

Saturn arrived at Siegel's Midheaven in 1956 at the same time that strictures of the Comic Code were imposed on comic books in America. It is generally considered one of the lowest points in the history of the comic book. It was a period during which Siegel was scrambling to find work. This was a scramble that would continue until transiting Saturn opposed natal Saturn and his secondary progressed Jupiter arrived at an exact square with his Ascendant. This is when Jerry got his second chance to write Superman. It must have seemed like a homecoming for him. Certainly, it was a steady job, until the old anger began to rise and Siegel got the urge to sue one more time.

In the end, we could say that Jerry Siegel won his battle with his publishers. At least he got his and Shuster's byline returned to the front page of every Superman comic and he got a pension and medical insurance to see him through the last ten years of his life. (Shuster died only a year after the settlement.) But it was a victory that cost Siegel thirty years of his life and brought great hardships on himself and his family.

SOURCES

Gerard Jones, *Men of Tomorrow: Geeks, Gangsters and the Birth of the Comic Book* (New York: Basic Books, 2004).

23

JIM BAKKER

American TV evangelist who built an empire with the faith and the money of other people

THE CHOICE

In November 1972, a young minister and talk show host named Jim Bakker heard God speaking to him. Though he was only thirty-two, Bakker had already enjoyed remarkable success. Along with his wife, Tammy, he had risen from an itinerant revival preacher, moving across the South from one poor church to another and living out of their car, to become a star on Pat Robertson's Christian Broadcasting Network. As the host of the nightly talk show, *The 700 Club,* Bakker had brought the glamour and sophistication of such secular television shows as *The Tonight Show* to the Christian market. More important, perhaps, using *The 700 Club* as his forum, he had shown a phenomenal ability to persuade viewers to send in donations, the lifeblood of the perpetually struggling Christian Broadcasting Network. His boss, Robertson, was duly impressed. Even though Bakker's salary at the time was nothing compared to such secular stars as Johnny Carson, it was substantial. Three years earlier, **when Saturn returned to its natal place**, Bakker and his wife had purchased a pricey home in an exclusive waterfront community.

239

All these accomplishments had not come without some conflicts. Bakker was frequently at odds with his boss. Recently Robertson had started hosting *The 700 Club* himself a couple of nights a week. Robertson had also brought in a new producer for the show who seemed intent on reining in Bakker's expansive vision for the program. There were also people at the station who complained about the way Jim and Tammy Bakker promoted themselves. They didn't like the fact that the couple sold Tammy's records and other merchandise after their morning children's show (which was also one of CBN's biggest hits). And then there were those who chafed at the Bakkers' lifestyle, their big house, fancy clothes, and jewelry. At one point Bakker had come to work in a brand-new Cadillac, and had been told by Robertson to get rid of it.

On that day in November, what Bakker heard God say was that it was time for him to break away from the restrictions imposed upon him by CBN and from his critics, and find a venue where he could express his particular view of the gospel without interference. Actually, Jim and Tammy had been feeling restless for some time. They had already put their house on the market. The decision Bakker made was that if the house sold, he would take that as a sign that God wanted him to leave CBN. Naturally, the house sold.

It is quite appropriate that Jim Bakker would look to the real estate market for a message from God at this point in his life. On November 8, the day he says God spoke to him, **Saturn was at 19 degrees of Gemini moving retrograde toward his IC at 16 degree Gemini. By the time this crucial transit was completed in the spring of 1973**, Bakker would be free of CBN and well on his way to launching a new television ministry that he would call PTL.

THE HOROSCOPE

Jim Bakker's horoscope is dominated by a T-square involving his Mercury, the conjunction of Mars with Jupiter in his 1st House and Neptune in his 7th. This T-square is particularly interesting because the combination of Jupiter and Neptune bring expansiveness and an appreciation for glitz and glamour that are quite foreign to Bakker's Capricorn Sun

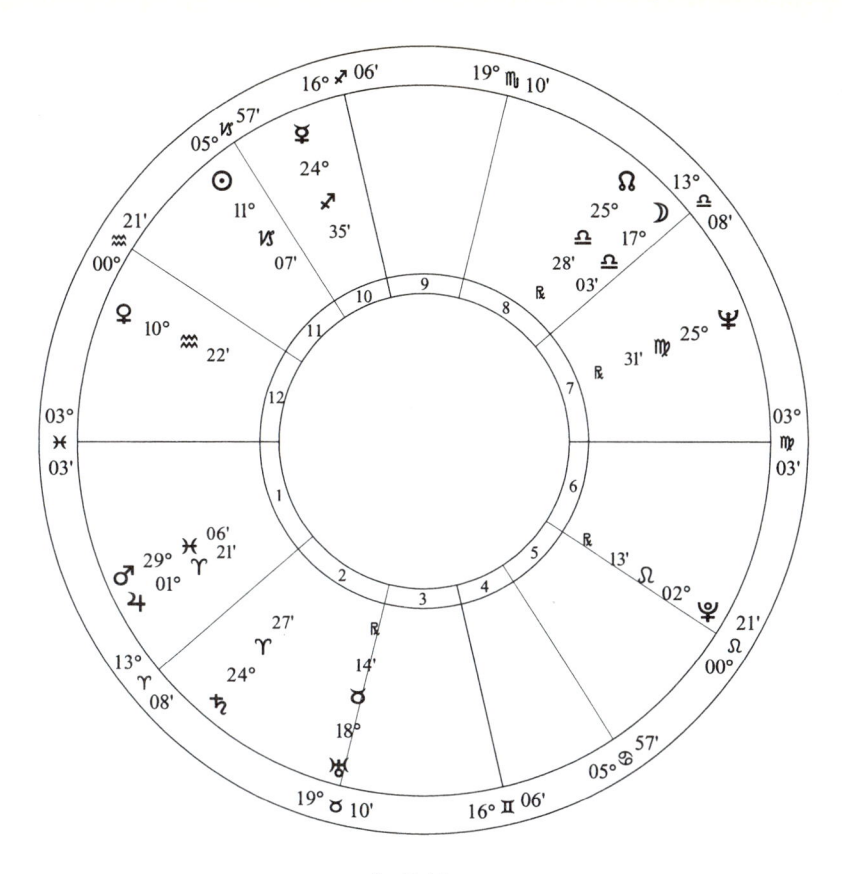

Jim Bakker

January 2, 1940, 11:00 AM EST

Muskegon Heights, MI, 43N12 86W

sign. As a Capricorn Sun, Bakker was a born initiator, organizer, and entrepreneur. This talent is further emphasized by a very close trine between his Mercury and Saturn. But Mercury is in Sagittarius, Jupiter's sign, and its square to Jupiter and his Pisces Mars, along with its very tight square to Neptune, speak of a dreamy and effusive personality, of salesmanship and showmanship, and grand visions that conflict with, and to some extent supercede, the gritty realism of his Capricorn Sun.

Religion was a natural fit for Bakker. Both Jupiter and Neptune have a spiritual side. Jupiter lends itself to a philosophical consideration of issues pertaining to the soul and the higher mind, while Neptune is the planet of mystical visions and spiritual epiphany. Also, since Bakker was brought up in a very religious home and in the Assemblies of God church, his religious devotion was the continuation of a family tradition, something that had to appeal to his convention-loving Capricorn nature. There is a tremendous amount of energy in this horoscope, with both the Sun and the Moon in active, Cardinal signs, and the conjunction of Mars with Jupiter, and religion would provide an apt vehicle for all this active, forward-looking zeal. Finally, with Pisces rising, Bakker was able to project a very warm, emotionally open persona, a persona that often did not agree with the more serious business-savvy qualities of his Capricorn Sun. This kind of emotionality, even at a superficial level, would be necessary for a man who sought to make his living as a charismatic preacher.

Unfortunately, all of these positive qualities carry with them some traits that can be problematic. The expansive energy provided by his Mars to Jupiter conjunction can lead to waste and the overstepping of bounds. Neptune also has problems with boundaries. The close square between Neptune and Mercury indicates thinking that can easily become skewed and out of balance. Fantasy can come to matter more than reality, and even the down-to-earth tendencies of his Capricorn Sun can become lost in self-deception. One other problem with Neptune in this horoscope is the close sesquiquadrate aspect it makes with Bakker's Venus in Aquarius. This is an aspect that indicates a loosening of boundaries relating to sex and love and, since Venus is in the 12th House, the possibility of a secret shame and scandal.

THE LIFE

Jim Bakker was brought up in a small town in Michigan, the youngest child in a family of meager means and strict religious devotion. When he was about eleven years old (with transiting Neptune conjuncting his Sun and transiting Uranus opposed to his Moon), he was molested by an older boy. In his autobiography, Bakker makes it clear that what disturbed him most was the fact that he so easily acquiesced to the boy's advances. This relationship lasted until Bakker was in high school and began dating girls.

Saturn crossed Bakker's Midheaven during his high school years, and during this time he made a surprising discovery about himself. He loved show business. When his school newspaper needed money, he organized a variety show. It was a hit and he was called upon to do it again the next year and the year after that. His ability to find talent and promote it, as well as his energy and organizational ability, earned him recognition from both his peers and adults.

The problem was that show business was not a likely career for a boy brought up in the Assemblies of God denomination. Even owning a television was considered liberal by some members of that church, including Bakker's grandfather. Even though Bakker's father favored a less strict route to God, he still frowned on dancing and the wearing of makeup. Bakker sought a way to accommodate this strict, religious upbringing within his innate showmanship. The first thing he did after he graduated and entered North Central Bible College in Minneapolis was to organize a show in a local theater with other divinity students. The second thing he did was to become acquainted with a talented young coed named Tammy LaValley. Tammy came from a poor, rural home in northern Minnesota and, at four feet-eleven inches, she was small enough to make the five foot-seven Bakker feel like a giant. She was also a musically adept Pisces Sun with a fine singing voice. On April 1, 1961, shortly after **Saturn squared his natal Saturn**, he and Tammy were married.

The young couple saw no reason to return to North Central Bible College. A few months after the wedding, they hit the road and began preaching at revival meetings, first in the Upper Midwest, and then in the South. Combining Bakker's flair for showmanship and his "good news" sermons with Tammy's singing and piano playing, the young couple was soon prosperous enough to buy a trailer. By 1963, they were very busy evangelists, traveling throughout the southern states, preaching and singing in churches large and small. Then, in 1964, when **Saturn made its first conjunction with his Ascendant**, Bakker was belatedly ordained as a minister. A short time later, as **Saturn again crossed his Ascendant**, Jim and Tammy were invited to host a children's program at a struggling Christian TV station. The gig was supposed to be temporary, but the charming couple proved so popular and did so much to improve the show that they were invited to stay. Suddenly Jim Bakker was a TV star.

Television proved to be a natural medium for Bakker. He was able to relate to both poor Christians and with people better off. He projected a sense that God cared as much about the physical and financial affairs of his faithful as he did their spiritual condition. Jim Bakker presented his viewers with a world in which faith could produce wealth, and he made sure every aspect of his program—from the clothes that he wore, to the set on which he stood—affirmed that vision. His message was that, for the devout Christian, wealth was not a distraction—it was his or her due. God wanted his people to be rich, to partake of his bounty. For the less fortunate Christians in his audience, this message brought hope of financial windfalls to come. For those who were already wealthy, the message was an assurance that rampant materialism could be godly.

Of course, all this hope and reassurance had to be paid for. As good as he was at organizing a show, Bakker found his true calling when it came to raising money. He possessed an unerring sense of drama and a gift for projecting palpable personal need across the air waves that seemed capable of opening every purse. The fact that he often stretched the truth in his appeals for donations, and that he frequently made promises and projections that were unlikely to be fulfilled, were not a problem for Bakker. After all, he was doing God's work for God's people.

A year after he made his decision to leave CBN, Bakker was debuting his PTL (Praise the Lord) show on a television station in Charlotte, North Carolina. A few months after that, and a few months before **Saturn squared his natal Saturn,** Bakker forced out his partners in the new venture and assumed complete control of the operation (with the support of a board of directors made up of his friends and admirers). Bakker immediately proposed a building spree. He wanted a new, state-of-the-art television studio. He also wanted to build a tourist attraction he called Heritage Village that would be patterned after old Williamsburg in Virginia. Many wondered how this fledgling television network could afford to undertake projects that were so costly, but Bakker refused to hear their small-minded cautionary concerns.

By the time **Saturn reached Bakker's Descendant** in 1978, Heritage Village was completed and Bakker had a new project. It was a Christian theme park and hotel he called Heritage USA. Even though the PTL organization had prospered since Bakker's arrival in Charlotte, the cost of this new project threatened to overwhelm it. There were massive layoffs within the organization that year and the local press began investigating the way money was managed by PTL. In particular, these reporters were asking questions about the expensive cars and houses that Bakker was buying.

On a more personal level, Bakker's almost compulsive attention to the details of the construction of the park put a strain on his relationship with his wife. Tammy felt neglected, and began seeking solace in the company of other men. How far these relationships went is debatable but, feeling Saturn's pressure on the region of his horoscope that deals with relationships, Bakker became convinced that his wife was having an affair.

During this period of estrangement between Jim and Tammy, the relationship between Bakker and certain male members of his staff took an odd turn. Some men reported that Bakker made sexual advances toward them. Others reported that he masturbated in their presence. Still others, who reported nothing, seemed to advance within the organization at a rate far in excess of their abilities. In general, people around Bakker excused their boss's behavior as evidence of the frustration and pressure he was feeling. After all, not only was he at odds with his wife, but he was also suffering through a grueling investigation by the FCC and continued sniping from the local newspaper. One of Bakker's friends thought he had the solution for the minister's sexual frustrations. In December 1980, while Bakker was in Florida helping raise money for a Christian television station, this friend arrived with a guest, a pretty young church secretary named Jessica Hahn.

In 1982, as **Saturn opposed natal Saturn,** Bakker and PTL got some good news for a change. The FCC closed its investigation with a lot of complaining about lax money management, but no decision to pull the network's license. Also, Bakker and Tammy had patched up their failing marriage after extensive counseling. Though the battles with the press continued, and money problems abounded within the organization, Bakker seemed free to continue his ministry and the high-flying lifestyle it funded. This peaceful interlude did not last, however. In 1985, as Uranus moved back and forth across his Midheaven, Bakker found himself threatened on two fronts. First, the IRS announced an audit of the tax records of the PTL organization. As a tax-exempt church, PTL was being asked to justify its involvement in profit-making ventures such as a theme park and new luxury condominiums that were under construction. Secondly, Jessica Hahn had approached the PTL organization, asking for money. She threatened to go to the press with a story of how she had been raped by Reverend Jim Bakker in December 1980 if she was not amply paid. In January 1985, Richard Dortch, Bakker's associate, delivered the payment to Hahn.

Even though Hahn had been silenced, rumors of the affair had reached the press and people within the ruling body of the Assemblies of God, including some of Bakker's rivals in the televangelist field. All they were waiting for was proof. Meanwhile, the IRS proceeded with its audit. In 1987, as **Saturn reached Bakker's Midheaven,** all the elements fell into place. Jimmy Swaggart, a powerful televangelist from Louisiana, launched a hostile takeover of PTL, citing evidence of Bakker's moral turpitude. At the same time, the story of Bakker's tryst with Hahn spread like a virus across the media. Bakker was forced to resign as head of PTL. A few months later, with **Saturn still crossing his Midheaven,** Jim Bakker was indicted by a federal grand jury on charges of fraud, tax evasion, and racketeering, thanks to evidence brought out by the audit. In October 1989, he was convicted.

Bakker was released from prison in 1993 and he found, to the surprise of many, that he was still beloved by many in the evangelical community. In 1994, as **Saturn crossed his Ascendant,** he began work on a book detailing the mistakes he had made during his years at PTL, and describing his struggle toward redemption while in prison. In 1998, **Saturn made its second return to its natal place** and Bakker, who had been divorced by Tammy while he was in prison, remarried. He and his new wife moved to the resort area of Branson, Missouri, and in January 2003, six months after **Saturn crossed his IC**, a quieter and more humble Jim Bakker began broadcasting a new Christian TV show.

SATURN AT WORK

In the case of Jim Bakker, the connection between Saturn's first passage across his Midheaven in 1957 and the second in 1987 seems compelling. During the first passage, he discovered that he had the organizational ability and the sense of showmanship necessary to bring a group of people together and put on a show. He discovered how he could make his own vision a reality and that his vision was in fact valued by the people around him. More importantly, he discovered he had control. He had control of his performers, he had control of his show, and through them he had control of his audience. For a Capricorn, particularly a Capricorn dealing with the sense of helplessness that comes from sexual molestation, this was an amazing and life-changing discovery.

Thirty years later, when his PTL empire collapsed and he was indicted, this sense of control was shattered. During his trial, Bakker suffered a complete emotional breakdown. He wept and crawled under a table while in the courtroom. It wasn't just that his wealth and luxurious lifestyle was being stripped from him or the fact that he was being convicted of bilking thousands of people out of money with false promises. He also was dealing with the loss of his sense of control. He had lost control of his show, of the organization that had grown up around it, and of the audience that had once adored him.

The key moment within this long and tragic cycle seems to have occurred at its halfway point, when Saturn crossed his IC in 1972 and 1973. When Bakker decided to leave CBN and go out on his own, he was removing his vision from any possibility of oversight or outside control. From this point on, his only boss would be his God. For an ambitious entrepreneur, this was a natural and necessary step. For a person with so much Neptune in his horoscope it was also an extremely dangerous step out into the real world. Neptune brings us visions, but it also brings us the possibility of self-deception and fuzzy, even delusional, thinking. Combine the influence of Jupiter in his chart with that of Neptune, and we get a vision so grandiose and unrealistic that it borders on fantasy.

Bakker desperately needed someone who could act as a censor and judge for his expansive vision. He needed someone who could say no. Unfortunately, during his years with PTL, Bakker systematically pushed out or demoted anyone who might have challenged his control of his vision. When the newspapers and people outside his organization offered criticism, he saw them as godless enemies of his divine mission. It took a federal grand jury and five years in jail to finally convince Jim Bakker that he was wrong.

SOURCES

Jim Bakker, with Ken Abraham, *I Was Wrong* (Nashville, TN: Thomas Nelson Publishing, 1996).

Charles Shepard, *Forgiven: The Rise and Fall of Jim Bakker and the PTL Ministry* (New York: Atlantic Monthly Press, 1989).

24

JAYNE MANSFIELD

American actress who used every means to become the next great "blond bombshell," but never quite got there

THE CHOICE

In 1959, an ambitious young actress named Jayne Mansfield took a hard look at her career and was not happy with what she saw. It had been nearly four years since she had gotten her big break in the Broadway play *Will Success Spoil Rock Hunter?* After this triumph, she had been given a contract by Fox Studios and starred in two hit movies, a Hollywood adaptation of the Rock Hunter script, and *The Girl Can't Help It.* Also during that time, thanks to her tireless self-promotion and hard work, she had become world famous, a virtual household name. And yet, more recently, Fox seemed unwilling to give her roles in big movies, preferring to use her as an ornamental draw for cheaper productions, or to rent her out to independent producers. Mansfield's career seemed stymied, and for this impatient Aries Sun who had come to Hollywood at the age of twenty-one, determined to become a major star within no more than six months, this was unacceptable. Changes would have to be made.

Also during 1959, **Saturn crossed Mansfield's Descendant three times,** in February, June, and November. This indicates that the changes would involve her relationships. Already, the year before, Mansfield had married Mickey Hargitay, a Romanian-born bodybuilder and former Mr. Universe, but there were other relationships that needed to be addressed.

The first thing Mansfield did in 1959 was break with her publicist, Jim Byron. Byron had helped organized Mansfield's first big publicity coup. He was responsible for getting her in on a photo shoot designed to draw attention to a new movie starring Jane Russell. The idea was to have a group of girls in bikinis line up around a swimming pool. Mansfield showed up early for the shoot and took the opportunity to charm the photographers as they set up their gear. Then, as she and the other girls jumped into the pool, the top of Mansfield's bikini artfully came off, displaying the full glory of her forty-inch bust to the hungry camera men. After that, no one seemed to care what became of Jane Russell, Debbie Reynolds, and the other "big" stars who were present.

The second thing Mansfield did was fire her agent, Bill Shiffren. Shiffren had gotten Mansfield her first contract with Warner Brothers, and when he saw that this studio wasn't interested in using his client, he got her the lead in *Will Success Spoil Rock Hunter?* Mansfield had balked at taking the role. She had always pictured herself as a movie star, and she had never even been to New York City, but Shiffren insisted that doing that play would greatly increase her stock in Hollywood, and he had been proven correct.

Ostensibly Mansfield was giving control of her career to her new husband, who was now acting as her manager, but both Byron and Shiffren knew that no one had ever managed Jayne Mansfield's career other than Jayne Mansfield. Byron had succeeded as her publicist mostly because he was as enamored of crazy, over-the-top publicity stunts as Mansfield was, and Shiffren had grown used to having his sage advice ignored with regard to the scripts she chose and the way she conducted her career. The truth was that the many mistakes that had thus far been made in the course of Mansfield's career had been, for the most part, her own, and by firing Byron and Shiffren she was simply freeing herself to make many more errors in judgment.

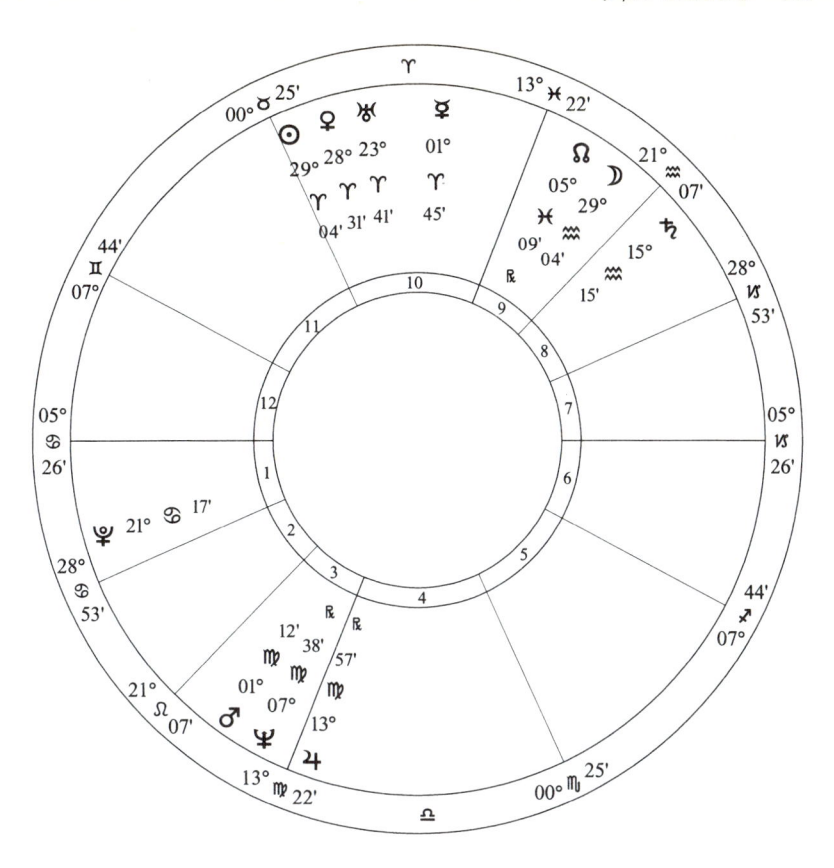

Jayne Mansfield
April 19, 1933, 9:11 AM EST
Lower Merion, PA, 40N02 75W18

THE HOROSCOPE

Even though Mansfield was born with her Sun in the last degree of Aries, it is hard to imagine a chart more full of Aries energy than this one. She also has Venus, Mercury, and Uranus in Aries—and Mars, the planetary ruler of Aries, trines the Sun, forms a quincunx with Mercury, and opposes her Aquarius Moon. All the Aries and Mars influence makes for a very dynamic, hard-charging, and highly competitive personality. This is the horoscope of a fighter, a person who needs the challenge and excitement of battle. Aries people always fight to win, but prizes and trophies interest them less than the physical thrill of victory. Often Aries folks become so embroiled in their battles, in their struggles to achieve, that they fail to notice when they have won or that their opponents have left the field. They just keep on fighting, without a purpose or a specific enemy.

One interesting feature of this horoscope is the placement of Jupiter directly on the IC. This is an extremely expansive and, some would say, lucky placement. It describes a larger-than-life personality, someone who can't help but be noticed. Knowing when enough is enough is the big problem with this strong Jupiter influence. There is a pronounced tendency to overdo, overextend, and overwhelm. What is particularly interesting about Mansfield's Jupiter is that it makes two nearly exact sesquiquadrate aspects, one to her Sun and one to her Venus. The Sun and Venus are in a conjunction, a fairly mild aspect indicating an appealing, easy-to-like personality with a tinge of narcissism. Jupiter's aspect to the Sun and Venus expands these qualities, as well as the natural egotism of Aries, to an extraordinary degree. It provides for an unwieldy surfeit of self-involvement and a tendency toward exhibitionism.

The most trying aspect in this horoscope is the opposition of Mars to the Moon. As well as adding to the combative tendencies of Aries, this connection also indicates a deep, emotional wound—a painful event or idea, a secret shame or failing, an unspoken anger or passion that will constantly eat away at the unconscious of the person. In many cases, such a wound can act as the impetus for extraordinary effort and great accomplishment, but pain will always remain. In Mansfield's case, since the Moon rules her Cancer Ascendant, that secret pain would become a big part of the persona she presented to the world.

THE LIFE

We do not have to look far for the source of Jayne Mansfield's secret anguish. When she was three years old and around the time that **Saturn moved across her Midheaven**, her father died suddenly of a heart attack. Her mother quickly remarried, and her stepfather was by all accounts a good man who loved little Jayne, but the memory of her lost father haunted Mansfield for the rest of her life.

Jayne's stepfather lived in Dallas, Texas, and it was here that Mansfield grew up. Her childhood was apparently uneventful. She was considered a remarkably generous and open-hearted girl. She had many friends but was not overly popular. One reason for this was her mother, who was very protective of her only child, particularly when it came to boys. Young Jayne could only actively flirt with boys when she was out of sight of her mother. This is what happened at a party in December 1949, when she attracted the attention of an older boy named Paul Mansfield.

Different accounts have been offered about what happened next. At one point, Jayne claimed she had been raped by an unknown man and chose to marry Paul to protect her honor. Another story has the couple marrying secretly a month after they met. In the most likely version, however, Jayne became pregnant by Paul out of wedlock. Paul did the right thing, and married her on May 6, 1950. The child, a daughter, was born in November. Uranus was conjuncting Jayne's Ascendant at this time, so it would be only natural that she sought to rebel from her mother's control. Also, **Saturn was passing over her IC**, making its final contact in June 1950, a month after she became a married woman.

As a married woman, no longer under the thumb of her mother, Jayne Mansfield seems to have discovered herself. For one thing, she became aware of the effect her remarkable figure had on men. She began to dress, and undress, in ways that showed off her bosom and she was proud that she could still turn heads even when she was pushing a baby carriage. For another, she discovered she could act. When her husband was drafted and she accompanied him to an army base in Georgia, Jayne began taking acting lessons and performing with local theater groups. When Paul was sent to Korea, Jayne returned to Dallas, where she continued to study and perform.

When Paul was discharged from the military in 1954, Jayne persuaded him to move to Los Angeles. She promised him that if she did not become a star in six months they could leave. By October, Paul was ready to go back to Dallas but Jayne was not. She was sure that success was just around the corner and she was right. In December 1954, **as Saturn squared its natal place**, she met Jim Byron, the publicist who would help launch her career. By the time this Saturn passage was completed, in August 1955, Bill Shiffren had landed her the role in *Will Success Spoil Rock Hunter?* that would make her famous.

In *Will Success Spoil Rock Hunter?*, Mansfield played the quintessential "dumb blond" starlet. She was bubbly, giggly, comically narcissistic, and proudly unintelligent. Her figure was a very important element of the role, and she made sure that it was frequently on display. This role soon became Jayne Mansfield. Though she was occasionally called upon play more serious characters in movies, her two biggest hits, *The Girl Can't Help It* and a motion picture adaptation of *Will Success Spoil Rock Hunter?*, were based on this particular persona. The press and the public began to see Jayne Mansfield as this character and Mansfield did everything she could to encourage this perception. She felt that success in Hollywood depended less on acting talent than upon projecting a personality that the public enjoyed seeing on the screen. If the public wanted to see an actress with an ultrawomanly body and the mind of a five-year-old, then that was what she would give them.

In reality, however, this persona had little to do with the real Jayne Mansfield. The real Jayne Mansfield was a worker and a fighter. Once she was aligned with Jim Byron, she had begun a relentless publicity campaign that would last for the rest of her life. Her daily schedule was awash with supermarket openings, product endorsements, interviews, nightclub performances, and appearances of all sorts. Nothing was too prosaic or too wacky for her to do if it resulted in publicity. There were many in Hollywood who found Mansfield's aggressive self-promotion vulgar and undignified. In New York, her busy schedule often made her late for rehearsals and detracted from her performances, causing the theater people to mark her as undisciplined and unprofessional. Bill Shiffren warned Mansfield about the dangers of becoming overexposed and advised her to "play it cool," but, for Mansfield, playing it cool was not an option (Saxton, 1975).

One reason Mansfield worked so hard to keep herself in the public eye was the fact that she felt she was in competition with several other blond movie stars, the most prominent of whom was Marilyn Monroe. Mansfield often compared herself to these other women in interviews, usually in order to emphasize her advantages. On one occasion, she attended a dinner held in honor of the busty Italian actress, Sophia Loren. Loren wore a low-cut gown. Mansfield wore one that was cut even lower, and kept adjusting the garment until finally her breasts were completely exposed. This stunt certainly drew attention away from Loren, but not in a manner favorable to Mansfield.

Mansfield's attitude toward her body was another problem. She was very frank about the degree to which her career depended upon her bustline and she seemed to enjoy displaying herself. Very early in her career, she began appearing in *Playboy* magazine and her poses became a little more risqué with each appearance. In 1963, **when Saturn made its return to its natal place**, she performed a nude scene in the movie *Promises, Promises*, becoming the first major Hollywood star to do so. When *Playboy* published stills from this scene, Hugh Hefner was taken to court as a pornographer. The movie was banned in some American cities.

The firing of Byron and Shiffren did not help Mansfield's sagging movie career. Neither did the nude scene in *Promises, Promises*. Mansfield was drinking to excess now and the publicity she got often involved drunken rows between her and Mickey Hargitay, her second husband. During the early 1960s, the couple separated several times and she had much publicized affairs with other men. She finally divorced Hargitay in 1964, and married a Brooklyn-born movie producer named Matt Cimber.

While both Paul Mansfield and Mickey Hargitay had been relatively passive figures in Jayne's life, Cimber was anything but. He took charge of Mansfield's career and began moving the emphasis away from movies and toward nightclub performances and television. It seemed like a wise choice. Personal appearances had always been Jayne's strong point, and on television talk shows her natural instincts for comedy were aptly displayed. At first Mansfield seemed ready to put her career in her husband's hands. Both Uranus and Pluto were crossing her IC, and she was ready for a fundamental change of direction. But in **1965, Saturn arrived at her Midheaven** and the marriage stumbled when Mansfield and Cimber had their first child. Cimber had strong opinions about how children were to be raised, and these did not include dragging the kids to movie locations and nightclubs or flaunting them in front of the press as Mansfield had done with her other four children. Cimber objected to the many lapses in the education of the other children and the way Mansfield used her oldest daughter as her personal assistant and occasional bartender. The marriage began to fall apart.

As Saturn made its **last contact with her Midheaven in early 1966**, Mansfield was starring in a play directed by Cimber in New York. People were lining up to see her and she was making a good deal of money, but she wasn't on Broadway and she wasn't lighting up the silver screen. It was obvious that the trajectory of her career was turning downward. A few months later, she and Cimber separated and began the process of an acrimonious divorce. Mansfield began an affair with her attorney, Sam Brody. Her fights with this new boyfriend frequently became violent and Jayne was seen sporting a black eye. In November 1966, Mansfield's son Zoltan was mauled by a lion while she was making an appearance at a zoo. She turned the tragedy into a publicity stunt, calling a news conference at her home so the press could see her welcoming him home from the hospital. Mansfield's secondary progressed Mars was making a square to her natal Sun during this period and violence, pain, and blood were becoming a dominant theme. This theme had its ultimate manifestation on June 29, 1967, as the aspect between progressed Mars and the Sun was just beginning to wane. While rushing from a performance in Biloxi to an interview in New Orleans, Jayne Mansfield, Sam Brody, and their driver were killed in a horrific car accident.

SATURN AT WORK

Early in the career of Jayne Mansfield, Saturn seemed to be working very much in her favor. As Saturn crossed her IC and she married and became a mother, she was able to escape the influence of her own mother and focus on what she really wanted in life—to become a movie star. Then, as Saturn squared her natal Saturn, and she joined forces with Jim Byron and Bill Shiffren, she was able to take some giant steps toward realizing that goal. By the time Saturn reached her Descendant in 1959, Mansfield had reached her goal. She had become a movie star. The downward spiral which began both in her career and her personal life after she separated from Byron and Shiffren in 1959 had much to do with her failure to recognize that, given her limited range as an actress, she had accomplished as much as she could realistically hope to accomplish and that it was time to set new goals and engage in new conquests.

When Saturn arrived at Mansfield's Midheaven, it seemed that she was on the verge of making this realization or of at least handing over the fight for her career to someone else. Matt Cimber may not have been the greatest manager, but he had a vision for Mansfield's future on the stage and on television that was attainable. He was putting her in a battle that she could win. The problem was that Mansfield could not be satisfied with winning at what seemed to her a lower level. She still longed for the high-profile victories of her youth.

At the same time, as often happens during Saturn passage, issues too long neglected rose to the surface. Mansfield had always made a great show of loving her children. Her determination to be both a hard-driving career woman and a good mother was one of her more endearing qualities. The problem was that, in this particular battle, she was losing badly. Her need to have the children with her when she traveled had caused them to be pulled out of school over and over again. Once they had accompanied their mother to these various locations, because of her frenetic schedule, they were frequently left in the care of strangers. Her oldest daughter, who was in her teens by this time, had become Mansfield's caretaker and was bearing the brunt of her mother's growing problems with alcohol. Rather than facing these looming realities, Mansfield chose to separate from Cimber, much as she had parted ways with Byron and Shiffren years earlier, and become her own manager once more. It was a poor decision both for her career and for her children. Three of her children were in the car with her when she died, though miraculously none of them were hurt.

As far as her career was concerned, if it weren't for the horrible, headline-grabbing nature of her death, it seems certain that Jayne Mansfield would have faded into obscurity after 1967. As it was, because of her shocking end, Mansfield's name is frequently spoken in the same breath as her chief Hollywood rival, Marilyn Monroe. In this sense, we could say that Mansfield won the big battle that she had been fighting all of her adult life. She had risen to the ultimate heights of Hollywood stardom, but at a terrible price.

SOURCES

Martha Saxton, *Jayne Mansfield and the American Fifties* (Boston: Houghton Mifflin, 1975).

PART 3
SATURN AT WORK FOR YOU

25

SATURN AT WORK ON THE MIDHEAVEN

When Saturn crosses your Midheaven, you will typically see Saturn as the high and powerful figure of authority sanctioned by society to pass judgment on your actions. Here you are called upon to prove your worth, display your talents, and show your abilities. Your strengths and your accomplishments are lauded while your weaknesses and your failings are subjected to withering criticism. It can be an exalting, triumphant passage, or it can be extraordinarily painful and disheartening. In either case, there is probably no point in your life where you can learn more about yourself, your ambitions, and the true value of your goals and your dreams.

Sometimes, as in the case of **Malcolm X**, this judgment is life-changing in a very positive way. During his Saturn to Midheaven crossing, Malcolm received recognition and a promotion from the honorable Elijah Muhammad for his hard work for the Nation of Islam. Likewise, **Albert Einstein** received the first acknowledgement of his groundbreaking work when he was asked by scholars to write a summation of his theory of relativity, a summation that included the first mention of the formula that would become his calling card to the world: E=mc². **Oprah Winfrey** won a beauty pageant and drew attention that would eventually land her a job as the news anchor on a local TV station. **Jim Bakker's** first Saturn to Midheaven crossing is another example. While still a high school student, Bakker received high praise for his organization of a charity talent show for his school. **Ralph Nader**, who graduated *magna cum laude* from Princeton during this crossing, provides us with yet another positive example.

However, when the judgment of Saturn turns negative during this passage, it can be very negative indeed. During his second Saturn to Midheaven crossing, **Jim Bakker** was found guilty of fraud and sent to prison. **Janis Joplin** was forced to endure the torturous teasing and disapproval of her fellow students in her conservative Port Arthur, Texas high school during her Saturn to Midheaven crossing. When Saturn passed over his Midheaven, **Bill Clinton** entered his first political race, a bid for the House of Representatives that he would eventually lose.

It should be noted that in all of these instances, the positive and negative, the judgment passed upon the subject opened the door to greater accomplishment. **Bakker** responded to the praise he received as a high school impresario by becoming one of the greatest showmen of Christian television. **Joplin** responded to the ill treatment she received at the hands of her peers by creating the tough-talking, irreverent rebel persona that would become her signature, and even though he lost the election, **Bill Clinton** established himself as an up-and-coming figure in the Democratic Party.

Sometimes the authority passing judgment on our goals and actions seems to come from a source both distant and beyond our control. **O. J. Simpson** found himself struck down with injuries early in his professional football career. **Thomas Merton**, still only a child, had to look on helplessly as his father was diagnosed with an incurable brain tumor. During his Saturn to Midheaven crossing, **Paul Gauguin** had his comfortable, middle class lifestyle ripped from beneath his feet by a sudden downturn in the French stock exchange, while young **Margaretha Zelle** (later known as **Mata Hari**) saw her happy childhood up-ended when her indulgent and free-spending father was forced into bankruptcy. All of these people had good reason to cry out, "No fair!" during this transit, but such an outcry would have been beside the point.

During such tough Saturn transits as these, what really counts is what we learn about ourselves, our strengths, our weaknesses, and our place in the world as we contend with these difficulties. This is where the judgment is really made. The suffering **Thomas Merton** endured with the early death of his father started him on a search for meaning that, after many years and a few missteps, led him to his vocation and the Catholic Church. **Paul Gauguin** responded to the crash of the stock market by devoting himself to becoming an artist. **O. J. Simpson** maintained his patience and his affable public persona and was, in time, able to achieve great things in his sport. **Margaretha Zelle**, on the other hand, may have learned some important lessons about self-reliance during her difficult Saturn transit over her Midheaven, but she obviously missed the one about the fleeting nature of material wealth.

In other cases, the judgment of Saturn comes to us through a very unlikely and even unwilling authority figure. Gianni Versace never aspired to become an important, judging personage in the life of **Andrew Cunanan,** but when he accepted the young man into his circle for a very brief period during **Cunanan's** Saturn to Midheaven passage, that's what he became. Likewise, as **Jayne Mansfield's** streetwise third husband, Matt Cimber seemed like an unlikely representative of Saturn, and yet his judgments with regard to her career and the upbringing of her children provided the actress with her last grasp at a sane existence. In both these cases, the psychological state of the subject gave the other party a level of authority and a power to judge that they otherwise would have never possessed and perhaps would have never wanted.

During its transit of the Midheaven, we expect the judgment of Saturn to relate strongly to our career and social standing, but this is not always the case. **Michael J. Fox** fell in love when Saturn crossed his Midheaven. It was only later in his life, when he was stricken with Parkinson's disease, that the strength of his companion, Nancy Pollan, would become crucial to his ability to move to a second career as an activist. The case of **Hermann Göring** presents us with another instance when love was the primary issue during a Saturn to Midheaven passage. **Göring's** affair with a Swedish countess certainly had an effect, mostly destructive, on his career aspirations, but the intense romantic attachment he displayed toward his lover was perhaps the most humanizing feature of the daring young pilot who would later become one of the most fearsome members of Adolf Hitler's inner circle.

So, which area of life is destined to be tested and judged during your next Saturn transit of the Midheaven? More than likely it will be that realm of experience in which you feel less than secure, that part of your life in which you have done the least work, made the worst choices, and have the least control. In other words, Saturn will bring its cold criticism and tough lessons to the area of your life where they are most needed. For example, **Britney Spears** entered her Saturn to Midheaven passage with expectations that her new album would become a turning point in her career. Instead, she found that the attention of the public had become much more focused on her personal life than on her music. Likewise, **Gloria Steinem** went to the National Women's Caucus during her Midheaven transit, expecting to work out a unified agenda for the liberation of women, and instead found herself battling a highly organized, highly motivated backlash to feminism from a conservative women's group.

Another person blindsided by the transit of Saturn across his Midheaven was **Bono**. He was appointed to a committee to study unemployment in Ireland during this passage. As a musician sitting at a table with a bunch of politicians, it is not likely much was expected of him, and yet **Bono** was not about to accept this inconsequential role. He derided the committee and left. Later in his life, **Bono** would find himself sitting at similar tables with similar politicians, but his role in the discussion would be far from inconsequential. It would seem that Saturn on the Midheaven is not always preparing us for the career we have right now. It may also be preparing us for the career we are going to have in the future.

It is also important to understand that even when this transit demonstrates itself in the most typical fashion, with a major triumph or accomplishment relating to your career and your self-esteem, there will also be some hard lessons to be learned. When Saturn is involved, success always brings greater responsibility, higher expectations, and more work. Being the winner can become as much a burden, as much a test and a challenge, as defeat. Even at its most positive, Saturn seldom brings us reason to celebrate. Rather, with Saturn, the victory of the moment is just a signal to prepare for new and probably tougher lessons further down the line.

26

SATURN AT WORK ON THE ASCENDANT

The things we do during this passage typically have a crucial bearing on the creation or perhaps re-creation of our self-image. At its most positive, the Saturn to Ascendant crossing marks a period during which you find and are drawn to those activities that give you the most joy, and the environments and people that make you feel most complete and fulfilled. It is as if Saturn holds up a mirror that magically reflects your highest hopes and fondest dreams for yourself, and shows you how they can be accomplished and made true. By the same token, however, that mirror can also reflect everything that is wrong and deluded about your self-image, and let you see in grim detail the true cost of the lies you tell yourself.

Among our examples, this transit coincides with many happy stories. The young **Bruce Lee** discovered kung fu and an esteemed master who could teach him its deepest secrets when Saturn crossed his Ascendant. **Lee Harvey Oswald's** mother remarried and rescued him from the orphanage during this period in his life, while **Thomas Merton** discovered the book that would eventually bring him into the Catholic Church. Likewise, **Jerry Siegel** wrote his first Superman story during this period, and **Jim Bakker** got his first crack at hosting a Christian television show. **Oprah Winfrey** found her calling when she was given her first talk show in Baltimore, and **Gloria Steinem** was feted at a huge birthday bash and fundraiser for the Ms. Foundation.

Sometimes we find our self-image at the same time we are projecting it to the public. Certainly this is what happened to **Oprah Winfrey** when she made her debut as a talk show host. This is also what happened to **Malcolm X**. Saturn passed over his Ascendant just as television was broadcasting his dark and angry message to an audience of nervous white Americans. It was an image of himself that seemed fitting, given the times and his role as a disciple of Elijah Muhammad, but it was also an image that he later sought to change.

We also have, within our group of examples, cases in which this Saturn to Ascendant passage was not so happy. It was during this passage that young **Margaretha Zelle** (**Mata Hari**) learned that her new husband valued neither her nor their marriage. This had to be a painful realization, but at the same time it was a realization that in many ways reflected Margaretha's own view of the marriage into which she had entered impulsively, mostly for the sake of being able to call herself a married woman. Likewise, we have the case of **Carl Jung**, who was forced to resume his position at Burgholzhi mental hospital during this passage. As a proud and self-confident Leo, **Jung** had assumed that the day-to-day grind of medical practice in the hospital was beneath him. By returning to this drudgery, he was forced to admit that his ability had not yet caught up to his high ambitions.

In some cases this Saturn to Ascendant crossing provides us with an opportunity at redeeming, repairing, or even redefining our self-image. During **Jim Bakker's** second Saturn to Ascendant crossing, he wrote his post-prison confessional, *I Was Wrong*, in which he tried to come to grips with the mistakes he had made as head of PTL, and the sexual abuse that had scarred him when he was a child. During this period of his life, **Michael J. Fox** resolved to stop drinking when his wife and three-year-old son discovered him passed out on the floor after a beer binge. Perhaps the most dramatic example of the redefining of a self-image during this transit is **Bill Clinton**. After entering the governor's office as the golden boy of the Democratic Party, **Clinton** proved too much in a hurry to bring reform to his home state and he made several political mistakes. When Saturn crossed his Ascendant he was voted out of the office after just one term. **Clinton** emerged from this defeat with a determination to do whatever it took to get the voters back on his side.

At other times, we are presented with an image of ourselves we would prefer to deny. **O. J. Simpson** was forced to recognize the end of his career as a football player during this passage, as a serious injury put a sudden end to his effectiveness as a runner. At the same time, **Simpson** was beginning his relationship with Nicole Brown and abandoning his marriage. When Saturn came around to **Simpson's** Ascendant a second time, his abortive attempt to make money from a hypothetical confession fell into the hands of his enemies. Likewise, **Jimmy Carter** was forced to abandon his chosen career as a naval officer and return home to Plains, Georgia to take over his father's business when his father died. **Janis Joplin** went to San Francisco seeking a career as a singer during this transit, but the image Saturn reflected back to her was that of an insecure and damaged young woman. Her attempts to cover up this self-image with tough talk and drugs derailed any opportunities she might have had to display her natural talent. And then there is the example of **Thomas Merton's** second Saturn to Ascendant transit, when he found his vow of celibacy challenged by an infatuation with a female nurse.

The key to this transit has less to do with the changes your self-image might undergo than with the way in which you deal with those changes. **Jimmy Carter** did not relish his new role as a small town businessman and peanut farmer, but he stuck with it and it became the image that he would carry into the White House. **Thomas Merton** made the difficult decision to break off his relationship with the nurse and continue his spiritual journey as a monk. **Carl Jung** used his position at Burgholzhi Hospital to further his own research, and eventually it became the place from which his career was launched. **Margaretha Zelle (Mata Hari)**, on the other hand, chose to remain in her broken marriage until it became so tragically dysfunctional that she absolutely had to leave.

In his classic text, *Astrology for the Millions*, Grant Lewi popularized the notion that the passage of Saturn across the Ascendant represented a seven-year period of obscurity. The examples present here do not confirm this notion. Certainly, for **Mata Hari**, the seven years following Saturn's crossing of her Ascendant would be characterized as obscure (she became famous just as Saturn reached her IC), but **Carl Jung** made great strides in his career during these obscure seven years, and the same could be said for most of our other examples. Perhaps the difference lies in the way in which you respond to the image of yourself that you see reflected in Saturn's uncompromising mirror. If you accept this image and are willing to acknowledge its shortcomings and correct its flaws (as we saw **Bill Clinton, Jim Bakker,** and **Michael J. Fox** do) then you need not fear any seven-year stretch of obscurity. If you do not, then obscurity may well become the least of your problems.

One thing that can be said about this transit is that we can't take for granted the success and good times it sometimes promises. Although we might feel a temporary burst of comfort and renewed self-confidence when we find Saturn reflecting back to us a self-image that we desire and want to make a part of our life, these euphoric moments will not last. We can be sure that **Jerry Siegel** felt a burst of creative joy when he and Joe Shuster created Superman, but it would be years before this brainchild would be published and he never received what he thought was adequate compensation for his new self-image as the creator of Superman. Likewise, young **Lee Harvey Oswald** was brought home from the orphanage to what would have seemed to him to have been the perfect home, with a loving mother and father, but the relationship between Oswald's mother and her new husband came to a quick and acrimonious end, a misfortune that **Oswald** resented for the rest of his life. The grand and very public birthday party thrown for **Gloria Steinem** when Saturn crossed her Ascendant might have built up her ego and let her know how many supporters her self-image as a crusader for women's rights had gained her, but these good feelings did not protect her from the decision she had to make three years later to sell *Ms.* magazine.

What this tells you is that, when Saturn crosses your Ascendant, it is not the approval or disapproval of some distant authority, or even the good graces of the fates, that matters. Unlike when Saturn crosses your Midheaven, you have no need to measure yourself against any socially sanctioned scale of accomplishment during Saturn's transit of the Ascendant. Winning, losing, success, and failure are not going to be your concerns. What matters during this transit is your ability to create an image of yourself that you can genuinely love and present to the rest of the world with pride.

27

SATURN AT WORK ON THE IMUM COELI

Since the IC represents the cusp of the 4th House of home and property, we might expect these passages to coincide with a change of residence or buying a house. In fact, only two of our examples (**Jerry Siegel** and **Jim Bakker**) were engaged in real estate transactions during their Saturn to IC crossings. Otherwise the events that coincide with this transit are extremely varied.

Some of these transits coincided with very positive events. For example, **Jayne Mansfield** got married. **Albert Einstein** became world-famous during this transit, as did **Margaretha Zelle,** who danced for the first time as **Mata Hari** and literally became an overnight sensation. **Gloria Steinem** also became famous during this transit for her article on Playboy Bunnies, and **Oprah Winfrey** was nominated for an Oscar and had her talk show go into nationwide syndication. **O. J. Simpson** was married shortly after Saturn crossed his IC and he was elected to the Football Hall of Fame.

Others examples are far less fortunate. **Carl Jung** was forced out of the Psychoanalytic Association by his erstwhile mentor, Sigmund

Freud, during his Saturn to IC transit. This break with the psychoanalytic community that had once nurtured him and accepted him as a leader sent Jung into a long period of personal reevaluation or—at least according to his detractors—outright psychosis. **Paul Gauguin** received news that his mother had died when Saturn crossed his IC. **Gauguin** had lost his father when he was still a child and his relationship with his mother was deep and complex. At the time of his mother's death **Gauguin** was only nineteen, and he was far away from home, working as a seaman on a merchant ship. His reaction to the news is unrecorded, but we can easily imagine his feelings of grief and loss.

To better understand what you might expect from this transit, it is necessary to go back to the two examples who did deal in real estate during this passage. The house that **Jerry Siegel** bought after the death of his mother was in a middle-class neighborhood in Cleveland. The youngest of six children, **Siegel** had lived with his mother until his marriage at age twenty-four, and many family members blamed **Siegel** and his marriage for his mother's sudden decline and death. By moving to a new neighborhood away from his disapproving family, **Siegel** was separating himself from a world in which he had always been seen as Mrs. Siegel's pampered and awkward youngest son. He was declaring, once and for all, his adulthood.

For **Jim Bakker**, the sale of his home represented a pact with God. **Bakker** had promised himself that if God allowed him to sell the ritzy home he had purchased with his wife, soon after he became a star on Pat Robertson's Christian Broadcasting Network, that he would leave the network. The house had long been a matter of contention between **Bakker** and his critics at the network, who saw it as evidence of the young minister's overly materialistic and lavish lifestyle. When the house finally sold, **Bakker** accepted this as a message from God telling him that it was time to go out and start his own Christian broadcasting network.

In both these examples, the transfer of property was less important than the way in which that real estate transaction represented a new start for the person involved. When Saturn crosses the IC, changes in your physical residence are far less important than changes in your attitude. House buying is not the issue. House cleaning, at a basic psychological level, is. With this transit, your old preconceptions and frames of reference are smashed, sometimes by good fortune, sometimes by ill, and you are forced to rebuild, repair, or at least rearrange your most fundamental expectations and beliefs.

When Saturn crosses the IC, even the most positive changes become wrenching. The year that **Oprah Winfrey** experienced this transit she had all the trapping of extraordinary success, but her rise to nationwide notoriety only served to make her more conscious of her excess weight. Likewise, when **Bruce Lee** landed the role of Kato in *The Green Hornet* during this transit, he was, in fact, making a huge compromise between the desire to take his martial arts skill to the widest possible audience and the odious task of portraying a stereotype. **Gloria Steinem's** sudden fame as the undercover Bunny caused her to be named in a lawsuit and cost her serious writing assignments, and **Einstein's** notoriety made him a target for Nazi repression in his native Germany.

Of course, there's an excellent chance that the event that causes you to clean your psychological house will *not* be sudden worldwide fame. For most people, the experiences of **Mansfield, Gauguin,** or **Seigel** might be a better model. Marriage, the death of a parent, moving out of your parental home, and other everyday transformations are more likely to be what you can expect when this transit comes your way. These humdrum events are just as capable of sweeping aside your useless preconceptions and out-of-date ideas as the sudden appearance of paparazzi at your front door. Saturn's work during this passage is primarily internal, and the important tests and the important choices you will experience during this transit will all be at the most personal and elemental level.

Nor are the changes you make during this transit always going to be immediately evident. Often the rearrangement of ideas and priorities this passage represents will take place at a level so deep within your psyche that it may take years to understand all of the ramifications. **Gloria Steinem** didn't understand the degree to which her experience as a Playboy Bunny moved her toward feminism until nearly twenty years after the piece was published. It took **Carl Jung** years before he accepted his exclusion from Sigmund Freud's inner circle and began expounding his own approach to psychology. Of all the Saturn transits, this is the one that goes the deepest. A full understanding of its meaning will not come quickly or easily.

As with every Saturn transit, Saturn's crossing of the IC will force you to make important decisions about your life, and the more you seek to hold on to those elements of your life that Saturn seems intent on sweeping away, the more difficult those decisions will become. **Margaretha Zelle** enjoyed her new life as an exotic dancer, but she had trouble accepting the fact that the price of becoming **Mata Hari** was her relationship with the daughter she had left in Holland. Her efforts to be reunited with her child and to once again become a mother caused the dancer immeasurable pain. Likewise, **O. J. Simpson** was no doubt glad to accept his election into the Football Hall of Fame, but the transition from being the star of the moment to being a part of history was not easy for him, and it is allegedly during this Saturn passage that he began abusing his soon-to-be wife, Nicole Brown.

On the other hand, if you are willing to accept the house cleaning that Saturn on the IC represents as good and necessary, if you are prepared to ditch the excess psychological baggage, abandon the roles and actions that no longer make any sense in your life, and put your priorities in a sane and practical order, then you can expect good things out of this transit. It is, even at its most quiet and mundane, a revolutionary passage. Handled correctly and with courage, this passage gives you a new start at living.

28

SATURN AT WORK ON THE DESCENDANT

Even though none of our examples got married during this passage (the Descendant marks the beginning of the 7th House of marriage), relationship issues are the predominant theme. As Saturn crossed his Descendant, **Bono** began dating the woman who would one day become his wife, and **Gloria Steinem** met her future husband during a Saturn to Descendant transit very late in her life. **Bill Clinton** broke up with his college girlfriend during this transit, and **Mata Hari** was forced to give up her relationship with the wealthy banker who had been supporting her for years when the unfortunate man went bankrupt. **O. J. Simpson** broke into the home of his estranged wife, Nicole, for the first time when Saturn crossed his Descendant, and **Jim Bakker** became convinced that his wife, Tammy, was having an affair with a famous gospel singer.

The relationships in question are not always romantic. It was as Saturn crossed his Descendant that **Hermann Göring** became estranged from the most important man in his life, Adolf Hitler. Likewise, **Jayne Mansfield** broke with two of the most important men in her life during this transit when she fired the agent and the publicist who were chiefly responsible for her fame. In another, very early Saturn to Descendant crossing, **Mansfield's** father died suddenly. **Thomas Merton** also lost a parent, his mother, during this transit, and **Gloria Steinem's** parents separated.

In some instances, the definition of relationships has to be expanded to include a completely new group of friends and associates. For **Oprah Winfrey,** this passage brought a whole new social world when she was transferred to a previously all-white school. Similarly, **Andrew Cunanan** was accepted at an exclusive San Diego high school, which allowed him social access to the wealthy people he so much wanted to imitate, and **Lee Harvey Oswald** was finally given the chance to live as a Communist when he was allowed to immigrate to the USSR.

Albert Einstein's Saturn to Descendant crossing demonstrates how challenging these aspects can be. During this period in his life, **Einstein** was faced with a choice between being with his pregnant fiancée and keeping alive any hope of landing a job at the Swiss patent office. Acknowledging a child conceived out of wedlock would have been seen as an unforgivable impropriety by **Einstein's** conservative Swiss employers and the job he had been promised in the patent office was his only hope of supporting a wife and family. On the other hand, the psychological damage done to his fiancée, who bore Einstein's child alone and in shame in her conservative hometown in Serbia, doomed their marriage.

Sometimes, rather than being the object of decisions made during this passage, relationships represent a catalyst for accomplishment and change. For example, when Saturn crossed **Carl Jung's** Descendant while he was still a child, he conquered his own debilitating neurosis through the exercise of his will. This feat was inspired by the concerns of his parents and his own unwillingness to remain dependent upon them. **Bruce Lee** was able to achieve great success with his marital arts films during this passage because he found that filmmakers in Hong Kong understood his concepts and were able to make and distribute the films quickly.

In some instances, it would seem that relationship issues are not the only matters of concern during this transit. Several of our examples experienced major accomplishments in other areas during their crossing. For example, **Paul Gauguin**, while still an amateur painter, had a painting accepted in the most prestigious art exhibition in France during his Saturn to Descendant transit, while **O. J. Simpson** became the star of his high school football team. **Michael J. Fox** won his first television role in Canada during this aspect, and **Britney Spears** signed a major record deal with Jive Records. **Bill Clinton** was awarded a Rhodes Scholarship under his first Saturn passage over the Descendant, and won his second term as president during the next one. But even in these examples, it is the area of relationships that is impacted. **Paul Gauguin's** success in the Salon convinced the young stockbroker that he could make a career for himself as a painter, a conviction that would later lead to the breakup of his marriage. **O. J. Simpson's** new role as a football star closed the door on his prior relationships with gangs and neighborhood thugs. Both **Fox** and **Spears** experienced a change in their relationship with their parents and elders in general once they became highly paid performers. We've already mentioned how **Bill Clinton** broke up with his girlfriend shortly before he won the Rhodes Scholarship. During his second Saturn to Descendant passage in 1996, **Clinton** broke up with another girlfriend, a young intern named Monica Lewinsky.

During this transit, new relationships and changes in your existing relationships often represent opportunities to make positive changes in your life if you are prepared to take advantage of the opening. A good example of this is **Oprah Winfrey's** transfer to a new school. For many people of this age group, such a transfer would have been a major trauma, and for an African-American going to a white school the trauma could have been much worse. On top of this, at around the same time that she started at her new school, **Winfrey** was being regularly subjected to sexual abuse at home—but the future queen of daytime TV was not deterred. She took full advantage of the educational opportunities afforded her at her new school and made friends with white classmates.

On the other hand, failing to recognize opportunities for positive change that are afforded us when our relationships change can be catastrophic. An example of this is the relationship between **Hermann Göring** and his Führer. The cooling in their relationship during Saturn's transit of **Göring's** Descendant came as **Göring** became increasingly aware of his hero's failings. If he had made the proper use of this change in their relationship, the Reich Marshall could have changed history and saved countless lives, but he didn't. Similarly, **O. J. Simpson** could have seen his first attempt at breaking into his ex-wife's home as an indicator that his obsession with her was out of hand, that he needed help. He could have taken the fact that he was never punished for the break-in as an opportunity to make a new start but, once again, this was not the choice that was made.

Even though it can represent the opportunity for positive change, the passage of Saturn across the Descendant can also be a very dangerous period. The impact of bad choices you make during this transit can be devastating—not just to yourself but also to the relationships you most value. For **Jerry Siegel**, the most important relationship in his life was the character he had created and named Superman. When he sued his publishers, he thought he was fighting to get a fair share of the profits from that remarkable character. Instead, when Saturn crossed his Descendant and the verdict came down, he learned that the lawsuit had cost him that very significant relationship. According to the terms of the settlement, **Siegel's** name was forever disassociated from that of his greatest and dearest creation.

Obviously, relationships are going to be the central issue when this transit arrives in your life. Even matters that seem totally personal and separate from your relationship will have an impact on this area. Care must be taken to protect the relationships you treasure most. You must also be aware of changes in your relationships and attuned to the opportunities the changes may provide you for personal growth. You might find it necessary to go with the flow in your relationship, and allow room in your life for relationships to develop and move to different levels. Be alert to what you can learn from other people and, more importantly, be alert to what you can learn from the way you relate to other people. Remember that finding and holding on to love and friendship are accomplishment in themselves. In fact, in some cases, these are the only accomplishments that really matter.

At the same time, you must also be aware that, during Saturn's crossing of the Descendant, relationships will become the arena in which you must expect to be tested. There will be challenges. There will be false hopes and irrational fears. There will be work that must be done. Entering this passage, it is important that you take no relationship for granted, that you have a clear idea of the value and true depth of each attachment. It is likely you will be called upon to master your feelings and deal with conflict. As always, expect Saturn to bring on tough choices and perhaps hard times. Even love is not exempted from Saturn's stern judgments.

29

SATURN CONJUNCT NATAL SATURN

This aspect occurs at least twice in the lifespan of most people: at about age twenty-eight and again around age fifty-six. The first transit is generally thought of as a time in which you are allowed, or perhaps forced, to take on the mantle of full adulthood. Among our examples we also see that it is often a passage during which we find our identity, when we settle on or discover an idea or a role in life that will become our calling card to the world. For example, **Malcolm X** was put in charge of the Black Muslim organization in Harlem. **Ralph Nader** quit his job as a small town lawyer and hitchhiked to Washington to begin his career as a consumer advocate. **Carl Jung** got his first big promotion and regular forum from which to expound on his ideas. **Oprah Winfrey** took over the *Chicago AM* talk show that would soon become *The Oprah Winfrey Show* and a worldwide phenomenon. **Bill Clinton** married Hillary Rodham, formalizing the union that would become a major force in American politics.

In all of these instances, we see a quality of youthful exuberance and budding self-confidence. These are people who are announcing themselves to the world, claiming their place, and preparing to take their first steps toward success, or at least fame. In other instances, however, this youthful enthusiasm and confidence is not so well placed. **Hermann Göring** met and was totally seduced by Adolf Hitler when this transit occurred in his horoscope. He made a decision and chose a role in life that would eventually lead him to disaster. **Jayne Mansfield** gained the dubious distinction of becoming the first major Hollywood star to perform a nude scene in a movie. For her, this transit came after her career was already well underway, and her decision to perform the scene only solidified **Mansfield's** public image as a cheap sex symbol. During his first Saturn to Saturn conjunction, **Jerry Siegel** made the ultimately disastrous decision to sue his publisher with the dubious assistance of an attorney he had met while in the army.

Sometimes what we discover during this passage is not thrilling. Sometimes it tells us more about our limitations in this life than our accomplishments. It was during this transit that **Michael J. Fox** began experiencing the first symptoms of Parkinson's disease. **Bruce Lee** learned that even his highly trained body was subject to physical limitations when he suffered a major injury to his back during his Saturn to Saturn conjunction. During her Saturn to Saturn conjunction, **Margaretha Zelle** discovered that even though dancing as **Mata Hari** had made her instantly famous and relatively wealthy, her triumph put her at a distinct disadvantage when her husband filed for divorce and deprived her of the right to visit her daughter.

What these examples show is that during your first Saturn return you can expect the call to grow up, take on the work or the role that will occupy your adult life, and face the limitations and problems that will define you as a person. It is a transit that is generally characterized by hard work, hard choices, and fateful decisions. Doors may be opened for you during this return, but these opportunities always come with heavy responsibilities and far-reaching implications. No Saturn transit should be taken lightly, but this one is particularly weighty. Missteps here almost always have major ramifications later on in life. Bad ideas take on an energy and momentum that is very hard to correct. At the same time, you have to be willing and ready to take advantage of opportunities that come to you during this transit, even the ones that at first glance don't seem all that promising or attractive. Small starts and incremental changes made during this transit have a way of becoming extremely significant as your life moves forward.

The second Saturn return, which occurs when the subject is about age fifty-six, is somewhat different. The circumstances of your life are not the same as during the first Saturn return. The major choices have already been made and your role in life either fulfilled or at least attempted. For this reason, this transit will often be a more personal, contemplative passage—a time to look back at your life and assess your accomplishments and mistakes.

At its best, this second Saturn return can become a time to revive and renew the identity you have created for yourself in the world. It gives you a chance to apply the wisdom and maturity you have gained since your first Saturn return, and to improve upon the choices and decisions you made in your youth. At its very best, it becomes a time during which you can redefine yourself and set off on a new and more fulfilling course in your life. **Jimmy Carter** did this after his disappointing presidency when he started his Carter Center during this passage. **Jim Bakker** remarried during his second Saturn return. In both of these cases, we see not only a new start being made, but also a search for redemption, a decision to put aside the mistakes and misjudgments of the past.

Of course, not all our examples are so hopeful. **O. J. Simpson** came up with the idea for his notorious hypothetical confession during this passage. He made a proposal to write a book and do a television special in which he was to give details of how the murder of his wife would have been carried out, if he had in fact committed the crime, a decision that did little to change the identity he had gained in the public eye as a cold-blooded killer.

As these latter examples indicate, this second Saturn return cannot be taken lightly. The changes taking place in your life during this passage must be viewed with due consideration and concern even when they seem more personal and are not so visible to the world. You can redefine yourself during this transit. You can find redemption and a sense of completion, but you must also recognize the possibility of making the wrong choice or perpetuating bad choices made in the past even more apparent. Also, you have to be aware that this crossing can bring you new challenges and new tests that can make this second Saturn return just as hard and laborious as the first so often is.

30

SATURN OPPOSED NATAL SATURN

Most of you can expect to experience this Saturn passage three times in your lives: at age fourteen, age forty-two, and age seventy. It is the first one that seems to cause most people trouble. Coming in the midst of the physical and emotional tumult of adolescence, it leaves few of us unscathed. Some of our examples suffered misfortunes far beyond the natural curse of adolescence during this period. **Thomas Merton's** father was diagnosed with a brain tumor. **Bono's** mother died suddenly of a brain hemorrhage. **Jerry Siegel's** father was shot and killed. **Margaretha Zelle's** parents were divorced. **Paul Gauguin** saw the role of his father, who by this time was long dead, taken over in an unofficial way by a wealthy Spanish businessman who became his mother's secret benefactor and probably her lover. **Janis Joplin** was transformed from a happy, freckle-faced child into a tormented outcast.

Of course, there are also happier stories. **Oprah Winfrey** won a college scholarship during this transit. **Britney Spears** spent her Saturn opposed Saturn passage feverishly promoting her first album. **Gloria Steinem** was making a splash at her new high school. But even these happy stories have a dark undercurrent. **Winfrey's** success came after years of sexual abuse and hardship. **Spears**' hard work would soon pay off in terms of record sales and fame, but the cost was her childhood. At the same time **Steinem** was impressing the girls at the high school with her wit and good looks, she was also busy dealing with a mentally ill mother and a rat-infested home.

Coming at about age forty-two, the second Saturn opposed Saturn passage typically coincides with what most people consider to be the prime years of their lives. The deterioration of old age has not yet arrived and the ignorance of youth has, hopefully, departed. Despite this fact, the second opposition of Saturn to its natal place can be just as traumatic and difficult as the first almost always is. In many of our examples it seems to bring trouble and worry and challenges. Nicole Simpson filed for a divorce from **O. J. Simpson** during his second Saturn opposition. **Albert Einstein** was confronted with proof of how dangerous it was to be a famous Jew in 1920s Germany when he learned that a prominent Jewish politician had been assassinated. **Michael J. Fox** testified before Congress in opposition to George Bush's limitation on stem-cell research and brought upon himself the ire of right-to-life extremists.

There are, of course, happier scenarios. **Paul Gauguin** moved away from the European conclave in Tahiti during his second opposition of Saturn to its natal place, and enjoyed a very pleasant and productive time among the more primitive natives of the island. **Bill Clinton** announced his candidacy for president of the United States and **Jerry Siegel** was persuaded by his wife to put aside his pride and his animosity toward the publishers of Superman and take a job as a writer for the series. In each of these cases, however, the positive nature of the event was shadowed by darker implications. **Gauguin's** joyful period among the natives only served to further alienate him from the Europeans on the island. Perhaps more importantly, this period cemented the painter's unsavory fondness for very young paramours. **Bill Clinton** entered the race for president with the knowledge that his past indiscretions with women would, at some point, be brought to light by the national press. **Jerry Siegel** used the money he earned during his second, uncredited stint as Superman's writer to finance a second ill-advised lawsuit against his bosses.

We have no examples involving the third and last Saturn opposed Saturn transit. This passage typically comes to us in our retirement, when changes in our lives are less public and more incremental. Generally, though, this transit would seem to be a period of woe in which even positive events can take on dangerous implications.

Of course, this is not exactly the case. The reason Saturn's opposition to its natal place often seems so hard on you is because the choices and challenges it brings come with so much extra baggage. In adolescence, you face these hard decisions at the same time that you are dealing with major changes in your physical body. During the second opposition, it is the weight of decisions and mistakes you have already made and committed that weigh you down. Unlike the conjunction of Saturn to its natal place, the opposition does not represent a fresh start. Instead it represents a turning point and a moment of decision in the ongoing issues that dominate our lives. It is the point where you see the fruition of your past efforts as well as your past failures. For that reason, this can often be the most complex and delicate Saturn passage you will face.

Perhaps the wisest course we can take during this passage is the one **Gloria Steinem** attempted. During her second Saturn opposed Saturn transit, she got a fellowship that allowed her to take a year off to write. In **Steinem's** case, this period of reflection was constantly interrupted by her obligations to *Ms.* magazine, feminism, and other social causes, but the desire she expressed to take a break from her hectic lifestyle may be your key to handling these troublesome transits. Instead of entering these passages with all engines burning, intent on adding to your accomplishments or making up for lost time, perhaps you should use this transit as a time of contemplation and evaluation. Perhaps the challenges Saturn brings you during its opposition to its natal place is the challenge to sit still for a while. Obviously sitting still is not a cure for the raging hormones of fourteen or the heavy responsibilities of forty-two, but neither is spinning your wheels as you try to grow up too fast, or indulging yourself with a midlife crisis. Knowing where you are and understanding what you want are achievements in themselves, and taking a moment or a week or a month or even a year to work on these insights is always worthwhile.

31

SATURN SQUARE NATAL SATURN

The first thing that needs to be understood about the square of transiting Saturn to its own place in the horoscope is that it happens more frequently than any other Saturn transit. For each Saturn return and each Saturn opposition you will experience, you will pass through two Saturn squares. Saturn squares natal Saturn every fourteen years, starting at age seven, which means that, if you live to be eighty years old, you will experience six of them. This is why it is so crucial that you learn how to deal with this transit.

We know that the first such square occurs at about age seven, when the child begins a variety of important physical, psychological, and social changes as she or he moves from the total dependency of infancy to the beginning of autonomy. Of course, not everyone gets off that easily with this passage. It was at this point in her young life that **Oprah Winfrey** made a fateful decision to stay with her mother in Milwaukee, while **Gloria Steinem** was under this aspect when she was forced to take on the role of caregiver for her mentally ill mother.

This second Saturn square, occurring at age twenty-one, the age when one becomes an adult in many legal definitions of the word, is often signified by important and highly visible changes. **Bono, Britney Spears, Jim Bakker**, and **Lee Harvey Oswald** all got married during this particular Saturn passage, and **Gloria Steinem** began dating a man who would later become her fiancé. **Jerry Siegel** received word that Detective Comics wanted to buy the Superman strip he and Joe Shuster had created. **Jayne Mansfield** met the publicist who would initiate her all-out assault on Hollywood. Of course, as with any Saturn transit, there are also much less happy tales to tell. **O. J. Simpson** suffered the first real setback in his athletic career when he was drafted by a team that had little interest in using his running ability, and **Bill Clinton** was struggling with a draft of a very different kind as he weighed his options in the face of the Vietnam War.

Later Saturn squares are more varied and far less predictable. For example, **Bill Clinton** won his spectacular comeback bid for governor of Arkansas during one of his later Saturn square Saturn passages. By the time the next one came along, **President Clinton** was waiting to see if Congress would vote to impeach him. Likewise, **Jim Bakker** took complete control of the PTL Christian Network during his age thirty-five Saturn square. When the next one came along, he was on his way to prison. Like Clinton, **Hermann Göring** also won an electoral victory during his mid-thirties square, when the Nazi Party rose from nowhere to become the second-most powerful group in the German parliament. Then, under a later Saturn square, **Göring** surrendered to the United States after Germany's defeat in World War II, only to find out that instead of being treated as a head of state he was going to be tried as a criminal.

As these examples illustrate, the reason that the influence of the Saturn square Saturn is so varied is because, like the opposition, it is typically part of an ongoing process. What happens to you during your Saturn squares, particularly the later ones, is a direct result of choices you have made and work you have undertaken during previous Saturn passages. Very often the Saturn square represents the next step, the inevitable outcome, the dropping of the other shoe. Even though events coinciding with the transit may be dramatic, they represent the completion of a process that was already underway.

In other instances, efforts may be started under a Saturn square, but they usually reflect long-standing interests and ambitions. Also this start is made in a limited way or on a small scale, although what is started under this aspect often grows into something of major consequence. For example, **Jimmy Carter** engaged in his first political battle during a Saturn square. As a part of the local school board, he took on a segregationist in his district and lost. Fourteen years later, under another Saturn square, **Carter's** long-standing political ambitions were realized when he won the Iowa caucuses and established himself as the frontrunner for the 1976 Democratic presidential nomination. Another example is **Carl Jung**. During his age twenty-one Saturn square, he experimented with spiritualism, using his teenage cousin as a medium. During his next Saturn square, **Jung** was using insights gained during these sessions as he forged a new, more spiritual approach to psychoanalysis.

It is easy to think of Saturn squares as little stepping stones in Saturn's grand journey, but don't underestimate their importance. Just like any Saturn passage, the square to its natal place will become a test. When **Jimmy Carter** tried to push his school district toward integration he was making a very hard choice between the demands of his conscience and his standing as a businessman and leader within the community, and when **Carl Jung** encouraged his cousin to act as medium for his scientific investigations, he was placing both the mental health of the girl and his standing within his family at risk. There is no such thing as a Saturn transit that lets you off easy. They all call for your best effort and your deepest wisdom.

APPENDIX

Abbreviated Ephemeris for Saturn 1990–2020

1990

Jan.—16 ♑
Feb.—19 ♑
Mar.—22 ♑
Apr.—24 ♑
May—25 ♑
S℞ May 5 at 25♑20
June—25 ♑
July—23 ♑
Aug.—20 ♑
Sept.—19 ♑
SD Sept 25 at 18♑42
Oct.—18 ♑
Nov.—20 ♑
Dec.—22 ♑

1991

Jan.—26 ♑
Feb.—29 ♑
Mar.—2 ♒
Apr.—5 ♒
May—6 ♒
S℞ May 17 at 6♒50
June—6 ♒℞
July—5 ♒℞
Aug.—3 ♒℞
Sept.—1 ♒℞
Oct.—0 ♒℞
SD Oct. 6 at 0♒11
Nov.—1 ♒
Dec.—3 ♒

1992
Jan.—6♒
Feb.—9♒
Mar.—13♒
Apr.—16♒
May—18♒
S℞May 30 at 18♒29
June—18♒℞
July—17♒℞
Aug.—15♒℞
Sept.—13
Oct.—12♒℞
SD Oct. 17 at 11♒49
Nov.—12♒
Dec.—13♒

1993
Jan.—16♒
Feb.—20♒
Mar.—23♒
Apr.—26♒
May—29♒
June—0♓
S℞June 12 at 0♓19
July—0♓℞
Aug.—28♒℞
Sept.—26♒℞
Oct.—24♒℞
SD Oct. 30 at 23♒38
Oct.—23♒
Nov.—24♒
Dec.—24♒

1994
Jan.—27♒
Feb.—0♓
Mar.—4♓
Apr.—7♓
May—10♓
June—12♓
S℞June 25 at 12♓3
July—12♓℞
Aug.—11♓℞
Sept.—9♓℞
Oct.—7♓℞
Nov.—5♓℞
SD Nov. 9 at 5♓40
Dec.—6♓

1995
Jan.—8♓
Feb.—11♓
Mar.—14♓
Apr.—18♓
May—21♓
June—24♓
July—24♓
S℞July 7 at 24♓45
Aug.—24♓℞
Sept.—22♓℞
Oct.—20♓℞
Nov.—18♓℞
SD Nov. 24 at 17♓59
Dec.—18♓

1996
Jan.—19♓
Feb.—21♓
Mar.—25♓
Apr.—29♓
May—2♈
June—5♈
July—6♈
S℞ July 20 at 7♈23
Aug.—7♈℞
Sept.—5♈℞
Oct.—3♈℞
Nov.—1♈℞
Dec.—0♈℞
SD Dec. 5 at 0♈ 36

1997
Jan.—1♈
Feb.—3♈
Mar.—6♈
Apr.—10♈
May—14♈
June—17♈
July—19♈
Aug.—20♈
S℞ Aug.3 at 20♈21
Sept.—19♈℞
Oct.—17♈℞
Nov.—15♈℞
Dec.—13♈℞
SD Dec. 18 at 13♈32

1998
Jan.—14♈
Feb.—15♈
Mar.—18♈
Apr.—22♈
May—25♈
June—29♈
July—2♉
Aug.—3♉
S℞ Aug. 17 at 3♉37
Sept.—2♉℞
Oct.—1♉℞
Nov.—29♈℞
Dec.—27♈℞
SR Dec. 31 at 26♈46

1999
Jan.—26♈
Feb.—27♈
Mar.—0♉
Apr.—3♉
May—7♉
June—11♉
July—14♉
Aug.—16♉
Sept.—17♉
S℞ Sept. 2 at 17♉10
Oct.—16♉℞
Nov.—14♉℞
Dec.—12♉℞

2000
Jan.—10♉℞
SD Jan. 12 at 10♉17
Feb.—10♉
Mar.—12♉
Apr.—15♉
May—19♉
June—23♉
July—27♉
Aug.—29♉
Sept.—1♊
S℞Sept. 13 at 0♊59
Oct.—0♊℞
Nov.—29♉℞
Dec.—26♉℞

2001
Jan.—24♉
Feb.—24♉
Mar.—25♉
Apr.—28♉
May—1♊
June—5♊
July—9♊
Aug—12♊
Sept.—14♊
S℞Sept. 27 at 14♊58
Oct.—15♊℞
Nov.—15♊℞
Dec.—11♊℞

2002
Jan.—9♊℞
Feb.—8♊℞
SD Feb. 8 at 8♊02
Mar.—8♊
Apr.—10♊
May—13♊
June—17♊
July—21♊
Aug.—25♊
Sept.—27♊
Oct.—29♊
S℞Oct. 11 at 29♊05
Nov.—28♊℞
Dec.—26♊℞

2003
Jan.—24♊℞
Feb.—22♊℞
SD Feb. 22 at 22♊08
Mar.—22♊
Apr.—23♊
May—26♊
June—29♊
July—3♋
Aug.—7♋
Sept.—10♋
Oct.—12♋
S℞Oct. 25 at 13♋14
Nov.—13♋℞
Dec.—11♋℞

2004

Jan.—9♋℞
Feb.—7♋℞
Mar.—6♋℞
SD Mar.7 at 6♋17
Apr.—7♋
May—9♋
June—12♋
July—16♋
Aug.—19♋
Sept.—23♋
Oct.—26♋
Nov.—27♋
S℞Nov. 8 at 27♋20
Dec.—26♋℞

2005

Jan.—24♋℞
Feb.—22♋℞
Mar.—20♋℞
SD Mar. 22 at 20♋23
Apr.—20♋
May—22♋
June—25♋
July—28♋
Aug.—2♌
Sept.—6♌
Oct.—9♌
Nov.—11♌
S℞Nov. 22 at 11♌18
Dec.—11♌℞

2006

Jan.—10♌℞
Feb.—7♌℞
Mar.—5♌℞
Apr.—4♌℞
SD Apr. 4 at 4♌22
May—5♌
June—7♌
July—10♌
Aug.—14♌
Sept.—18♌
Oct.—21♌
Nov.—23♌
Dec.—25♌
S℞Dec. 6 at 25♌04

2007

Jan.—24♌℞
Feb.—22♌℞
Mar.—20♌℞
Apr.—18♌
SD Apr. 19 at 18♌09
May—18♌
June—19♌
July—22♌
Aug.—25♌
Sept.—0♍
Oct.—3♍
Nov.—6♍
Dec.—8♍
S℞Dec. 19 at 8♍34

2008

Jan.—8♍℞
Feb.—6♍℞
Mar.—4♍℞
Apr.—2♍℞
May—1♍℞
SD May 3 at 1♍40
June—2♍
July—4♍
Aug.—7♍
Sept.—11♍
Oct.—15♍
Nov.—18♍
Dec.—20♍
Dec. 31 at 21♍46

2009

Jan.—21♍℞
Feb.—20♍℞
Mar.—19♍℞
Apr.—16♍℞
May—15♍℞
S℞May 17 at 14♍54
June—15♍
July—16♍
Aug.—19♍
Sept.—23♍
Oct.—26♍
Nov.—0♎
Dec.—3♎

2010

Jan.—4♎
S℞ Jan. 13 at 4♎39
Feb.—4♎
Mar.—2♎
Apr.—0♎
May—28♍
SD May 30 at 27♍50
June—27♍
July—28♍
Aug.—0♎
Sept.—4♎
Oct.—7♎
Nov.—11♎
Dec.—14♎

2011

Jan.—16♎
S℞Jan. 26 at 17♎13
Mar.—16♎℞
Apr.—14♎℞
May—12♎℞
June—10♎℞
SD June 13 at 10♎26
July—10♎
Aug.—12♎
Sept.—15♎
Oct.—18♎
Nov.—22♎
Dec.—25♎

2012

Jan.—28♎
Feb.—29♎
S℞Feb. 7 29♎30
Mar.—29♎℞
Apr.—27♎℞
May—25♎℞
June—23♎℞
SD June 25 at 22♎45
July—22♎
Aug.—24♎
Sept.—26♎
Oct.—29♎
Nov.—3♏
Dec.—6♏

2013

Jan.—9♏
Feb.—11♏
S℞Feb. 18 at 11♏31
Mar.—11♏℞
Apr.—10♏℞
May—8♏℞
June—6♏℞
July—4♏℞
SD July 8 at 4♏49
Aug.—5♏
Sept.—7♏
Oct.—10♏
Nov.—13♏
Dec.—17♏

2014

Jan.—20♏
Feb.—22♏
Mar.—23♏
S℞Mar. 2 at 23♏19
Apr.—22♏℞
May—20♏℞
June—18♏℞
July—17♏℞
SD July 20 at 16♏38
Aug.—16♏
Sept.—18♏
Oct.—20♏
Nov.—24♏
Dec.—27♏

2015

Jan.—1♐
Feb.—3♐
Mar.—4♐
S℞Mar. 14 at 4♐55
Apr.—4♐℞
May—3♐℞
June—1♐℞
July—29♏℞
Aug.—28♏℞
SD Aug. 2 at 28♏17
Sept.—29♏
Oct.—1♐
Nov.—4♐
Dec.—7♐

2016
Jan.—11♐
Feb.—14♐
Mar.—16♐
S℞Mar. 25 at 16♐24
Apr.—16♐℞
May—15♐℞
June—13♐℞
July—11♐℞
Aug.—9♐℞
SD Aug. 13 at 9♐49
Sept.—10♐
Oct.—11♐
Nov.—14♐
Dec.—17♐

2017
Jan.—21♐
Feb.—24♐
Mar.—26♐
Apr.—27♐
S℞Apr. 6 at 27♐47
May 27♐℞
June 25♐℞
July 23♐℞
Aug.—21♐℞
SD Aug. 24 at 21♐10
Sept.—21♐
Oct.—22♐
Nov.—24♐
Dec.—27♐

2018
Jan. 1♑
Feb. 5♑
Mar. 7♑
Apr.—8♑
S℞Apr. 18 at 9♑08
May—9♑℞
June—7♑℞
July—5♑℞
Aug.—3♑℞
Sept.—2♑℞
SD Sept. 6 at 2♑32
Oct.—3♑
Nov.—5♑
Dec.—8♑

2019
Jan.—11♑
Feb.—15♑
Mar.—17♑
Apr.—19♑
S℞Apr. 10 at 24♑21
May—20♑℞
June—19♑℞
July—17♑℞
Aug.—15♑℞
Sept.—14♑℞
SD Sept. 18 at 13♑54
Oct.—14♑
Nov.—15♑
Dec.—18♑

2020

    Jan.—21 ♑

    Feb.—25 ♑

    Mar.—28 ♑

    Apr.—0 ♒

    May—1 ♒

    S℞ May 11 at 1 ♒ 57

    June—1 ♒ ℞

    July—29 ♑ ℞

    Aug.—27 ♑ ℞

    Sept.—25 ♑ ℞

    SD Sept. 13 at 25 ♑ 32

    Oct.—25 ♑

    Nov.—26 ♑

    Dec.—28 ♑

BIBLIOGRAPHY

Amburn, Ellis. *Pearl: The Obsessions and Passions of Janis Joplin*. New York: Warner Books, 1992.

Bair, Deirdre. *Jung: A Biography.* Boston: Little Brown, 2003.

Bakker, Jim, with Ken Abraham. *I Was Wrong.* Nashville, TN: Thomas Nelson, 1996.

Bentley, Toni. *Sister of Salome*. New Haven, CT: Yale University, 2002.

Brown, Kevin. *Malcolm X: His Life and Legacy*. Brookfield, CT: Millbrook, 1995.

Buckhorn, Robert F. *Nader: The People's Lawyer.* Englewood Cliffs, NJ: Prentice-Hall, 1972.

Chunovic, Louis. *Bruce Lee: The Tao of the Dragon Warrior.* New York: St. Martin's Griffin, 1996.

Crowley, Evelyn. "Gloria Excelsis: Flashback Gloria Steinem," *W* 35.6 (June 2006): 32.

Dalai Lama XIV. *Freedom in Exile: The Autobiography of the Dalai Lama*. New York: Harper Collins, 1990.

Davis, Don. *Fallen Hero*. New York: St. Martin's, 1994.

DeCaro, Louis A. *On the Side of My People: A Religious Life of Malcolm X*. New York: New York University, 1996.

Echols, Alice. *Scars of Sweet Paradise: The Life and Times of Janis Joplin*. New York: Henry Holt, 1999.

Fenjves, Pablo, with O. J. Simpson. *If I Did It: Confession of the Killer*. New York: Beauford Books, 2006.

Fox, Michael J. *Lucky Man: A Memoir*. New York: Hyperion, 2002.

Gold, Todd. "A Summer Surprise: Britney Spears and Fiancé, Kevin Federline, Talk About the Ring, the Proposal and the Need to Nest," *People Weekly* 62:2 (July 12, 2004): 52.

Hamilton, Nigel. *Bill Clinton: Mastering the Presidency*. New York: BBS Public Affairs, 2007.

Harris, Jennifer, and Elwood Watson, editors. *The Oprah Phenomenon*, Lexington, KY: University Press of Kentucky, 2007.

Harvey, Mary. "Women Investors Take Back *Ms*." *Folio: The Magazine for Magazine Management* 28.1 (January, 1999): 12.

Heilbrun, Carolyn G. *The Education of a Woman: The Life of Gloria Steinem*. New York: Dial Press, 1995.

Helliger, Jeremy. "A Major Minor: Singer Britney Spears, 17, Flexes Her Muscles in the Booming Teen Music Market." *People Weekly* 51:6 (February 15, 1999): 71.

Higgins, Michael W. *Heretic Blood: The Spiritual Geography of Thomas Merton*. New York: Stoddart Publishing, 1998.

Howe, Russell Warren. *Mata Hari: The True Story*. New York: Dodd, Mead, 1986.

Irving, David. *Göring: A Biography*. New York: Wm. Morrow, 1989.

Isaacson, Walter. *Einstein: His Life and Universe*. New York: Simon & Schuster, 2007.

Johnson, Haynes. *The Best of Times: America in the Clinton Years*, New York: Harcourt, 2001.

Jones, Gerard. *Men of Tomorrow: Geek, Gangsters and the Birth of the Comic Book*. New York: Basic Books, 2004.

Jung, C. G., recorded and edited by Aniela Jaffe. *Memories, Dreams, Reflection.* New York: Vintage Books, NY, 1989.

"Kissing Madonna Upstages MTV Awards." *Broadcasting and Cable* 133.35 (September 1, 2003): 2.

Krohn, Katherine. *Oprah Winfrey*, Minneapolis: Lerner, 2005.

Larkin, Michael. "Parkinson's Disease Research Grant Available." *The Lancet* 360.9332 (August 17, 2002).

Maraniss, David. *First in His Class: A Biography of Bill Clinton.* New York: Simon & Schuster, 1995.

Martin, Justin. *Nader: Crusader, Spoiler, Icon.* Cambridge, MA: Perseus, 2002.

Maryles, Daisy. "'Lucky Man,' Says He." *Publishers Weekly* 249.15 (April 15, 2002).

Mazlish, Bruce, and Edwin Diamond. *Jimmy Carter: A Character Portrait.* New York: Simon & Schuster, 1979.

Morris, Kenneth E. *Jimmy Carter: American Moralist.* Athens GA: University of Georgia, 1996.

Munro, Neil. "Cloning Begets Diverse Factions." *National Journal* 34.17 (April 27, 2002).

O'Leary, Kevin. "How Did This Happen?" *Us Magazine* 668:52 (December 3, 2007).

Orth, Maureen. *Vulgar Favors: Andrew Cunanan, Gianni Versace and the Largest Failed Manhunt in U.S. History.* New York: Delacorte, 1999.

Posner, Gerald. *Case Closed: Lee Harvey Oswald and the Assassination of JFK.* New York: Random House, 1995.

Robbins, Sarah. "A Look Back With Oprah." *Shape* 25.8 (April 2006): 32.

Russell, Lisa. "Oprah Winfrey: Issues and Answers? She Gives Voice to Both." *People Weekly* (March 15, 1999): 143.

Saxton, Martha. *Jayne Mansfield and the American Fifties.* Boston: Houghton Mifflin, 1975.

Shepard, Charles. *Forgiven: The Rise and Fall of Jim Bakker and the PTL Ministry.* New York: Atlantic Monthly Press, 1989.

Spears, Britney and Lynn Spears. *Britney Spears' Heart to Heart.* New York: Three Rivers, 2000.

Stern, Sydney Ladensohn. *Gloria Steinem: Her Passion, Politics, and Mystique.* Secaucus, NJ: Carol Publishing Group, 1997.

———. "After Insisting She Wasn't the Marrying Kind Feminism's Golden Girl Finally Took the Plunge." *People Weekly* 54.27 (December 25, 2000): 68.

Sweetman, David. *Paul Gauguin: A Life.* New York: Simon & Schuster, 1995.

Tagliaferro, Linda. *Bruce Lee.* Minneapolis, MN: Lerner, 2000.

Tyrangiel, Josh. "Constant Charmer, The Inside Story of How the World's Biggest Rock Star Mastered the Political Game and Persuaded the World's Leaders to Take on Global Poverty; And He's Not Done Yet," *Time* (December 26, 2005): 46.

Wall, Mick. *Bono: In the Name of Love.* London: Seven Oaks, 2005.

———. "Bono's Campaign for Africa: After Years of Lobbying the Rock Star Helps Rid the Continent of More Than $40 Billion in Debt." *People Weekly* 63.23 (June 27, 2005): 54.

Wheelwright, Julia. *The Fatal Lover: Mata Hari and the Myth of Women in Espionage.* London: Collins & Brown, 1992.

Yuan, Jada. "Bullying Rush OK With Fox: Helps Stems." *New York* 39.42 (November 27, 2006).

Zackheim, Michele. *Einstein's Daughter: The Search for Lieserl.* New York: Riverhead Books, 1994.

Free Catalog

Get the latest information on our body, mind, and spirit products! To receive a **free** copy of Llewellyn's consumer catalog, *New Worlds of Mind & Spirit,* simply call 1-877-NEW-WRLD or visit our website at www.llewellyn.com and click on *New Worlds.*

LLEWELLYN ORDERING INFORMATION

Order Online:
Visit our website at www.llewellyn.com, select your books, and order them on our secure server.

Order by Phone:
- Call toll-free within the U.S. at 1-877-NEW-WRLD (1-877-639-9753). Call toll-free within Canada at 1-866-NEW-WRLD (1-866-639-9753)
- We accept VISA, MasterCard, and American Express

Order by Mail:
Send the full price of your order (MN residents add 6.5% sales tax) in U.S. funds, plus postage & handling to:

> Llewellyn Worldwide
> 2143 Wooddale Drive, Dept. 978-0-7387-1493-6
> Woodbury, MN 55125-2989

Postage & Handling:

Standard (U.S., Mexico, & Canada). If your order is:
  $24.99 and under, add $3.00
  $25.00 and over, FREE STANDARD SHIPPING

AK, HI, PR: $15.00 for one book plus $1.00 for each additional book.

International Orders (airmail only):
  $16.00 for one book plus $3.00 for each additional book

Orders are processed within 2 business days.
Please allow for normal shipping time. Postage and handling rates subject to change.

All Around the Zodiac
Exploring Astrology's Twelve Signs

Bil Tierney

A fresh, in-depth perspective on the zodiac you thought you knew. This book provides a revealing new look at the astrological signs, from Aries to Pisces. Gain a deeper understanding of how each sign motivates you to grow and evolve in consciousness. How does Aries work with Pisces? What does Gemini share in common with Scorpio? *All Around the Zodiac* is the only book on the market to explore these sign combinations to such a degree.

Not your typical Sun sign guide, this book is broken into three parts. Part 1 defines the signs, part 2 analyzes the expression of sixty-six pairs of signs, and part 3 designates the expression of the planets and houses in the signs.

978-0-7387-0111-0, 480 pp., 6 x 9 $21.95

To order, call 1-877-NEW-WRLD
Prices subject to change without notice
Order at Llewellyn.com 24 hours a day, 7 days a week!

Cosmic Karma
Understanding Your Contract with the Universe

MARGUERITE MANNING

Marguerite Manning invites you on a spirited ride through the stars to see your soul's evolutionary journey. Based on astrology, *Cosmic Karma* can help you navigate the karmic crossroads and gain fresh insights into your soul's spiritual agenda.

Where has your soul been and what are your karmic obligations in this lifetime? All the answers are in a celestial map of planetary energies—your birth chart. The Sun's house will help you figure out your "cosmic calling"—what you're meant to accomplish, while Saturn, the humorless taskmaster, reveals karmic lessons you need to learn. Lastly, peek inside the forbidding and intoxicating twelfth house—where you can explore precious experiences, painful memories, and all your past deeds.

978-0-7387-1054-9, 216 pp., 7 x 7 $15.95

To order, call 1-877-NEW-WRLD
Prices subject to change without notice
Order at Llewellyn.com 24 hours a day, 7 days a week!

Cycles of Life
Understanding the Principles of Predictive Astrology

Rod Suskin
Foreword by Noel Tyl

Change is an inevitable part of life. Major life changes can propel us toward exciting growth or painful setbacks. Astrologer Rod Suskin provides a cosmic roadmap that predicts these developmental phases and offers advice for using these times to our advantage.

Cycles of Life describes how the planets are implicitly connected to important transitions in our lives. Easy-to-follow tables and worksheets help readers track planetary cycles and interpret the results. From there, individuals can gain a new understanding of the past and begin preparing for future life changes. The author also shares how the planets affect many aspects of life, including relationships, money management, business, and daily living.

978-0-7387-0659-7, 264 pp., 6 x 9 — $16.95

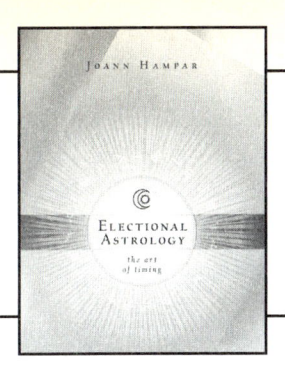

Electional Astrology
The Art of Timing

JOANN HAMPAR

Planning a wedding? Scheduling surgery? Buying a house? How do you choose a date and time that offers the best chance of success? The odds are in your favor when you plan life events using electional astrology—a branch of astrology that helps you align with the power of the universe.

Professional astrologer Joann Hampar teaches the principles of electional astrology—explaining the significance of each planet and how to time events according to their cycles. Readers will learn how to analyze the planetary alignments and compile an electional chart that pinpoints the optimal time to buy a diamond ring, adopt a pet, close a business deal, take a trip, move, file an insurance claim, take an exam, schedule a job interview, and just about anything else!

978-0-7387-0701-3, 216 pp., 6 x 9 $14.95

To order, call 1-877-NEW-WRLD
Prices subject to change without notice
Order at Llewellyn.com 24 hours a day, 7 days a week!

Identifying Planetary Triggers
Astrological Techniques for Prediction

CELESTE TEAL

This technical approach to prediction is for intermediate and advanced astrologers who want to build upon the themes in progressed charts using planetary return charts, transiting aspects, and other little-known but extremely accurate secrets.

One chapter is devoted to each planetary return, from the Moon through Saturn, where chart illustrations and commentary lead you step by step through the process. Learn various calculation techniques of the returns, such as whether or not to precess a chart and what the underlying difference is. Several special charts are introduced, including the Anlunar, Sunrise chart, and Diurnal chart.

What's more, the classic reference on transits by Dr. Heber Smith is reprinted in its original form, instilling an understanding of how the transiting planets function. The significance of the nodes of the moon, their transits, and aspects are followed by a table of the nodal positions from 1935 to 2054.

978-1-56718-705-2, 384 pp., 7½ x 9⅛ $17.95

To order, call 1-877-NEW-WRLD
Prices subject to change without notice
Order at Llewellyn.com 24 hours a day, 7 days a week!

Lunar Nodes
Discover Your Soul's Karmic Mission

Celeste Teal

Are you an old soul or a young soul? Will this life be filled with cosmic blessings or karmic sacrifices? The story of your evolving soul—through the past, present, and future—can be read in your lunar nodes.

No other book on the market offers such in-depth information on the lunar nodes—the points where the moon's orbit crosses the sun's path. Nationally-renowned astrologer Celeste Teal explores numerous ways to interpret the north and south nodes—in relation to houses, ruling planets, aspects, signs, the Part of Fortune, the Vertex, and more—in the natal chart. As your karmic path is revealed, you'll learn which personality traits to leave behind, where spiritual growth is needed, and where opportunity for rewards may be found. This comprehensive guide will also help you gain insights into relationships, make predictions, and understand how fate may be impacting your life.

978-0-7387-1337-3, 240 pp., 7½ x 9⅛ $27.95

To order, call 1-877-NEW-WRLD
Prices subject to change without notice
Order at Llewellyn.com 24 hours a day, 7 days a week!

Mapping Your Soul's Purpose
Discover Your Karma & Destiny

ANNE WINDSOR

As we ride the soul train from life to life, we are bound to stop and wonder: Why am I here? What am I meant to do in this lifetime? Where am I heading? What if the answers to these vital cosmic questions lie in the stars?

Astrology offers a bounty of clues in determining the heart's desires, the soul's intentions, goals of past lives, and the karmic lessons we're meant to learn in this lifetime. *Mapping Your Soul's Purpose* makes it easy for anyone to peer into the cosmos for a glimpse of their spiritual path. No previous astrological knowledge is required. Included with the book is an easy-to-use CD-ROM, which makes it a cinch for beginners to start mapping their karmic journey.

978-0-7387-0673-3, 216 pp., 7½ x 9⅛   **$19.95**

To order, call 1-877-NEW-WRLD
Prices subject to change without notice
Order at Llewellyn.com 24 hours a day, 7 days a week!

Solar Arcs
Astrology's Most Successful Predictive System
NOEL TYL

The first major treatise, in the history of astrology, on Solar Arcs.

Now available to all: *Solar Arcs*—the simplest of astrological prediction systems that harness the individualized symbolism of the Sun in the mechanics of future times. And with the computer, no more problems stand in the way of learning and applying Solar Arcs.

Noel Tyl, astrology's foremost analyst, writer, and teacher, presents the entire power potential of *Solar Arcs* with many case studies; he shows the work of Solar Arcs that is essential to authoritative rectification.

The book is also filled with bonus material: Tertiary Progressions, Rectification (with an exciting example using Sir Edmund Hillary), a 100-year quick-glance ephemeris, and Tyl's analytical synthesis of every one of the 1,130 possible Solar Arc and Solar Arc midpoint pictures.

978-0-7387-0054-0, 480 pp., 7½ x 9⅛ $19.95

To order, call 1-877-NEW-WRLD
Prices subject to change without notice
Order at Llewellyn.com 24 hours a day, 7 days a week!

Synastry
Understanding the Astrology of Relationships

ROD SUSKIN

Synastry puts relationships under the cosmic microscope of astrology—offering an insightful perspective on the dynamics that drive all personal interactions.

Rod Suskin, the author of *Cycles of Life*, blends traditional methods with modern techniques in this introduction to synastry. His step-by-step approach begins with interpreting an individual's birth chart to pinpoint relationship needs and behaviors. Next, you'll learn chart comparison techniques—involving the elements, inter-chart aspects, planets in aspect, the fifth house, dignities, and other astrological factors—to determine the compatibility and longevity of a relationship. *Synastry* will help you explore many critical issues that affect relationships: communication habits, values, feelings of self-worth, sex drive, life goals, attitudes toward money and children, karma, and more.

For the professional astrologer, there is also advice for conducting client consultations with sensitivity and objectivity.

978-0-7387-1255-0, 264 pp., 7½ x 9⅛   **$21.95**

To order, call 1-877-NEW-WRLD
Prices subject to change without notice
Order at Llewellyn.com 24 hours a day, 7 days a week!